EXILED

EXILED

*Voices of the Southern Baptist
Convention Holy War*

Edited by Carl L. Kell
Introduction by Samuel S. Hill

The University of Tennessee Press / Knoxville

Library of Congress Cataloging-in-Publication Data
Exiled : voices of the Southern Baptist Convention holy war / edited by Carl L.
Kell ; introduction by Samuel S. Hill.— 1st ed.
p. cm.
Includes bibliographical references and index.
ISBN 1-57233-448-7 (hardcover)
1. Southern Baptist Convention—History—20th century.
2. Baptists—United States—History—20th century.
3. Baptists—United States—Doctrines.
4. Church controversies—Baptists—History—20th century.
5. Fundamentalism—United States.
I. Kell, Carl L.

BX6462.3.E95 2006
286'.132'09045—dc22

2005011123

To my friend and coauthor

L. RAYMOND CAMP

Who, in his integrity and love for the human spirit,
at work in crisis and in conflict, embodies all that is good
in rhetorical scholarship.

CONTENTS

FOREWORD
Carolyn Crumpler

xi

FOREWORD: EXILED, INDEED
James Dunn

xxv

PREFACE
xxxiii

ACKNOWLEDGMENTS
xli

INTRODUCTION
Samuel S. Hill

1

SOUTHERN BAPTIST WOMAN IN EXILE
Eleanor B. Williamson

13

MY STORY: A PERSONAL ADVENTURE IN UNHOLY RIGHTEOUSNESS
Joe Yelton

17

A TRUSTEE WHO COULD NO LONGER TRUST
George Steincross
21

FROM BAPTIST TO BAPTIST
Frank Kendall
25

NO MORE KNOCKIN'
Rachel Smith Childress
29

GETTING MY HEAD ON STRAIGHT
Cecil E. Sherman
31

STILL A BAPTIST WOMAN
Gladys S. Lewis
39

MY DEPARTURE FROM THE SUNDAY SCHOOL BOARD
Alan G. Jolly
51

STRANGERS IN MY HOUSE
S. L. Harris
55

YESTERDAY'S DREAMS, TODAY'S REALITIES
Lavonn D. Brown
59

ONE LAYMAN'S RELUCTANT JOURNEY TOWARD HIGHER GROUND
Wayne C. Bartee
63

EXILED FROM THE SBC
June Brown
67

FREEDOM HAS NEVER BEEN SO PRECIOUS
Michael K. Olmsted
71

A LOT LIKE DYING
Gregory L. Hancock
77

THE TEXAS TWO-STEP
Rick McClatchy
81

A LIBERAL BAPTIST'S STORY OF EXILE FROM THE SBC
C. Fred Werhan
87

EXILED: SOUTH CAROLINA–STYLE
E. C. Watson
93

A SEPARATE PEACE
Ronald D. Sisk
99

EXODUS FROM THE SOUTHERN BAPTIST CONVENTION
Michael R. Duncan
103

FINDING A VOICE IN EXILE
Paul D. Simmons
107

THE HIJACKING OF THE SOUTHERN BAPTIST CONVENTION
W. H. Crouch
121

INSIDE THE GATLINBURG GANG
Edwin F. Perry
123

THE SKIRMISH OF FIRST BAPTIST CHURCH, JAMESTOWN, NORTH CAROLINA
Pascal L. Hovis
127

I AM IN EXILE. I AM HOME: EXILE OF INNOCENCE
Tracy Dunn-Noland
133

"EXILE OF INNOCENCE"

Dawn Darwin Weaks
Tracy Dunn-Noland

135

WITHDRAWAL AND EXCLUSION: DOING THE RIGHT THING

J. R. Huddlestun

139

PHOENIX RISING

Reba Cobb

143

POSES

Mark Fleming

145

EARLY RETIREMENT

Joe E. Trull

147

APPENDIX: COMPARISON OF 1925, 1963, AND 2000 BAPTIST FAITH AND MESSAGE

153

BIBLIOGRAPHY

181

CONTRIBUTORS

185

INDEX

191

FOREWORD

Carolyn Weatherford Crumpler

Exiled: Expulsion from one's native land or home by authoritative decree. As I read this definition in *Webster's College Dictionary*, I tried to apply it to myself. I could not make personal application. So, I went back to another word. *Obliterate: to blot out or render indecipherable: efface.* Aha! That's it. I was not expelled from the Southern Baptist Convention. I left happily, by taking early retirement from Woman's Missionary Union, SBC, to marry J. Joseph Crumpler, Southern Baptist pastor from Alabama, who had gone to Ohio from seminary during the time that Southern Baptists were focusing on moving into the Great Lakes area. He had begun a church in Defiance, and after a few years had moved to the old Mt. Carmel Baptist Church in Cincinnati, which was founded in 1822 and became Southern Baptist in the mid-1950s. I left the platform for the parsonage. The effacing, or the obliteration, happened in the year following. Let me tell you my story.

I was born in the rural community of House, Mississippi. My parents both were from that area, but had lived in Florida since their marriage. Deciding to return to my mother's home place to "make a crop" during the Depression, they put their only child, my brother, in first grade at the consolidated school, and welcomed my birth in January 1930. By the time summer came, they had decided to return to Frostproof, Florida, where we were joined by a sister in 1931.

Life in this small town in the citrus/cattle area of south Florida was centered in the First Baptist Church, the Frostproof public school, and the family home on West B Street. Daddy was a deacon. Mama was the teacher, then director, of the primary department. She also led the Girls' Auxiliary (GA), so she taught my sister and me in Sunday school and in the missions organization when we reached the age of nine.

I "joined the church" when I was nine years old, during a revival, when the children were brought into "big church" to hear the evangelist. What I remember about his sermon was, "Do you want to go to hell? Of course not!" When the invitation was given, I went to the front of the church. My parents and my pastor sensed that I was not really ready to accept Christ personally, so I was not baptized. It was later, when I was thirteen, that my Sunday school teacher, also my pastor's wife, stopped me after class and talked with me about my personal salvation. In the morning service I made my public profession of faith, and that afternoon was baptized in Clinch Lake, just blocks from my home. It was several years later that we finally got a baptistery in First Baptist Church.

Several of my teachers were Baptists, and members of my church. The one who stands out most vividly in my mind was my high school biology teacher. Gwen Boyette was just out of college, and among the things she did in my church was to get BTU (Baptist Training Union) started. When our pastor was caught in an affair with one of the church women, she was the one who helped the youth through the difficult time. She taught only one year, then went to the old WMU Training School and became a Baptist Student Union director.

When I was in the tenth grade, my pastor came to talk with my parents. He asked if they would be willing for me to be a Sunday school teacher. He said the Junior boys were in critical need of a teacher, and he thought I could do it. My parents agreed, and I had my first experience teaching the Bible. I also had my first experience of leading a person to Christ—one of the boys in my class.

In addition to BTU and Sunday school, the missions organizations were very important in my life. When I moved from Junior GAs to Intermediate GAs, my mother suggested that I lead the younger girls, and she would continue with the older girls. Then I met the second influential woman in my life, Elizabeth Provence, the state WMU young people's secretary. She came to Frostproof to lead a workshop, and I'm sure she was quite surprised to see the girl who met her bus and helped get her boxes to the church. She also convinced my mother that it would be a good thing for me to go to Ridgecrest Assembly for Young Women's Auxiliary Week. They agreed, and the church helped with the expenses for my best friend and me to make the trip. We rode the Greyhound bus to Jacksonville, where we joined the chartered bus to Ridgecrest. It was during this week that God really opened the world to me. Although I had learned from books about the Southern Baptist Convention, and I knew what the Cooperative Program was, the week at Ridgecrest brought me face-to-face with the men who led the Convention. I got their autographs. I've always remembered how impressed I was that these four men, the leaders of the four convention boards, had given their time for a meeting with high school and college girls. I met many missionaries. I met Kathleen Mallory, Juliette Mather, and Alma Hunt, leaders of Women's Missionary Union.

At the end of the week, during the time of decision, I went to the front of the auditorium with many other girls, committing my life to full-time Christian service. I could hardly wait to get home to tell the folks there about the meeting and about my decision. My very wise pastor told me, "A call to serve is a call to prepare. Let's get you prepared." In my senior year in high school I had three major jobs at church: I was the BTU director; I became the choir director (because we had a music school led by a state worker who said I could beat time better than anybody else!); I continued teaching the boys in Sunday school. Also, my pastor enlisted me as an associational Training Union worker, so I added associational work to my load.

By the time I graduated from high school, I was a full-fledged, card-carrying Southern Baptist. I could name the agencies of the Southern Baptist Convention, and I knew what percentage of the Cooperative Program pie each received. I knew the names of the people who led. I knew about Baptist organization from my church, to Orange Blossom Association, to the Florida Baptist Convention and its agencies. But I was soon to learn about another wonderful, important work, the Baptist Student Union. Not being able to afford the private Baptist school in Florida, I enrolled at Florida State University. Adjacent to the campus was the BSU House, where a brilliant, committed young woman, Faith Jones, was the director. I moved my church membership from First Baptist Church, Frostproof, to First Baptist Church, Tallahassee. BSU became my home away from home, and helped me to transition from my small town to the huge university.

CAROLYN CRUMPLER

My goal was to become a high school teacher. I changed majors every quarter, seeking just the right match. At the end of my sophomore year, a member of First Baptist Church stopped me one Sunday. He was the dean of the new School of Library Science. He told me that he had noted how I often I had changed my major, and also had noted that I stuck with secondary education. He asked, "Why don't you come into the library school?" So I did. That decision led me to five years in the public schools of Florida, first as the only librarian in a small high school in central Florida, and then as one of three librarians in a large high school in Tampa. In both schools, my principals were Christians, both Baptists. In Eustis, I joined the First Baptist Church, which was just recovering from a major split, so I had my first taste of Baptist controversy. In Tampa, I joined Seminole Heights Baptist Church, a large, older church from which six missionary couples had gone to foreign fields, two had become seminary professors, and several were home missionaries.

I became a "state-approved worker" with the Florida Baptist Convention, leading conferences in stewardship, in Training Union work, and in WMU. I taught Sunday school in both churches, sang in the choir, and worked in other areas. In Tampa, I served two summers as youth director at my church. I was comfortably settled as a full-time volunteer in my church. I had not forgotten the commitment I had made at Ridgecrest, but it was not uppermost in my mind. Then we had a revival. Dr. Charles Howard, the visiting evangelist, really touched my heart in one of his messages, and I realized that I had not carried out my intent. From that point I began making plans to go to seminary. Years later, I saw Dr. Howard, and told him of the impact of his message. He hugged me and said, "Thank you for telling me that. I've always thought of that revival at Seminole Heights as a major failure. You've just let me know it wasn't."

The big question became: which seminary? Every pastor I knew, plus two of my special Baptist women mentors, had gone to Louisville—to Southern or to the WMU Training School. Faith James had graduated from Southwestern. Somehow that didn't seem to fit me. I prayed about it. I read catalogs. Then, at a state YWA meeting, I met Gladys Keith, a Baptist home missionary working in New Orleans at the Rachel Sims Good Will Center. I determined that my place would be New Orleans Baptist Theological Seminary, and I began to make my plans to attend.

It was good news to be reminded that through the Cooperative Program most of my fees would be taken care of. Withdrawing my teacher's retirement, I left for New Orleans with an abundance of hope and enthusiasm. Of course, I tried to enroll in the School of Theology. After all, I had studied all those study course books about church work, and I wanted Bible study. How shocked I was to discover that, because I was a female, I could not make that choice. I could choose between the School of Music or the School of Religious Education. In spite of my being able to "beat time" better than anybody else at First Baptist Church in Frostproof, I chose religious education. Helen Falls, who would later move to the School of Theology, taught missions education and became a good friend. Margaret Leverette taught social work, and because she had grown up in the church in Tampa where I was a member, we had a good connection. John Price, Kelva Moore, and John Durst were excellent teachers, though I already knew most of what they taught.

The very good news was that I could take all my electives in the School of Theology, and that I did. My first New Testament class was under Dr. Frank Stagg. My first Old Testament class was under Dr. Olen Strange. I decided I would remain with the two of them, rather than changing, so I confess that my New Testament is Stagg-ology and my Old Testament is Strange-ology. The best news of all was that as I arrived in New Orleans I was immediately contacted by Harriett Mather, who was the directress of Mather School of Nursing at Southern Baptist Hospital, and sister of Juliette Mather of the national WMU. She had learned that a librarian was coming to the seminary, and she wanted to recruit me to work for her. Although the school was established in 1929, thirty years later its library had not been set up. For the two years I was in seminary, I worked almost full-time at Mather. There I saw firsthand another ministry of the Southern Baptist Convention. I joined First Baptist Church, and the preaching of Pastor J. D. Grey blessed my life. There, too, I was given a Sunday school class to teach—senior high school girls.

I lived in the women's dormitory, and the house mother was Sybil Brame Townsend, a former BSU secretary, now widowed and rearing her three children on the campus. She later left to marry Dr. C. C. Warren. Mrs. Townsend and Dr. Durst were very much interested in my going into Baptist student work. Dr. Falls was very much interested in my going into missions education. Miss Leverette wanted me in social work!

Near graduation I had some interesting offers—one to work in a state Baptist college, another to be youth director in a university church, with double duty of being assistant to the BSU director on campus. The offer I felt led to take was to join the staff of Alabama Women's Missionary Union, and I moved to Montgomery following graduation. There I learned from a pro—the late Dr. Mary Essie Stephens. My two and a half years under her direction formed the excellent preparation I had for the work to follow. During my time in Montgomery, I attended a missions week in the city, where Dr. Baker James Cauthen was the keynote speaker. During one of his messages he kept repeating, "If the Lord has not told you *not* to be a missionary, perhaps he wants you *to be* one." I began making application with the Foreign Mission Board for missions service, and because of what became a persistent physical problem I was told to "come back later."

When I was invited to join the staff of Florida Women's Missionary Union, I felt that this was a wonderful opportunity to return to my home state, while waiting for further guidance about foreign missions. I came to understand that my call was to missions education, and from that point I was committed to that calling. After three years I returned to Alabama as Dr. Stephens' associate director. After four years with Alabama WMU, I was offered three positions with WMU—one to join the staff as an associate in the national office, another to join the staff of another state WMU, and the third, which I took, was to return to my home state as WMU executive director.

The retirement of Josephine Jones from WMU coincided with the retirement of the state executive, John Maguire. Harold C. Bennett succeeded Maguire; I succeeded Miss Jones, and thus began another time of learning from a professional. For seven years I led Florida WMU and experienced the leadership of Dr. Bennett. The major decision that we made during that time was to change our status from auxiliary to the state convention to that of a department of work. That was the best plan for Florida at the time, and WMU earned a respected position in the state network. It also gave me an excellent position in which to become acquainted with the leaders in the Southern Baptist Convention, as they visited our state and always included me in the plans. It was a very difficult choice I had to make when I was asked to succeed Alma Hunt as executive director of WMU, BSU.

To this point, you have seen Carolyn Weatherford as an active member of a Southern Baptist church and an active participant in associational and state Baptist work. Now we will move her to the national area, as she becomes the executive director of Women's Missionary Union, auxiliary to Southern Baptist Convention.

My election took place at the annual meeting of WMU in Dallas, Texas, in 1974. Immediately I was besieged by the press, a foretaste of things to come! My biggest blunder was when a reporter asked me if I were a feminist. I said, "No, of course not. I am a humanist!" I meant, of course, that I was for human beings, laypeople, men and women, not a "secular humanist," the enemy of the day. I was a quick learner, and I never had as hard a press conference again. Baker James Cauthen was head of the Foreign Missions Board at the time, and he said, "Carolyn, keep your passport in order; I want you to visit the missionaries around the world." Dr. Arthur Rutledge, head of the Home Mission Board, countered with, "I want to take you on a home mission tour, as soon as possible, but before March. I want you to have fresh stories to tell during the week of prayer." Both men were true to their word, and before I retired fifteen years later, I had visited missionaries in ninety-seven countries, and had been to every state and territory of the United States. I saw missions firsthand. I loved the missionaries, and they loved me, and together we had a great story to tell.

My greatest circle of friends were the men who made up the Inter-Agency Council, a group that no longer exists as such. I was the only female member, just as Alma Hunt before me had been the only female. But the seminary presidents, the board presidents, and the executives of the other agencies accepted me as one of them, and I learned so much about the Convention I thought I knew so well already. My position earned me a seat on the General Council of the Baptist World Alliance, and my Baptist world grew as I learned how many other Baptists there were in the world.

Then things began to happen. I made a speech in Columbia, South Carolina, in a meeting planned by an organization in that state to look at the role of women in the church. When I returned to my desk on Monday, I had a call from Baptist Press. "Did you say . . . ?" "Oh, yes," I responded, "and let me tell you the other good things I said!" He listened patiently, then said, "But that's not newsworthy. This is." So to the state Baptist papers went the headline: "WMU leader smacks the Total Woman." This was in 1976—two years into my tenure at WMU. The letters began to come in. The wife of a prominent pastor who would, in several years, become president of the Convention, called. She said, "You don't know me, but . . ." I said, "Of course I know you!" and told her of our previous contacts. With this first bashing from the public over a speech I made in public, I was very disturbed. I called my pastor for counseling. Catherine Allen, WMU's public relations director at the time, told me not to worry, but that didn't help. After it was all over, however, we counted the letters. I had received 129. Only 31 of them were negative. I began to feel better.

In 1976, Southern Baptists celebrated the nation's bicentennial in Norfolk, Virginia, and there we began to see what would become the takeover of the Convention. It was rumored that Adrian Rogers would be nominated as president, but it didn't happen that year. Dr. James Sullivan, who had retired as president of the Sunday School Board, was elected. The following year, Dr. Jimmy Allen was elected. In 1979, Adrian Rogers was elected; thus, the "conservative resurgence," as "they" called it, had begun. That also was the beginning of the exile for many Southern Baptists in leadership. I vividly recall walking up the steps after the election, certainly with a long, sad face, when I was stopped by one of the seminary presidents. He said, "Cheer up, Carolyn. It won't last." He was among the first exiles. People in the churches would not stand for a "takeover." But they did.

The president of Women's Missionary Union at the time, Mrs. A. Harrison Gregory of Virginia, and I spent many hours talking about the situation. We were in agreement that we were going to "stick to our knitting," that Convention politics was not our business, and that we would keep WMU on course. Even so, we were attacked at times, viciously. The worst attacks came after the convention in Kansas City when the resolution on women as "first in the Edenic sin" passed. Many men worked with us to try to defeat the motion. Alma Hunt agreed to go to the platform to speak against the motion. She was greeted warmly by one of the "guards," who said, "Of course, you've come to speak *for* the motion." To which she sternly responded, "Of course, I have to come to speak *against* the motion." She was never recognized, and the passing of the motion, with debate cut off, is part of our history. During the weeks of prayer, always planned and promoted by Women's Missionary Union for the support of home and foreign missions, we received many letters and phone calls from pastors and other church leaders rebuking us for being "feminists."

When Bill Tanner resigned from the Home Mission Board, one of the members of the search committee for his successor called to tell me he was putting my name in the pot as president of the Home Mission Board. That was an interesting bit of information, soon followed by a call from another member of the search committee who definitely understood that this was not the Lord's will for me, and wanted to be certain that I, too, understood that! This second man is one of the current agency leaders. Of course, I was not considered for the position. The old Christian Life Commission decided I should be recognized with their Distinguished Service Award for Leadership in Christian Ethics and Moral Concerns. I had almost forgotten that it had been mentioned to me, when I received a phone call from a reporter in Atlanta. He had just come from the CLC meeting, and asked, "Are you going to accept the award from the Christian Life Commission?" I asked, "Are they giving it to me?" He said, "Oh, yes. But there was opposition." "How much," I asked. "The vote was sixteen for, thirteen against." I said, "Then, of course I'll accept it!" Later, I heard that one of the board members had said, "I don't even know Carolyn Weatherford." (He was a deacon in a church in which I had spoken twice in recent years.) Another member, a woman, said, "Well, I know her, and I don't like her!" But you know what? I accepted the plaque at the 1987 SBC meeting. I still have it. I think I earned it!

At this time, Pope John Paul II visited the United States. An ecumenical panel of Christian leaders was invited to meet with him in South Carolina. I accepted, to the horror of many Baptist leaders. I had letters and phone calls. One pastor assured me that if I thought it would be an opportunity to "convert" the Pope, I should know that there were many preachers who were better equipped to do so. My favorite letter came from a pastor in Louisiana who wrote, "Dear Carolyn Weatherford, in the last ten years you have did many things that made me say Oh, No! But this time you have outdid yourself." I loved that one!

A year later, Southern Seminary gave me the E.Y. Mullins Denominational Service Award. Again, there were horrified responses. One trustee, who later became, for a short time, president of one of the seminaries, wrote to the WMU board member from his state, demanding that I be disciplined! He said that the only reason I received it was that Dr. Honeycutt, the Southern president, and I were the same kind of liberals that were ruining Convention.

This happened in 1988, in San Antonio, just after the magnificent Centennial Celebration of Women's Missionary Union in Richmond. Apologetically, the personnel committee of the WMU board "called me in" while in San Antonio and shared with me the message from the disgruntled pastor. They apologized profusely for having done so.

In 1989, when the Convention met in Las Vegas, my wedding plans were complete, and everybody knew that I would take early retirement from WMU after my wedding in August. A young pastor from Georgia came to me and asked if he could nominate me for vice-president. My husband-to-be, seated beside me, assured me that would be good. So, I was nominated, though defeated. This was my first venture into the political arena, but it was not to be my last. After returning from our wedding trip in Europe, I joined the church where my husband was pastor, and began to settle into the role of pastor's wife. My settling was soon disturbed, however, by a phone call from Daniel Vestal, asking me to run for first vice-president at the convention in New Orleans in 1990. Again, Joe told me to do it. He reminded me that this was the strategic time for me, while I was still close to what was happening. I asked Joe to go with me to Columbus, where I could talk personally with the state convention executive, Tal Bonham, a friend from the days when he was in Oklahoma and I was in Birmingham. It was Dr. Bonham who had invited me to speak at the Ohio state convention, where the WMU director had arranged for Joe to take me to dinner. We met Tal for lunch, and I told him that I wanted him to hear the news from me. He thanked me for that. He said he would vote for me, but he couldn't nominate me. I assured him that the nominator already had been selected. With the public announcement began erasure from Southern Baptist life. Although I wrote to all WMU leaders explaining why I had chosen to run, and not asking for their endorsement, a public statement was made by the president that "WMU has not endorsed Mrs. Crumpler for vice-president." I received a call from Jimmy Draper at the Sunday School Board denying one of the statements I had made about Women's Ministries, a new activity of the Sunday School Board, that I felt was in direct competition with WMU. From Florida I had the news from my good friend Roger Knapp, retired missionary, who told me he was going to run against me. He said it was because being vice-president would give him the opportunity to tell the missions story. History indicates, of course, that this missionary had no voice as a vice-president. I have not heard from him since. Interesting mail began to arrive. One letter from a woman in Kentucky said, "How could we let you lead WMU all these years and you don't believe in the Bible?" I talked with Joe about how to answer questions about the Bible. Interestingly enough, no one ever, in the "campaign," asked me any questions about the Bible.

In New Orleans, as I was seated with my husband and friends from our church, a man walked up to our row and asked if he could speak with me. He said that he had a word from the Lord for me. The word was that I should withdraw my name from the ballot, that it was divisive, and that if I would do that he himself would nominate me the next year. I assured him that the Lord had spoken directly to me, and that I would not withdraw. You know the rest of the story. We were defeated. The next morning we met for what was to have been a celebration breakfast. It became, instead, a time for planning a meeting in Atlanta, when we would gather and look to the future. Joe and I were not present, for we were in Seoul, South Korea, where he was preaching in several churches. We attended the Baptist World Alliance. There I was employed as director of the North American Baptist Fellowship, one of the regional fellowships of the BWA, and at the close of the meeting Joe and I were joined by three dozen folks for a tour of Lottie Moon's China. That meeting in Atlanta became the Cooperative Baptist Fellowship. Joe and I have been active in that organization since the beginning. I was named to the global missions committee. I served as moderator (president) for one term, and Joe has led our North Central Region CBF. Then the "erase her from our Convention" campaign really began. My employment by the BWA for the North American Baptist Fellowship was immediately misinterpreted. Confused with the meeting in Atlanta, it was said to be a "new organization for liberals."

The church where Joe was pastor voted to allow members to designate gifts to the Cooperative Baptist Fellowship. He began sooner than I to designate around the Cooperative Program and Lottie Moon and Annie Armstrong offerings. I designated around CP, but couldn't bring myself, for awhile, to discontinue gifts to Annie and Lottie. That changed abruptly, in 1993, when the Foreign Mission Board took money designated for the seminary in Ruschlikon from that school. From that point on, my financial support for missions has gone totally through the Cooperative Baptist Fellowship. That's when I removed myself from the Southern Baptist Convention. My church membership is still in a Southern Baptist church, the one where my husband was pastor for thirty years before retirement. But I no longer have any opportunities that are Southern Baptist.

Soon after I moved to Ohio, Tal Bonham died, the state leadership changed, and that erased me from the state Baptist activities. One director of missions in Ohio called to tell me, "I'm sorry we lost you," to which I responded, "You didn't lose me; you never found me." I was invited by the women to participate in a state meeting, and later was called by an apologetic friend who said, "I'm sorry, but I must dis-invite you. The state evangelism man said we can't have you." A similar invitation came from the wife of the director of missions in Chicago. I asked her if she were sure, that in some places I was "not allowed." She assured me that they could do what they wanted to do. Several months later a lovely basket of fruit and flowers arrived at my home with a note from her, indicating that I had been right. As a trustee of the American Bible Society, I was asked to arrange for an interpretation meeting in our state. I wanted it to be in a Baptist church, but I was told that we had too many requests for "parachurch" groups to meet, and while I could, if I chose, contact churches directly, the association could not provide a meeting place. I sadly chose a church of another denomination, sorry that my Baptist friends would not have the opportunity to host such an important gathering.

The SBC Ministers' Wives organization had been an interesting relationship for me while I was with WMU. We helped them with their meeting places; we provided the opportunity for officers to meet at the WMU offices each year. Several years after I married, the officers asked if I would accept the Mrs. J. M. Dawson Award, which had been given annually to a pastor's wife. I agreed, and it was announced that at the next year's SBC meeting in New Orleans the award would be presented to me. By then, the leadership of this organization had changed, and many of the women in New Orleans were unhappy with the selection. Baptist Press carried stories about it; there were many phone calls and letters, but the decision was made to "go ahead and give it to her." It was something less than an enthusiastic presentation!

While in Birmingham, I was a frequent writer for *Open Windows*, and was delighted to be asked to write again after my marriage. Although that assignment was printed, I was told that I would not be asked again. Meanwhile, although I continued to be invited to WMU annual meetings and to meetings of the executive board, in the twelve years since my retirement, I have never been asked to serve in any capacity, with one exception. I was asked to write *Prayer Patterns* for the adult magazine, a task I had enjoyed frequently. That didn't last long, though, because "we need to give some other folks a chance." I later was informed by a staff member that it was because of my involvement with CBF. Although other former executives and presidents have served on committees and in other capacities, I remain "obliterated," and many current women do not know there was anyone who served between Alma Hunt and Dellana O'Brien.

The funniest story, however, I must tell here. It is illustrative of how little current leaders know of our Southern Baptist past. One evening I answered the telephone in the kitchen. It was Dr. Bill O'Brien, calling from Birmingham. I went to another phone, since grandchildren were eating popcorn in the kitchen. When I got to another phone, his wife, Dellana O'Brien was also on the phone, so I called Joe in to join us. Bill said, "I just have to tell you this story."

He had called Dellana's office, but she was not in. Reva, Dellana's administrative assistant, had answered the phone for her and said, "She's not back yet, but I must tell you about the phone call I've just had. It came from a pastor in Florida who was very angry about something that Dellana had said. After he vented for a while, he then said 'Now let me tell you about that other woman!'" Through questioning, Reva determined he meant Carolyn Weatherford Crumpler. He said, "That's the one," and began venting his anger toward me. His final charge: "and to top all that, she went and married that man Lottie Moon turned down!"

You can be sure, dear reader, that since that time friends have often said to me, "How's your toy?" Legend has it that Lottie Moon turned away the romantic interests of seminary professor Crawford Toy. In the "good old days" of Southern Baptists, every pastor would have known that Lottie Moon died in 1912, almost eighty years before this telephone conversation.

Well, my friends, that's my story. I am not exiled from home. The Southern Baptist Convention, as it is today, is no longer my home. I have been obliterated! That happened because I was not willing to give up the fragile freedoms of Baptists for the narrow, restricted, power-control SBC of today.

I am grateful for the years I grew in, learned from, loved, and supported with my life the Southern Baptist Convention. I was saddened by its demise. But I'm over that, and I've found that there *is* life after the SBC!

Now let's read the stories of others—exiles, obliterated—whatever!

CAROLYN CRUMPLER

FOREWORD
EXILED, INDEED
James Dunn

In the early 1930s, the president of Southwestern Baptist Theological Seminary in Fort Worth, Texas, called the three men who taught in the School of Sacred Music to his office. Sad news! The full force of the Great Depression had hit giving to the seminary. Dr. L. R. Scarborough informed the professors, who with their wives were the entire music school faculty, that the school would be closed. There was no longer money for their salaries.

They protested. They had not come to the seminary, Southern Baptists' largest, for the paycheck. They were there to prepare men and women (men mostly) for ministry. The three, B. B. McKinney, I. E. Reynolds, and Edwin McNeely, said, "We will stay and teach without pay."

They did. They lost their homes. For three years they had a tough time, but the School of Sacred Music survived and became one of the great graduate schools of music in the nation. I know this story quite well because the daughter of the McNeelys, Marilyn, is my wife. She was born while her parents were living in Fort Worth Hall, the dormitory into which they were moved when they lost their home. But that is just the beginning of the story, merely a hint of the dedication and devotion of folks at Southwestern to keep it alive, and to make it the successful and respected institution that it became.

They were also utterly committed to make it the distinctly Baptist scholarly seminary that, with full accreditation and educationally sound principles, led it to become the largest and one of the most productive entities in higher education for ministers. A powerful irony obtains merely because of the location—Fort Worth, Texas—not the heart of progressive religion. In fact, J. Frank Norris, partner of W. B. Riley and one of America's most virulent fundamentalists, was pastor of Fort Worth's First Baptist Church.

Yet, Southwestern produced great biblical scholars, H. E. Dana, Charles B. Williams, L. R. Elliot, Ray Summers; the church historian, A. H. Newman; and father of training for religious educators, John Milburn Price. W. T. Conner studied with Walter Rauschenbusch at Colgate Rochester and at the University of Chicago and returned to Southwestern with a sort of Southern-fried version of the social gospel. T. B. Maston did his second doctorate with H. Richard Niebuhr at Yale, and when he came back to Texas brought with him an understanding of the best of neoorthodoxy, a perspective on theology and the world that takes sin seriously and believes the Bible.

The Southwestern Baptist Seminary of these years turned out a generation of future leaders who are theologically biblical, soundly spiritual, missionary in spirit, and evangelistic in the best sense. Without listing their job histories, most Baptists know their names: Keith Parks, Bill Pinson, Randall Lolley, Milton Ferguson, Jimmy R. Allen, Foy D. Valentine, R. H. Dilday, William R. O'Brien, Browning Ware, Bill D. Moyers, and dozens of others. Yet these are the very denominational loyalists who were rejected, libeled, and treated shabbily by the takeover crowd.

Back to Mac—Edwin McNeely. My late father-in-law is the source of many of the stories regarding the struggles with fundamentalists for control of Baptist life in Texas, that from which many of us have been exiled. He became the target of some of the nastiest little stunts by Norris and his minions. During the difficult years economically, Norris would send the McNeelys rotten fruit and vegetables. The "greathearted leader" of the Baptist World Fellowship, Norris, would send hecklers out to the Seminary to harass the chapel speakers. He did, until Dr. McNeely, himself a hefty human, rounded up some of the biggest bruisers he could find among the theologs and physically threw the uninvited guests off the campus.

All this has relevance because it reveals the true nature of the mean-spirited fundamentalism that returned, replicated in the henchmen of the right-wing politicians in the 1979–99 era. It is no accident that the large meeting hall at First Baptist, Fort Worth, on Throckmorton Street was dedicated to John Birch. They, like the society that bears his name, follow an any-means-is-justified-by-our-divinely-dictated ethic. I know; I have been one of their designated hittees for more than twenty years.

The usefulness, if there is any, in the entire venture of this book is to put a human face on the events of the takeover. Heresy trials are seldom evaluated from the perspective of the heretics. There is some value, it seems, in an up close and personal look at the developments that have led the Southern Baptist Convention from bordering on being a mainstream denomination in the 1960s and 1970s to returning to a marginalized, ultra-conservative sect status. There is also some significant justification in looking at Texas Baptists who have resolutely refused to go along with the power play that has disenfranchised the pastors and laymen of many of the strongest and healthiest churches in the late great SBC. As Jerold McBride, pastor of the First Baptist Church, San Angelo, Texas, said early in the unpleasantness, "The Baptist General Convention of Texas is not a farm club of the Southern Baptist Convention."

How can it be? How can these "cowboy Christians" in Texas save a bundle of basic Baptist beliefs when the voting majority at the national conventions do not care about being authentically Baptist anymore? I hear the shock all the time from Baptists in Virginia, North Carolina, and Georgia who have their preconceptions about Texas Baptists challenged or even destroyed.

Several obvious answers pop up. Texans still possess a frontier mentality of rugged individualism or individual ruggedism that refuses to conform. We identify with a *very* Baptist trait exhibited by Roger Williams as one of the "otherwise-minded." "Ain't nobody but Jesus gonna tell me what to believe" is about as close as we come to a creed.

Then, there is the lengthened shadow of Baptist giants who knew what a Baptist is and why and taught hundreds of students the same. W. W. Barnes, Robert A. Baker, and William R. Estep interpreted history and did not merely recite events in their classes. I knew them all, heard them preach, asked them questions. No one could possibly find them sympathetic to fundamentalist rigidity. E. Leslie Carlson loved to refer to the Norris gang downtown as the "funny-mentalists." W. T. Conner insisted that, while Jesus Christ is the same yesterday, today, and forever, "each new generation must rewrite its own theology." One of his favorite aphorisms when dealing with biblical literalists was "The Bible does not mean what it says; it means what it means." Such talk is utterly confounding to the dedicated biblicist. All these role models were not at "The Seminary." There were great teachers who had a grasp of the whole gospel for the whole person at Baylor, Hardin Simmons, Howard Payne, Wayland, and other Texas schools. I personally knew many of them. It was hard to find a fundamentalist among them.

One cannot make too much of great leaders like George W. Truett and J. M. Dawson, who consistently and winsomely proclaimed the truth as Baptists have defined it and defended it. The famous Truett speech on the steps of the U.S. Capitol in 1920 set the stage for the Baptist perspective on church-state separation in the twentieth century.

Next, there was the negative example of hard-core fundamentalism found in the Frank Norris movement. Many people cannot begin to comprehend what a powerful factor this laboratory experiment was right under our noses. Some scholars today are utterly at a loss to explain why Baptists in Oklahoma, Arkansas, Louisiana, and New Mexico are so vastly different from Texas Baptists. You had to have been there.

The Norrisite fundamentalists did not simply leave the Texas Convention in protest. They started another loosely knit denomination. It was a Baptist fellowship hotly dedicated to most of what was worst in Baptist life. They boasted that their churches used "English Bible Only," or even King James only. They focused on a brand of premillennialism that was forever finding "THE anti-Christ," predicting the end times, and reveling in an effete eschatology. Practically, they denied women places of recognized leadership, brought Jim Crow right into the church house, and refused to cooperate with other Christians of any sort. All of this would not have made such a difference, except that the Bible Baptist churches, the Baptist World Fellowship churches, the J. Frank Norris churches were exceedingly "missionary." They had an "Independent" Baptist church (aren't we all?) in every county. They started "Bible" Baptist churches in every town and village. They fed on discontent in the not-so-aggressive churches. They actually "planted" people in the Baptist General Convention churches to split them. In many instances they succeeded. They were soon in towns and cities from Dalhart to Port Arthur.

This is not "preaching." I am telling you the truth. I was there. I knew many of the people involved. I heard Norris preach and foster hostility toward every other kind of Baptist. When I was a pastor in Weatherford, Texas, a second cousin of mine was pastor of the fundamentalist church a half mile away. We never came to blows.

The aspect of this story that has been sorely neglected is the failure of historians, commentators, and analysts to see and understand the impact of the fundamentalist phenomenon in Texas. The demography, the sociology, the economics of the parallel but vastly different breeds of Baptists in Texas produced the Baptist General Convention of Texas that we know today. The presence of usually struggling Independent churches with generally poorly trained preachers, often in poorer sections of town, presented a genuine missionary outreach that was nonetheless "another way to do church." More importantly, the brand of Baptistness presented there was more often than not literal in biblical interpretation, caught up in eschatology, angry about the evil "social gospel," opposed outright to any form of ecumenism, and suspicious of higher education.

Thus, the Norris brand of fundamentalism, so similar to the faith of the folks now in charge of Southern Baptist life, gave Texas Baptists an alternative. In good all-American fashion, those who preferred the competition went to the independent churches. This left a more compatible crowd in the Convention churches. I grew up in Evans Avenue Baptist Church in Fort Worth. It was one of those that Norris tried to split. I knew the would-be splitters. And, as was often the case when there was some dribbling away in the 1940s and 1950s, no serious split took place.

From my perspective, the cooperation-inclined Baptists were blessed with a great catharsis. Our churches were spared many a fight over arcane doctrine and actually were beginning in the postwar period, 1950–80, to join the human race, if sometimes kicking and screaming.

Something like this may be one other explanation that Texas Baptists are so different. Yet, as one of those exiled, I would be a poor steward of the story as I know it if I did not share some of the insights from the wise older prophets I have known well—stories that only I can tell and that will never be told otherwise. Our exiledness is characterized by their words.

J. M. Dawson was in his nineties. The Christian Life Commission took him with us as our major speaker on a retreat for graduate students in ethics. W. A. Criswell had just announced that for five thousand dollars a little bronze statuette had been cast of the main building of the First Baptist Church of Dallas. On top of the church, which served as a base, there was the statue of Dr. Criswell holding an open Bible in his familiar preaching posture. We sat at the dinner table. We thought Dr. Dawson was asleep. He had been quiet for a long time, nodding occasionally. One of the students asked, "Why in the world would any pastor allow something like that to happen in his church?" Dr. Dawson came to life enough to answer, "Ego, massive ego."

Alas, "ego, massive ego" on the part of those who won the battle for control is and has been a factor. Hear their personal pronouns related to

JAMES DUNN

the vindictive management of their spoils—I, me, my, mine, we, us, ours. Just listen.

Abner V. McCall, former president of Baylor, former Texas Supreme Court justice, former FBI man, understood power politics. When the denomination was far gone down the slippery slope toward creedalism, he visited the offices of the Baptist Joint Committee. As was so often the case when old-timey Baptists got together—Baptists who believed in soul freedom, personal interpretation of scripture, and other such historic doctrines—we reflected on what was happening. This crowd was unwilling to order anyone around, get them to sign a political pledge card, or tell them what they *had* to do. Abner opined that he could tell us in two simple words the nature of the problem. He saw what was taking place after the annual Southern Baptist conventions. His two-word analysis: "gutless preachers."

Lack of courage on the part of those who had the responsibility to report to the churches was surely part of the problem. Many otherwise admirable pastors confessed that they were intimidated, unsure, afraid . . . in a word, "craven." "I have to think of my wife and kids, my future, my job." An old sad song that was heard too often.

Acker C. Miller, first secretary of the Texas Baptist Christian Life Commission, first secretary of the Southern Baptist Christian Life Commission, lived well into his nineties and seemed to see things with each passing decade of his long and useful life. Dr. Miller went with the staff to most CLC meetings. We heard repeated reports of his historic reading of what was happening to the Southern Baptist Convention. In a phrase he saw it all as a "return of the old Landmark revision of Baptist emphases." He could make the case: "the takeover crowd valued a rigid Calvinism, narrowness of spirit, ignorance rather than courageous engagement with critical scholarship, refusal to fellowship with or even acknowledge the faith of other brands of Christians, a fixation upon the by-and-by rather than the here-and-now." He was right.

T. B. Maston, the first professor of Christian Social Ethics at Southwestern Seminary, also lived and wrote into his nineties. He continued to the very end of his life to have hope for some of "his boys." He knew their fathers. He wrote them long, serious letters. They wrote back assurances of their love and respect for him. He kept hoping for the best. Some of us continued to hope that he would catch on to the true goals and ambitions of the conservative cabal that was now taking over the institutions that he had loved and served faithfully. On a beautiful day not long before he died, he and I walked and talked in Mommie's garden. "You know," he said, "these boys who think that they can keep women 'in their place,' who think they can keep women from being ordained and serving as pastors, are just as wrong as they can be." He paused, grinned that mischievous grin of his, tapped me on the chest as he sometimes did, and said, "Trying to deny women who believe they are called of God their place in ministry is sort of like telling the sun not to come up in the morning. It's coming."

So, the conflict has been between tradition and modernity, anti-education and education, large churches and small, willing political fighters and those who disdain all power plays, the ins and the outs, rapid progress toward ecumenism, acceptance of the pluralistic realities of our day, a desire to return to yesteryear—in many ways, simply a crass battle for control. But the measure not taken has been the human toll.

The denomination was entirely too dear to many of us. We know that now. Our churches were more than just the places we worshiped. They were the center of our lives, our social identity, the glue that held our lives together, our extended families. We, like many of our black brothers and sisters, found in the beloved community all sorts of support, encouragement, hope, and help. We found in the denomination, as well, a way of shaping life to try to make it conform to God's will for ourselves. We found in the institutions of the denomination, especially the seminaries, a gateway to sharing the gospel with the world in word and deed. That's gone. We are exiles, indeed.

Back to Mac . . . In the early 1920s, with Mother Williams of the Missionary Training School standing over him "helping," Edwin McNeely planted the pecan trees on the campus of Southwestern Baptist Theological Seminary. Now a band of brothers with a different vision have taken over. From my view they have a truncated theology, an accommodated approach to church-state separation, smallness of spirit, a propositional religion, a sick sort of Calvinism, an absence of vision for social justice, and a dozen or so other basic flaws. Other than that they are fine. They are closer to the J. Frank Norris brand of Baptist than to their predecessors at Southwestern.

Perhaps these flashes of vision from moderate victims of the takeover will reveal the sense of alienation—the awareness that we have, indeed, been exiled.

Hey, guys, spray and water the pecan trees, will you?

JAMES DUNN

PREFACE

One of the major news stories of religious life in the twentieth century was the takeover, or takeback, of the Southern Baptist Convention. The SBC began a steady turn to the right in 1979 with the election of Adrian Rogers of Bellevue Baptist Church, Memphis, Tennessee, as president. In an unbroken succession of conservative-fundamentalist presidents, the SBC leadership expended considerable rhetorical effort to move the Convention to a sure and steady rightward course, directed by the Bible and led by powerful rhetor-preachers. Now, some twenty-five years later, the SBC is a purified denomination, but not without considerable collateral damage.

The SBC is the largest Christian, non-Catholic denomination in the United States. With approximately 16 million members and forty-two thousand congregations, the SBC is positioned to continue as the most powerful voice in religious life in the Southeast and in many other areas of the United States. Professor Samuel S. Hill affirms these facts when he writes that "in the case of the Southern Baptists, a whole denomination quite seriously entertains the notion that it is Christianity's purest expression since apostolic times."[1] As the SBC moves with focus and purpose in the coming

---

1. Samuel S. Hill, *Southern Churches in Crisis Revisited* (Tuscaloosa: The University of Alabama Press, 1999), 29.

years, the conflict and controversy that has been at the center of Baptist life may or may not go silent.[2]

In the twentieth-century history of the SBC, there have been contentious debates over scripture, society, race, and all matters of church life. But never has there been a war of words like the fundamentalist vs. moderate battle over the nature of the Bible.

The 1979 leadership of Paul Pressler, then a Houston, Texas, appeals court judge, and Paige Patterson, then president of the Criswell Center, Dallas, Texas, set in motion a political agenda to secure the successive elections of conservative presidents of the SBC. These presidents would set a second plan in motion, as a function of their office, to replace members of boards and trustees of Convention entities with new conservative leadership. The new leadership would support the concept of an inerrant Bible (that the Bible is true and accurate in every respect). Over the twenty-five-year history of the process, the Pressler-Patterson initiative came to pass.

The controversy over the inerrant nature of scripture and the rhetorical character of the messages broadcast to the membership at the annual SBC meetings, as well as in the Convention states, captured the attention of scholars and the secular press. As of this writing, there are scores of books on the subject ranging from personal memoirs to academic analyses from every imaginable angle. For this writer, the rhetorical/persuasive nature of the SBC controversy best captures the humanity and the hubris of the battle for the Bible in a manner unlike any other analysis. *Exiled* is a small part of a large-scale rhetorical study designed to evaluate the greatest religious success story of the twentieth century.

This book is the second in a three-volume initiative to study the rhetorical history of the conservative resurgence of the SBC. The first book dealt with the discovery of the theories of argument employed by the presidents of the SBC (1979–1994) as well as by other men of consequence in the SBC. Professor Emeritus Ray Camp, North Carolina State University, and I wrote the first book, *In the Name of the Father—The Rhetoric of the New Southern Baptist Convention* (1999).

Ray and I contended that there are three bodies of argument to be discovered in the battle for the Bible among Southern Baptists. First, there is the master rhetoric of fundamentalism, that is, that the Bible is inerrant or true in all of its verses. Second, the rhetoric of inerrancy develops a com-

---

2. Walter B. Shurden, *Not a Silent People—Controversies That Have Shaped Southern Baptists* (Macon, GA: Smith & Helwys Publishing, 1995).

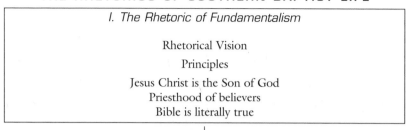

THE RHETORICS OF SOUTHERN BAPTIST LIFE

I. The Rhetoric of Fundamentalism

Rhetorical Vision

Principles

Jesus Christ is the Son of God
Priesthood of believers
Bible is literally true

II. The Rhetoric of Inerrancy

Rhetorical Vision

Principles

Argument from definition
"Bully pulpit"
Bible is literally true

III. The Rhetoric of Exclusion

Rhetorical Vision

Principles

Attack-expulsion paradigm
Fear-comfort argument
Liberal attack

prehensive set of arguments, with scripture as proof warrants, to affirm the Bible as accurate in all matters. Third, we showed that these two rhetorics were forged into a third rhetoric: the rhetoric of exclusion.

The third body of argument, the rhetoric of exclusion, has as its goal the disenfranchisement of any member or church that denies the inerrancy of the Bible. The groups targeted for exclusion are women as ordained leaders, liberals of any persuasion, homosexual church members, and churches that accept homosexuals in their membership.

From 1980 to date, the Southern Baptist Convention has systematically held the line on biblical inerrancy. In that time, approximately one hundred churches have formally dissolved their relationship with the Convention. Additionally, untold numbers of church members have been exiled in profoundly direct and indirect ways. Similarly, untold numbers have simply walked away from the denomination of their youth or adulthood because they could not stop the conservative changes in their church.

The exiled members of the Southern Baptist Convention are victims of the largest takeover or recovery of a Christian denomination in the twentieth century, now extending into the twenty-first century. Ray Camp and I determined in late 1999 that the story of displaced Southern Baptists would serve as the focus of our second book on the SBC controversy, but an unforeseen health matter derailed our plans.

In early January 2000, I received word from Carolyn Camp, Ray's wife, that he had suffered a massive stroke. Along with so many other hopes and dreams in the Camp family, I had lost the best coauthor and scholar I had ever known. The project was shelved and the momentum gained from *In the Name of the Father* was derailed, but not for long.

The *Exiled* project was dramatically revived in the late spring/early summer of 2000 with an infusion of resources and the encouragement of fellow rhetorical scholars in the South. With the assistance of the leadership of the moderate Southern Baptist group—the Cooperative Baptist Fellowship (headquartered in Atlanta, Georgia)—I met with a CBF regional coordinator, Bill Bruster, in Dallas, Texas. With his assistance, I compiled a list of approximately two hundred "exiles" who might (or might not) agree to write their story for the book. Little did I know that I had struck a chord that would resonate across the landscape of moderate Southern Baptist life.

From the spring of 2000 through the fall of 2003, the search for Southern Baptist "exiles" intensified. People of national consequence and people known only to their home church area were contacted, often with little more than "I have a friend you need to contact." Twenty-nine Southern Baptists ultimately agreed to tell their story of displacement, disappointment, and eventual discovery of a new place in life to "do church."

As I read their essays singularly and as a collective body of work, it became clear to me that these representatives of the exiled community of Southern Baptists had created a fourth rhetoric—"The Rhetoric of the Exiled." To a person, each writer affirms the "priesthood of the believer" standard of Southern Baptist life—that is, each person is capable of interpreting the Bible, without an intermediary, as directed by the Holy Spirit.

Referring to themselves as "free" Southern Baptists, the writers in this book are at odds with the inerrant nature of scripture, the position on women as ordained professionals, the rightward leaning of Baptist educational institutions, and the "creedal" nature of the 2000 Baptist Faith and

THE RHETORIC OF THE EXILED

Rhetorical Vision

A free Southern Baptist can affirm the SBC dictum "The Priesthood of the Believer"—as his or her victory over conservative Southern Baptist policies.

The master counterargument to victimage

is

Freedom

thus:

The Metaphors of Freedom

1. As a free Southern Baptist, members are considered by the SBC as:
   - An *enemy*—cast as an *outsider* if they choose to defy SBC guidelines.

2. As a free Southern Baptist, they speak of themselves as:
   - *Grieving*—Speaking of themselves as adrift from a familiar SB home that was beneficial and supportive at one time.

   - *A War Refugee*—Speaking of themselves as adrift from a *place* to which they can no longer return.

   - An *Expatriate*—Speaking of themselves as seeking/finding a *new* place to worship and serve in a new life as a Southern Baptist outside the constraints of the Southern Baptist Convention.

Message (See Appendix for a three-part comparison of the 1925, 1963, and 2000 Baptist Faith and Message).

The stories of *Exiled* are compassionate summaries of the anguish and anger felt by the larger community of sincere, honest, and committed Southern Baptist victims of the "holy war." At the same time, these writers reflect the strength and power of their faith as they struggled against the leadership of the Convention. To their credit, they not only survived, but now flourish in their exilic journey.

It is our hope that this collection of stories serves to warn of the dangers of obsessive fanaticism while calling Southern Baptists to a common rhetorical ground where all can stand firm in their private faith. The history of the controversy over an inerrant Bible would suggest, however, a contrarian perspective.

In every essay, you will read how each writer was cast as the enemy, even an outsider. Then, he or she was set adrift to grieve over a church place they once called home. As refugees of the "holy war," many writers speak of their refugee status in terms of "church shopping," still attending their home church, withdrawing from their home church, or even moving to a new denomination.

Finally, every writer has had an epiphany—a moment of revelation in which they came to accept their status as an expatriate, a banished citizen of Southern Baptist life. This moment in their lives serves to free them from the guilt of being a victim, and transitions them into a new life as a "free" Southern Baptist. No longer in a modern-day Babylonian captivity, the exiles of the Southern Baptist Convention are now set on a course of no return. The Southern Baptist experiences of their present are now relegated to their past.

The church home these writers once knew is no more. Still, as Professor Hill notes in the Introduction, "once a Southern Baptist, always a Southern Baptist." For the exiles, there is a new home somewhere that each can be the Southern Baptist of their dreams and their convictions.

Southern Baptist scholar Kenneth Chafin, writing in *In the Name of the Father*, said it well when he stated that "I also know many of the victims—individuals who have been injured, institutions that are being destroyed, and Baptist principles that are being laid to rest. The victims who touch my heart most are people whose lives have been, and still are being, damaged. . . . One reason the takeover movement was so successful was in how it dealt with those who dissented. Those who disagreed with the takeover leaders were attacked, labeled, isolated, and banned."[3]

The clear message of this book is that, in the twenty-first century, the exiled have a new voice: a rhetoric of freedom and a spirit of hopefulness for the future. For them, there is a new and exciting promised land. They are no longer in captivity; they are free. But their freedom came in the crucible of a Convention at war with itself and its history. It is to the history of Southern Baptists that we turn to learn from whence they came and whither they are bound.

In their Forewords, Ms. Crumpler and Dr. Dunn have borne witness to their stories of national disappointment and subsequent journeys as exiles. In the Introduction to follow, Professor Hill sets the historical scene in motion. Then the twenty-nine writers reveal the central message of the book: dissent brings expulsion that brings renewal and freedom.

3. Carl L. Kell and L. Raymond Camp, *In the Name of the Father—The Rhetoric of the New Southern Baptist Convention* (Carbondale: Southern Illinois University Press, 1999), xv.

The third and last volume of rhetorical history is under way. *Against the Wind—The Moderate Voice in Southern Baptist Life* will chronicle and evaluate the earliest expressions of the voices of Southern Baptists and show how the typical members and dominant leaders learned a new language and found a new voice to counter the voices of change in Southern Baptist life. The completion of this initiative is for another day.

There is mutual agreement between Southern Baptists on both sides of the controversy. Both factions see their special calls to personal soul winning and missioning the world for Jesus Christ. From the earliest days of Convention life, there have been countless bumps in the road regarding soul winning and missions. In spite of their problems, Southern Baptists have prevailed on both fronts and from both sides of the aisle—conservative and moderate.

Exiled tells a different story—stories of casualties and stories of renewal and release along the way to the realm of God. In the larger context of Southern Baptist life, these are stories from the margins, far away from the bright lights of Convention life. These are bittersweet expressions of what contributor Gregory L. Hancock says is "a lot like dying." *Exiled* is not a "pretty" book, yet it is a book of hope. In that spirit, all of these writers are heroes of Southern Baptist life.

There are many ways to tell the Southern Baptist story of controversy, conflict, and crisis. Professor Samuel S. Hill graces this book with a personal and professional analysis of the Southern Baptist "holy war" in the larger context of Southern religious history. Writing for all of the contributors, we thank him for setting the tone for *Exiled—Voices of the Southern Baptist Convention Holy War.*

ACKNOWLEDGMENTS

First, I am grateful to my Western Kentucky University colleagues and the agencies who have supported and sustained the work of rhetorical scholarship in the study of the takeover of the Southern Baptist Convention. I appreciate the leadership and encouragement of Dr. Sally J. Ray, Department Head, Department of Communication. Next, I received valuable support from Dean David Lee, Potter College of Arts, Humanities, and Social Sciences. Year in and year out, as *Exiled* took shape, these two colleagues sustained my efforts with release time from instruction and the resources necessary to complete the manuscript.

Second, I am indebted to Dean Elmer Gray, dean of graduate study and chair of the WKU Faculty Scholarship Council, and to Dr. Phillip E. Myers, director of Sponsored Programs, for their financial support, without which *Exiled* could not have been completed. The costs of scholarship are high and require administrative support and patience. These two colleagues have supplied all of the resources necessary for the work at hand.

Third, I am indebted to my good friends Bill Sumners and Jean Forbis of the Southern Baptist Historical Library and Archives, Nashville, Tennessee, for their assistance over the years.

Fourth, I am honored by the contribution of Dr. Samuel S. Hill, professor emeritus of religion, the University of Florida. Dr. Hill's *Southern Churches in Crisis* (1960) helped to establish southern religious history as a field of scholarly inquiry. Some forty years later, *Southern Churches in Crisis* continues to be widely read, quoted, and cited. Professor Hill's Introduction to this volume captures the scope and sentiment of the exilic journey away from the conservative resurgence of the Southern Baptist Convention.

I was convinced during the research phase of *Exiled* that I would need stories from men and women of national consequence in the takeover struggle who suffered personal and professional losses. Two names came immediately to mind, and they agreed to write at length about their experiences.

I am grateful to Carolyn Crumpler and Dr. James Dunn for their in-depth stories in the Forewords to this book. Taken together, Dr. Hill, Dr. Dunn, and Ms. Crumpler provide a unique perspective on the takeover of the Southern Baptist Convention that is second to none on the bookshelves of Southern Baptist history.

Most of all, I am forever indebted to the twenty-nine men and women, selected from among two hundred potential contributors, who agreed to participate. For those who declined to contribute, their decision was marked by an often agonizing, always interesting letter, phone message, or e-mail. From them, I learned about the pain of being part of a denomination and/or a local church that had turned them away. I am convinced that the stories of these Southern Baptists are representative of thousands of others who experienced an involuntary displacement from their denominational home. Of the thirty-one contributors to this book, I have met only four. That these twenty-seven men and women would agree to write for and trust a total stranger is a testimony to the psychological and spiritual release of telling their stories of exile.

Finally, my wife, Mary Anne, deserves the last and best credit. For twenty-five years, she has supported my efforts in researching the rhetorical strategies of the takeover of the Southern Baptist Convention. If my work was wrongheaded, I was always set straight. If my critical analyses of rhetorical events were correct, I was always encouraged to look deeper. I was made to understand that truth is hard to come by. In all matters, she would ask, "Is that what you really want to say?" When I demurred, she was the voice of clarity and realism. No critic or husband could ask for more.

ACKNOWLEDGMENTS

For every book in the marketplace, there is an extraordinary professional guiding every line and correcting every error. My profound thanks to Zee Evelsizer of the office staff of the provost and vice-president for academic affairs of Western Kentucky University. She is as good an assistant as any writer could expect to find in the precise world of scholarship.

To my mentor, Ralph T. Eubanks, retired, University of Arkansas, my best regards and thanks for opening the world of southern oratory to a young man in love with the South. I was taught that the spoken word can lift the soul to heaven or save it from hell, whether from the pulpit or the political stump. Ralph T. Eubanks placed me in the audience of these orators of the South, then and now, where I learned to listen, reflect, and evaluate the thrilling rhetoric of the times.

In the final hours of manuscript preparation, I learned of the passing, on July 10, 2004, of Eleanor Williamson. Ms. Williamson was the first contributor to agree to have her story in print. My regards to her immediate family are but a small recompense to the "Everywoman" of *Exiled*. Ms. Eleanor speaks for her church, her gender, and her generation in words both eloquent and sweet, unlike any other I have encountered. Thank you, Ms. Eleanor.

To all of these important players in the development of *Exiled*, thank you and God speed you on your road to freedom.

INTRODUCTION

Samuel S. Hill

I might well have been one of those interviewed for Carl Kell's voices of people "exiled" by the radical changes that have recently occurred in the Southern Baptist Convention. That is true despite the fact that my church membership shifted away from SBC affiliation more than three decades ago. Like the thirty-one people whose statements we have here, I too feel excluded and suffer from a sense of loss.

What sense does it make for a person who formally left the Baptist ranks so many years ago to consider himself a candidate for exilic status? The explanation lies in the truism, "Once a Southern Baptist, always a Southern Baptist." Such loose, seemingly frivolous generalizations certainly do not apply to all denominational switching. But they often do to people who move from the SBC, the Roman Catholic Church, the Mormon Church, and other communities of faith with similar strong identification so that, particularly in the cases of professional adherents or those nonordained members nearly so, your whole life is bound up.

Why so, wherein? For one thing, the message of religious groups with powerful self-identity that instill in you what to believe and how to live is presented forcefully and repeatedly. In those cases, your hearing is attuned and your mind is shaped. For another, the style of preaching and worship is distinctive, rendering all other approaches—to the same Christian message even—seem almost foreign. Switchers from such bodies as these experience great difficulty in feeling at home anywhere else.

Specifically in the Southern Baptist case, the most important reason is that membership affords you a kind of Total Culture. The denomination is held up as possessing a special destiny, uniquely gifted and responsible, as being something akin to God's last and best hope for Christianizing the entire world and almost, it sometimes seems, to civilizing the whole world. The SBC is a highly self-conscious denomination, regarding cooperating with other Christian communions as really unnecessary even if somewhat desirable, at least for most clergy and a large company of faithful lay members. The momentum always tilts towards isolation. Being a part of the SBC provides you with so much: home, friends, friends of friends, mannerisms, styles of speech and a vocabulary, theological and cultural perspectives, and a proud heritage—all of that in league with its sense of destiny. It speaks a different language—not just a southern accent—from other bodies, even Baptist and evangelical ones. It really does.

The contributors of testimony that make up this book reveal the power that the denomination holds for them. We can expect that the pain of exclusion will be acute for ministers and persons employed by the SBC, but it cuts just about as deeply into the hearts of many who are Sunday school teachers, deacons, faithful attenders of Wednesday night prayer meeting, and officeholders in congregations.

The recent disruption of this particular Total Culture, thus, is having a seismic-like effect, somewhat comparable to developments in the Roman Catholic Church in the wake of the Second Vatican Council. The SBC disruption issues from the struggle initiated by a brilliantly organized, militant, take-no-prisoners sector of pastors and determined lay leaders in the late 1970s. Their driving force? To take back the Convention from generations of leaders who were too loose in holding to the "truth once for all delivered to the saints."

The rescue party was initially referred to as "fundamentalists," a term that they rather gladly claimed; those opposing them, perpetuators of the SBC leadership and outlook long in positions and offices that enabled them to give broad direction to the body, were called "moderates." A few years later, the titles evolved, respectively, to "fundamental conservatives" and "moderate conservatives." While this wording probably carries the greatest accuracy, it too phased out, so that the reigning usage applied to the two camps is "conservatives" and "moderates."

What was/is the struggle all about? A glimpse at their history provides illumination. Despite its popular reputation as a "fundamentalist" denomination, despite its standing as a curiosity to the general public that just can't figure them out—so large and so wealthy, so much at home in their world, yet so standoffish and so distinctive—the Southern Baptist Convention has not been fundamentalist. In fact, it has been rather progressive and very much (southern) culture-affirming. (Classical fundamentalism has been either hostile or indifferent to human culture.) Also this body, notwithstanding its massive size, has displayed considerable diversity, not in ethnic or racial terms, but in outlook and temperament. These devout Christians for a long time managed to subordinate their differences, in the words of a term close to their hearts, to a single cause: "evangelism and missions." Also, they thought of themselves as family, a unit in which severe fractures were intolerable. With these principles consistently before them, they rarely allowed differences to fester and burst, except under especially turbulent conditions. This dual agenda and their sense of family and destiny have been their life force; a notable cooperation was forged long ago around those twin goals in that constituency where unity was very highly prized.

All that has changed. Beyond any doubt, all that has changed. Tolerance, even respect, for differing theological positions is an attitude that has been declared intolerable by the conservative ("fundamentalist") sector. That company has shown unyielding determination to establish correct belief as the test of faith and the supreme characteristic of true biblical understanding. Correct belief is the number-one requirement. Stated baldly, they have insisted on unexceptionable subscription to certain basic doctrines, or absolute obedience to absolute truth definitively understood. They share with some other conservative Protestant bodies the commitment to testing and proving. Each person's affirmation of faith must be tested for authenticity and proved to be in line.

The issue of authority, thus, has overwhelmed all other concerns. Battle lines have been drawn between biblical inerrancy, the conservatives' watchword, and biblical infallibility, held to by the moderates. This distinction refers to "the biblical text is without error at all, in any respect" in the case of inerrancy, and to "the authority of the biblical message" as the sole basis of faith and truth, spelling out the meaning of infallibility. Heavy, even tortured, as such discussion may seem to many men and women of other churches (and more than a few insiders), it forms the outline of a life-and-death struggle within the SBC.

SAMUEL S. HILL

These conservatives do resemble classical fundamentalism in one important respect. They are as conscious of error as they are of truth, as directly on the attack against heresy as they are aggressive about the truthfulness of scripture. Their program is equally given over to the negative and the positive. They identify enemies of God's truth and wage war vigorously. Chief among the enemies that provoke their onslaughts are, sadly, fellow Southern Baptists—the moderates who, they reckon, have every reason to know better but have succumbed to modern ways of thinking generally described as "the cancer of liberalism." They fear that the SBC, called to be a (the) special people of God, will follow the liberal mainline denominations, such as Presbyterians, Methodists, Episcopalians, and Lutherans, down into compromise and spiritual death.

Purity is their aim. It is also their claim. To be precise, they exalt *rational* purity, total allegiance to God's truth absolutely grounded and perfectly set forth in the inerrant scriptures.

Between the mid-1970s and 1990 or so, the annual meeting of the Southern Baptist Convention was a virtual donnybrook. From the beginning of this series of clashes, it was pretty clear that the conservatives would prevail. Their ranks were tightly and efficiently organized, and they formulated a crystal-clear message that generated a powerful attack. From winning the office of Convention president (meaning the power to nominate officers), they advanced to controlling the various Convention agencies and the personnel in the six theological seminaries. At one point a Peace Committee was created to seek to facilitate conversation between the factions, but this too failed; indeed, its efforts to build bridges and to work toward reconciliation only succeeded in highlighting how divergent their two paths were. For the past dozen or so years, the moderate constituency has been conspicuous by its absence from the annual meeting. The conquest is complete. There is nothing excessive about characterizing their annual deliberations as rubber-stamp events.

This wide gap separating the conservatives from the moderates in the SBC must be seen for what it is; a comparative perspective can help us understand. When looked at that way, the observer can only conclude that anything resembling historic Protestant liberalism is all but unknown in this setting. Truth be told, both groups are conservative. They do differ, but not along lines describable as liberal and conservative. In both cases, nothing but the Bible possesses authority for the message preached and lived. In both cases, the God revealed in Christ is presented as calling for obedience and worship; also, with particular emphasis, the people are called to experience this God, to "know the Lord in their hearts." The hallowed twin themes of evangelism and missions are magnified in both companies. Both display Southern Baptist qualities and styles unmistakably. Other kinds of Baptists (and evangelicals in general) find themselves not quite at home in either setting, conservative or moderate. We must be clear that this is a family struggle, internecine strife.

The old adage, blood is thicker than water, seems to apply. Claims and counterclaims have been hurled back and forth. A once unified, if hardly united, Southern Baptist Convention now is in a shambles. Conversation across this great divide has become impossible. Of course, the party in power does not recognize this condition, because they have been led to the disenfranchisement of all others—in obedience to divine leading.

The conservatives stand by a nonnegotiable set of doctrines and an unexceptionable principle of knowing—namely, unswerving subscription to rational propositions. They give ultimate credence to the status of doctrinal formulation as much as to doctrines themselves. In historic terms, this is some version of Aristotelian epistemology, not Platonist in the manner of St. Augustine (and Southern Baptists' most celebrated theologian, E. Y. Mullins), or nominalist as Martin Luther understood the biblical message. Denominationally, the SBC conservatives show more epistemic affinity with, say, the Dutch Reformed tradition (though hardly in all its manifestations) and Roman Catholicism (which requires much more than proper belief) than with classical Protestantism. When we see clearly this characteristic of the conservatives, we draw close to their central issue: the epistemic imprecision practiced by the moderates leads to indefensible accommodation to prevailing cultural currents, and putative Christians who behave this way are sounding the death knell. Just look at the decline in membership totals—a criterion of the greatest significance to the SBC—of Lutherans, Presbyterians, and Episcopalians, they point out. The body that turns in a liberal direction has doomed its cause.

Understanding truth in that way, while far from dominant in the denomination's past, has been elevated to the standing of sine qua non. Those who are not faithful on *how* the truth is known are simply living in error. (Of course, there is always correlation between the "how" issue and *what* is known, no matter the epistemic route taken). It follows that the moderates' deviance must be opposed and destroyed, and that no negotiating what biblical teaching is can be permissible; any such procedure would amount to unfaithfulness, to compromise, which is the most unsavory of all traits.

SAMUEL S. HILL

We need to address the observation that this way of knowing is far
from dominant in their past. To be sure, this godly company has always
been staunchly committed to the exclusive authority of the biblical text—
that is, to the infallibility of the biblical message. Moreover, these Christians have been doubt-free with respect to the total reliability of the texts
in that huge collection of writings. If "literalist" is too strong a designation of their way of reading scripture, it is so only in some technical way.
Emphatically they have not regarded it as referring to eternal truth in
some figurative or symbolic manner. They have stood foursquare against
any reader's tinkering with the text's meaning, with any imposition of
human (manmade) interpretations on the divine revelation. They have
resisted many "latest" and "hottest" new ways of discerning the message
of the Word of God. Or, to state the matter in a way these devout believers in scripture would find familiar, they just believed what they had always
believed, what they had always heard: the plain, pretty self-evident teaching of the Bible.

Well then, one may ask, why can't we say without equivocation that
the Southern Baptist people, alike in the pulpit and the pew, have been
"literalists"? Partly because they have been little interested in any debate
on the nature of biblical authority. All have always declared: if the Bible
says it, I believe it. Moreover, the *status* of formulations has not been any
kind of concern; instead they have turned to scripture to hear God's message to the world. (Aristotelian modes of thought have been recessive.)
They have had small reason to ask any "first principles" questions, mostly
because very few challenges have been hurled at these Bible-believers
either in church or in the culture. Busy reading it devotionally, given to understanding better what they already knew, they have assumed that there
are many more miles to be traveled along the road to a thorough grasp of
the Bible's meaning. At the same time, they have never doubted that they
were on the correct path. Something more, rather than something different, is the goal to which they have seen themselves as led.

The pervasive Southern Baptist understanding of the Bible has thrived
in the realm of personal experience, as a matter of the heart more than of
the head. In one role, they have read it as evangelists, a people called to
bear witness to the unsaved, the lost, persons at home and abroad who
have not yet trusted Christ as their personal savior. In practice, this particular mandate has applied more to pastors than to people in the congregations. But the latter could hardly have read it without noting—and being
constantly reminded of—that theme in many passages of the New Testa-

ment. Whether or not they have been personally given to soul-saving, they study the Bible as a saved community, individuals who now are called to embody the fruits of the redeemed life. Of course, that condition has a great deal to do with ethical living. What the scriptures of both testaments direct godly people to do, how to live their lives, bulk large as incentive to thoughtful study.

Just as basic, however, is a devotional (or pietist) reading of the text. The longing for inspiration, for a vibrant sense of God's presence in their lives as lived out daily in such settings as family and neighborhood, has dominated those "sweet" moments when they hold the sacred text in their hands and concentrate on feeling the reality of God in their hearts.

In all probability, if you were to ask these servants of the Lord, most Southern Baptist people throughout their history, whether they were biblical literalists, the response would likely be, why, yes. Or, really, why do you ask? What else is there, what other faithful way to read scripture? Their minds, in most cases anyway, might briefly ponder what, if any, devout alternatives there are to literalism. They have no other intention than to let the Bible speak for itself. That point notwithstanding, the strongest lure of Bible study has had to do with personal devotional life, with knowing certain key texts, a number of whole psalms and book chapters, and familiarity with biblical stories that offer the concerned soul practical help in steering through the rapids of life in a turbulent world that too often dishonors God. They have turned to it for guidance, for challenge, to pray for the healing of sick persons and those confused and distressed, for gaining the spiritual power to live faithfully, for courage to make demanding decisions. In short, intimate knowledge of the Bible affords inner equipping to enable the person redeemed by Christ's blood to live worthily and victoriously.

This son of that tradition offers these descriptions as coming close to capturing the attitudes of most earnest Southern Baptist people, no less now than before the eruption of the warfare over what the Bible is (more than what it says), the concern that has roiled the body during the past quarter-century. The public face of the denomination, of course, suggests otherwise. The spotlight has shone on the public policy statements, those top-level decisions of the SBC ruling sector that give priority to the concern to define the precise message and mission of the churches, then mandate conformity to those definitions. What the faithful read in the media and what they hear from the most prominent voices all refer to orthodoxy, "straight thinking." But one suspects that what occurs in Sunday school classrooms and around family tables devotes more attention to the application of biblical teaching to life in the world. Moreover, one hopes that such smaller group gatherings demonstrate a gentleness and a quietness in a spirit of open inquiry that do not characterize official meetings and public pronouncements. To underscore that point, gentleness is a missing quality in the language and spirit of the conservatives.

Personal piety has been replaced by rational purity, correctness of belief. The Convention's preoccupation has turned away from cultivation of godly living to defense of doctrinal propriety. In this huge Baptist fellowship where the action historically has been local, that is, in individuals' lives and in nearly forty thousand congregations—large, small, and medium, in cities, towns, and the countryside—there has been a shift to a centralized structure in which the defining of a message to hold the line against heresy and preventing the encroachment of cultural perversions now supersedes everything.

The thirty-one exiles telling their stories in this book reveal the classical Southern Baptist love for the Bible in the Psalmist's words as God's "lamp to my feet and light to my path." What they are hearing from the central leadership—and increasingly are likely to hear from the pulpit of the neighborhood church now that revised seminary education is informing rising generations of pastors in the new way—has to do with prolegomenon, a version of a here's-what-you-are-reading manual, with details on how-you-MUST-understand-it. The "first principle" has upstaged the meaning of the text itself.

That, of course, is not the traditional Baptist way, certainly not the Southern Baptist way, and it is far removed from classical Protestantism's insight that "God has yet more light to break forth from his holy word." The shift from assurance that each reader's "soul competency" (a powerful theme enunciated by past Southern Baptist leaders), acknowledging the capacity and responsibility of individual Christians to interpret scripture, to the insistence that scripture's meaning is thus-and-such as asserted by a virtual Baptist creed—itself a historical contradiction—is disturbing. Far more, it threatens to destroy the biblical basis of their piety. The category of truth has overwhelmed the category of persons. To paraphrase a saying of Jesus, with its logic turned upside down, they find themselves hearing that the Bible was not made for man but man for the Bible.

Hardly less disruptive, especially for ministers and denominational agency leaders, is the shattering of this body that has served as Total Culture in the ordering of their lives. I recall pointing to this particular current in Southern Baptist life, when I confidently declared in 1983 during a lectureship at the body's oldest seminary (of which my father and I both are graduates) that the movement to set the denomination straight, then gaining strength, was destined to fail. "You don't turn your back on Mother" are the exact words that I used in assuring my hearers that unity would prevail. If there are degrees of wrongness, my prediction was the wrongest it could be.

The severity of my miscalculation comes nowhere near rivaling the anguished pain—and incredulity—of hundreds of thousands of the faithful such as the voices heard in the following pages. "Mother church," a Roman Catholic term poorly suited to Baptist ecclesiology (but not without some practical merit), has been subverted; the Total Culture that has provided so much has vanished. Southern Baptist readers will understand such extreme language, as will some from other Christian bodies. But you do have to take serious note in the Southern Baptist case of regional culture and society as a salient factor. The American South from the Civil War following (with roots dating back a few decades) has been the setting, the home, a sustaining company to the people of the SBC.

This is nowhere better demonstrated than by observing how southern culture (now in the secular sense) has been shaped by this one massive religious body. Other center-to-right Protestant groups, notably the Methodists and Presbyterians, have felt the influence in their methods and emphases of this larger-than-life company. More than a few Episcopal leaders have noted how hard they have had to work to teach their parishioners wherein their version of the Christian tradition is different. Overstating the Baptists' influence on southern life and society would amount to quite a stretch. Ask any man or woman running for elective office. Note the wording of prayers offered at the opening of a new business or, at least still in certain locales, before public events. Open the subject with newcomers to southern cities who moved there from "the North."

A number of efforts, some one hundred books and many essays, have been offered in an effort to account for this dramatic change in Southern Baptist ways of thinking and organizing their formal denominational life. One prominent effort has been to tie this religious change to the breakup of the once recognizable, pretty solid southern culture. That such a disruption of the "southern culture" long taken for granted by most citizens of Dixie has occurred is acknowledged by almost everyone—and lamented by more than a few. Familiar ways of relating to other people, earning a living, coexisting in neighborhoods, carrying on conversations, and many more everyday conventions have been challenged. Public schools, once quasi-Protestant establishments, have been transformed in size and have been consolidated; that is, they are no longer coterminous with neighborhood or town, *and* they have become interracial. The courts have been raising troubling questions about the suitability of prayer in the classroom and at commencements and athletic events. The display of the Ten Commandments in public buildings is being prohibited. What then, many thousands are wondering, may we look to as the foundations for orderly living? Equally fundamentally, what holds this regional people together, or for that matter, any regional people? Are there today any books that everybody knows (most notably the Bible), traditions that identify a citizenry, jokes and tales that resonate broadly, points of connection that assist in making graceful efforts to develop acquaintance with new people? How do you open a conversation? Can you talk about church and beliefs, so long a conversation starter and a matter of genuine concern? (Summing up, is there a specifiable region anymore? Do you know where you are, culturally speaking, and does that matter anymore in the kind of world we are becoming?)

In cities and larger towns, unfamiliar ethnic groups have been appearing for some years. For one thing, persons with heritages other than Anglo-Saxon are one's neighbors. Besides national ethnicity—European, Asian, Latino, and so forth—American regional ethnicity is an issue. Many life patterns fall outside familiar ways and forms. Black people are present in new ways. They now prefer being referred to as African American. Those longtime fellow citizens live near by, certainly nearer by; their children share the same school classrooms, and you shop and recreate in the same settings. Yet, not enough deep-level interaction seems to be occurring; very little church life sharing appears possible. And so on. Repeating, is there a specifiable region anymore? Do you know where you are? Inevitably, people begin to ask, so what? Perhaps familiar cultural ways are no longer possible, and maybe that doesn't matter so much? But what is replacing that? And how do I adjust?

Redirecting the subject without changing it, certain Southern Baptist leaders, perhaps always conservative, wake up to see that their world is damaged, threatening to fall apart. Familiar cultural ways have disappeared; the automatic "owning" of people, customs, and values by Baptist (and similar) churches has ceased. Something seems horribly awry. Disaster has struck. The time for action has been thrust upon sensitive religious leaders. We, the responsible leaders, one hears them think, must yield not another inch to forces of modernity. And now that we think about it, they continue, our seminaries and many "progressive" pastors show signs of accommodating too readily to the ways of a changed and, surely, dissolute world.

The litany becomes: We must hold the line, we must work hard to regain our cultural sway, we must firmly pursue a strategy that brooks no departure from biblical orthodoxy. Just getting along cannot be a premium virtue. Compromising in the interest of denominational unity is intolerable. Any such attitude is, ultimately, an offense to Almighty God.

This kind of social/cultural analysis is appealing because it points to the situation on the ground. No institution or tradition surrenders easily when the loss of its prominence or power is threatened. And there is no doubt that the information age with all its attendant traits is becoming as powerful in the South as elsewhere. The small town or rural area, or even the metropolitan area once made up of country people moved to town— none of these forms of life together has been normative for the South for a generation. Thus, the urgency to refuse to give in anymore runs deep.

But the persuasiveness of this sociological kind of analysis tells only part of the story. Curiously, it underrates the very modernness of the conservative leaders themselves. These men and women see life in the large, not simply their state or region. The whole world, Western and developed at any rate, has fallen under error's spell. Postmodernism and relativism have gripped the existing and emerging human cultures in their foul clutches. The changes they aim for in the American South must encompass the entire world. Here is where the high-powered Southern Baptist engine kicks in. From the aftermath of the Civil War forward, the southern devout have inclined to see their mission as universal, their responsibility as urgent. While the American people at large have tended to think of the nation as God's new Israel, the faithful people of the southern region, in displaying the highest degree of dedication and purity to embodying an Israel-like calling, have raised that designation to the highest power. The twenty-first century is seen as the age for which God has been preparing the Southern Baptist people all along. They are commissioned to hold the line against error and compromise; they are called to bring the world to the truth; they are instructed to practice the unique calling that the Almighty has issued them.

It is surely difficult—to the point of impossibility—for people in the rest of the nation, much less in Europe and elsewhere in Christendom, to grasp the gravity, grandiosity, and degree of the Southern Baptist vision of itself and its divine vocation. In fact, most are not aware of it. Whether they have seen it or not, there really is a high-powered engine that is now revved up. The leaders are deadly serious. Their first community of influence is the denomination and its homeland, for certain, but they have set their sights on the entire human population. They must obliterate the ways of thinking that date back to the Enlightenment. A broader way of practicing "go ye into all the world," as their central New Testament passage impels Christians to do, has been laid at their feet.

The tragedy of this new condition is that the perspectives of many thousands of Southern Baptist people, represented in these pages by the contributors to Carl Kell's valuable collection, are repudiated by these earnest leaders. More painful by far is their rejection, their total exclusion from the mission, once so widely shared, of being servants of God in building churches, homes, and lives. Some of the testimony givers have been banished from positions of leadership. Many more have been deprived of voice and vote as their congregations have been stigmatized as "liberal," meaning in actuality heretical, even traitorous toward the truth. Responses that originated as incredulity, then anger, have modulated to anguish, the deepest pain.

As you read, be sure to listen, to feel, and to capture both their sense of rejection and their longing, if anything now increased, to return from exile to membership in communities of faith.

There will be no returning. The body they once loved, in which they served, does not exist anymore. Not well equipped by their comfortable past to find a home setting anywhere else, they must nevertheless endeavor to locate one. More likely, they will join forces with others among the dispossessed to generate new forms of traditional southern Baptist life. That they will do, so great is their dedication, but not without continuing anguish over what happened to "home." The era of new beginnings is before them.

SOUTHERN BAPTIST WOMAN IN EXILE

Eleanor B. Williamson

When Susan B. Anthony first began her fight for women's rights in the nineteenth century, she saw a union threatened by the practice of slavery. In addition to this abusive injustice, Anthony saw another type of bondage. Just as slaves belong to their masters, wives belong to their husbands. That's the way the law read—Blackstone's old English common law that bluntly stated, "The husband and wife are one, and that one is the husband."[1]

In America, that meant that a married woman could not own property, make contracts, sue or be sued, or among other inequities be the guardian of her own children. If women worked outside the home, they were required to give the money to their husbands. Further, women could not attend college (there were none for females), and of course they could not vote.

During her lifetime, Anthony worked tirelessly to reverse this wrong and to win women's suffrage and other rights. Fourteen years after her death in 1906, the Nineteenth Amendment gave women the right to vote. That was eighty-one years ago, and today there is something about the *new* Southern Baptist fundamentalist movement that sounds like the old English law. Women who reject this subjugation find themselves in exile from the world's largest Christian denomination, in which they once had great faith.

---

1. Lynn Sheer, *Failure Is Impossible: Susan B. Anthony in Her Own Words* (New York: Random House, 1995), introd.

When the takeover of the Southern Baptist Convention began in 1979, one of the fundamentalists' first objectives was to gain control over its eight million female members. Thus the infamous and existing tradition that Southern Baptist women could not preach was intensified with the warning that they were not to speak from the pulpit nor any *man's space*.

Another existing tradition was women's role in missions work (which functioned as a separate entity). Through the years, it was not uncommon for Southern Baptist clergy to resent the strong and auspicious Women's Missionary Union. When the fundamentalists gained authority, it was extremely painful for them to share their newfound fame with anything controlled by women. Subsequently, the walls of the century-old WMU began to crumble. When *they* dusted off Blackstone's old English law book and added the statement, "Women should submit to their husbands," in the 2000 Baptist Faith and Message, it also meant women were to remain "silent in the church even on the subject of missions."

Another new test for Southern Baptist women and men was to affirm the inerrancy or belief that the Bible is without error. Any debate over access to scripture interpretation was overruled. This mandate was a strong repudiation of religious liberty as Southern Baptists previously knew it. When the rumor spread that the fundamentalist movement sought to infiltrate and to take over the First church in every city, I became frightened. Even more frightening was the fact that my church peers didn't seem to care. They just "wanted to keep the church *pure* and as it had always been." It didn't matter that the autonomy of the local church grew less important each year and that our seminaries and other agencies were being taken over by the strong arm of fundamentalism.

My Baptist heritage came mostly from my mother. When she was expecting me, she was concerned that she would miss teaching her Sunday school class a few times. In that mid-Missouri Southern Baptist church atmosphere of childhood missions, I dreamed of being a missionary and going to a foreign country. When the time was right, I accepted God's Plan of Salvation and joined the Southern Baptist Church—which I thought were one and the same. In retrospect, it was a great time to be a Southern Baptist child.

The dream of being an overseas missionary didn't materialize, but I did have the good fortune of graduating from then–Southwest Baptist College at Bolivar, Missouri. It was there that I learned about the Cooperative Program, other Southern Baptist entities, and about great Southern Baptist men as George W. Truett, Herschel Hobbs, and B. H.

Caroll, to name a few. Learning Missouri's Southern Baptist history was also in the mix.

Much later as a divorced mother, I was a likely candidate for all that was alleged to be wrong with righteous Southern Baptist women. It didn't matter that I was a dedicated Christian mother and public school teacher. In addition, I raised four young and impressionable children during the turbulent sixties and seventies. Still we had many good times. When we needed spiritual help and a church home, we found both at Springfield's FBC. Thus, when we were not at school, the church was the *good news* in our lives.

After retirement, I lived five years in the Pacific Northwest. In my church there, I met the widow of Southwestern Seminary graduate Leonard B. Sigle, the man who was mostly responsible for returning Southern Baptists to the Northwest in 1946–47. We agreed that I would write his story. What a story it was! Due to an 1895 Comity Agreement in which North and South Baptists stayed in their own territory, Southern Baptists were in retreat from 1939 Oregon and California. Subsequently, Sigle joined the Landmark, later Missionary Baptist Church. For over ten years, he worked with them, started their kind of churches and prayed for Southern Baptists' return to the Northwest. But before his prayers were answered, the influence of World War II caused California to reopen its doors to the SBC; Oregon and Washington followed. When the Sigle biography was finished, I understood what it meant to be a man of true Southern Baptist principles. (I often speculate what Sigle would think of the fundamentalist takeover of his beloved Southern Baptist Convention.)

When the Cooperative Baptist Fellowship first appeared in the early 1990s, FBC Springfield and others allowed members to send their missions money to CBF. However, this was threatening to the ruling power, and war clouds fell over our church. Speculating without facts, some church members accused the CBF as being pro-abortion and pro–gay rights, among other things. After three open meetings in 1997, the congregation voted to exclude CBF from the church and thus to send its members into exile.

I cried for weeks; my pain exists today for the fellowship and freedom I once enjoyed with the FBC, SBC, and more recently the Missouri Baptist Convention. Presently, I belong to University Heights Baptist Church in Springfield, Missouri, which allows members to follow historic Baptist principles. They believe in the Bible, separation of church and state, priesthood

ELEANOR B. WILLIAMSON

of the believer, and local congregation autonomy. In addition, they believe men and women are equal in God's sight and allow women to be deacons. Finally, they support the WMU and its World Mission goals.

From the womb to almost my grave, I faithfully served what I felt was the world's foremost denomination. In the twilight of my life, I search for the meaning of what happened to my cherished Convention, its people, and its future. Right now, I am in exile and realize the situation will probably not change in my lifetime.

MY STORY:
A PERSONAL ADVENTURE IN UNHOLY RIGHTEOUSNESS

Joe Yelton

Like most children reared in southern tradition mixed with Baptist participation, I rarely gave much thought to what it meant to be Baptist. In fact,
I was beyond childhood before noticing that Baptist is spelled with a *p* and
not a *b*. The sign outside my home church, First Baptist of Asheville, North
Carolina, was the instructor. The usual mix of Sunbeams, RAs, and youth
activities flavored a rich tradition of preaching and teaching. I was Baptist
and felt good about it.

My unassuming Baptist world would be changed forevermore when my
pastor, Dr. Cecil Sherman, returned from the 1979 annual meeting of the
SBC, warning of ominous clouds on the horizon. I believed him, but was
certain that there must be some exaggeration to the thoughts given over
a coming "Convention-wide split." After all, the SBC was too large to split,
and the Cooperative Program was too perfect to leave. Or so I thought.

I attended my first SBC annual meeting in 1981. It was held in Los
Angeles. This would be the first of ten in a row. The 1990 Convention

meeting in New Orleans would not assuredly be my last. Frankly, it was not the political outcomes of those conventions that drove me away. I can lose with grace; after all, I am a Democrat. It was the feeling, year after year, that I had been congregationally and politically raped that tapped the final coffin nail. Upon my return from national Convention meetings, I would be out of sorts for weeks, trying to piece together why it is that I am a proud Southern Baptist. Witnessing brutish power in the name of God was and is a hard pill to swallow. Determining God's will based on majority vote was sickening.

During the early 1980s, I led the church I pastored to move our Co-operative Program giving to 22 percent of our annual budget. Though a small-town church, this sacrifice was a gladly received opportunity. We understood we had to give more to make up for the SBC megachurch leadership who gave either nothing or token contributions.

By this time, I not only knew that Baptist was spelled with a *p*, I also understood something of our rich heritage and our historic belief in soul competency and local church independence. I watched year by year as the uncompromisable was compromised. Churches were told how to select ministers, women were told how to serve and not serve God, and those who had given their life's blood in service to God through the SBC were shown the proverbial door.

Oddly enough, it was two events that occurred in the SBC annual meeting in San Antonio that sealed for me the reality that my tenure within the SBC was concluding. No matter what the armchair quarterbacks back home said about this being strictly a "preacher's fight" that would never directly impact them, I knew from these events that it was much, much more.

The first happened outside of the convention center when a Criswell Bible College student noticed a lapel pin I was wearing. Apparently, he was offended. With his big smile and backslapping "Howdy," we began a dialogue. In this discussion, he would aim most of his darts at the liberalism within Southeastern Baptist Theological Seminary. He was particular in his analysis and scathing in his review. Specific, he was not. He could call no names, no locations, only a litany of stories about what one liberal professor had taught about the virgin birth, and what another had said about homosexuality.

I asked him how much time he spent on the campus to achieve this information. As it turns out, he had never been to North Carolina. I then told him that I had three years invested there, and later my wife fulfilled her two-year commitment. I told him that we were never recipients of such data. He insisted that he had the data "back home." At this impasse, I gave him my card and asked that he mail me the information. Of course, that was the end of that. But from the experience there was solidified for me the reality that truth is of little consequence to these masters of the takeover. What matters is results, and if stories concocted or distorted assisted in this quest, so be it and to God be the glory.

The second lesson came inside the convention center. When the report was being given to the convention regarding a new chair for the Nominating Committee, the Reverend John Reid stood to challenge the nomination. He cited that the proposed candidate was pastor of a non–Southern Baptist Congregation. To this, the convention president countered, "What's your point?" After a moment's hesitation, Reverend Reid responded, "My point Mr. President is, it would seem that in a denomination of thirteen million members, we ought to be able to find at least one of us who is able to chair our Nominating Committee." At this point, he was ruled out of order and was booed as he left the microphone. His point had been made to those of us who were again witnessing the blatant misuse of the president's platform power to propel a personal agenda. To the majority of those in attendance, however, the issue he took with a non–Southern Baptist chairing the Nominating Committee was apparently a non-issue.

That evening, I sat by the hotel pool and struck up a conversation with a stranger. This layman was gentle and kind and quite grandfatherly in his persona. After determining that I, like he, was a messenger to the annual meeting, he said, "Wasn't that mess about the chairman of the nominating committee a disaster?" I assured him of my agreement. But then I realized that we both saw the action as a car wreck, but were at odds over which driver was at fault. He said, "Yes, that man who spoke up about the chairman not being a member of the Southern Baptist Convention was only nit-picking and trying to stir up trouble." It was there that I realized that the Convention of my youth was gone. It was there that I discovered that the chasm separating moderates and conservative/fundamentalist Baptists was too wide and stony to be breached.

In 1992, the church I pastored officially left the SBC. By 1998, I was serving a new congregation, and they too have officially cut all ties to the SBC. Am I proud of this action? No, but I am immensely proud of the congregations who took it. Did we lose anything in the process? We lost nothing that had not already been terminated in the 1980s. Will I look back? No, because I move on to brighter and better ways of cooperatively doing missions. I wish the SBC well. Many good people remain steadfast there. I pray that as the new generation of SBC leadership assumes responsibilities, they, more than their predecessors, will be more intent on truth, kindness, forbearance, scriptural integrity, and righteousness.

A TRUSTEE WHO COULD NO LONGER TRUST

George Steincross

It all commenced in the mid-eighties during my first years as pastor of the Second Baptist Church of Liberty, Missouri. Michael Willett, a person called to missions service by God and prepared for that task at two of the finest Baptist institutions of higher education—William Jewell College of Liberty, Missouri, and Southern Baptist Theological Seminary of Louisville, Kentucky—was in language training. At typical bull sessions in the late hours of night, he entered into various conversations about life, faith, and works.

Interestingly, the Foreign Mission Board called him on the carpet for some of those conversational statements—not intended to be formal statements of theological beliefs but, rather, the give-and-take of a young theology student committed to a search for truth. It seems that another of the students in that language training who had already established truth on every matter had "reported" Michael to the authorities that be.

The Foreign Mission Board sent Michael home and denied him the opportunity to serve God and his denomination in missions theological education. In an effort to bring insight to such devious goings, Michael's pastor of two decades and major Bible professor in college met him at the airport in Atlanta to indicate that what was happening was wrong. In actuality this refusal-to-let-serve was an indictment of a historic Missouri Baptist church and college, to say nothing of the mother seminary of Southern Baptists which had granted him the earned doctorate. That meeting resulted in nothing. It was a wake-up call that persons could and were successfully turning in others in Gestapo fashion and bringing ruin to the good that was happening.

A few years later, the dean of Midwestern Baptist Theological Seminary, Dr. Larry Baker, accepted the call to become the executive director of the Southern Baptist Christian Life Commission. We of Second Baptist Church knew Larry and his family to be people of fruitful Christian faith and works. However, it was not long until he, too, became persona non grata among those who had the truth on every issue and, therefore, as one who refused to say it their way he had to hit the highway.

The crucial issue in this case was abortion. It seems that though the various views about abortion may not have been that far apart, the problem was that Larry would not use the words they wanted him to use. Thankfully, Larry's ministry continued then and now as a beloved pastor of a local church, first in Louisiana and now in New Mexico. The episode was another strong piece of evidence that persons whom we at Second Baptist Church knew to be genuine Christians and historical/mainstream Baptists were not welcome in the new Southern Baptist Convention.

By this time, two specific things were happening in my life. Our church had in operation a Denominational Study Committee that was bringing recommendations for church action as various entities of the Convention were being intentionally taken over and changed. As pastor, it was gratifying to observe laypeople evaluate their faith and how it was, or was not, being affected by a movement gaining strength in its announced intentions to take over their denomination from the inside. At the same time, I was a trustee of the Southern Baptist Theological Seminary. Though Second Baptist Church was only twenty minutes from Midwestern Baptist Theological Seminary, and many students, faculty, and staff were members at Second, my personal witness of what was happening was more stark at Southern.

Things began to change ever so slowly at Southern when Wayne Allen came on the Board of Trustees as an avowed and vocal fundamentalist. As the years went by, more and more fundamentalist trustees were named to the Board. They commenced meeting in caucus sessions.

Those supposedly clandestine meetings were not known for their quiet decorum. One night, a trustee, not included in the caucus, was rooming next door and heard them call Adrian Rogers to receive their marching orders for the next day.

I wish we would have, early on, taken the bold step to declare ourselves independent from the Southern Baptist Convention and what it was becoming, while at the same time emphasizing our dependence on the Bible and our Baptist history for making theological decisions. However, voices that thought this only a pendulum swing and feared a legal battle won the day. Dr. Roy Honeycutt's voiced and clear efforts to maintain Southern as a "centrist" seminary in a diverse Baptist setting were noble but of no avail once the fundamentalists had the votes. Suddenly, they no longer just wanted "parity" and "balance"; they wanted it all.

So much happened during the years of the fundamentalists getting stronger and stronger on the Board. A first-year trustee, at his first trustee meeting, shamefully accused Dr. Honeycutt. A huge document was prepared questioning many professors about statements they had made or written, many taken out of context. In contrast, students who really knew the professors from classroom and life experiences attempted to express themselves in a variety of ways, but no attention was paid to them.

The bottom line was that at the meeting of transition of the presidency from Dr. Honeycutt to Al Mohler, I and three others resigned in protest. I stated at that time that Southern Seminary, my alma mater, was no longer a place in which I could place my trust. It had been deliberately thrust into a direction of change that would eliminate its role as a leader in theological education. Subsequent events have proven that to be altogether too true for Southern as well as for the other entities of the Southern Baptist Convention.

FROM BAPTIST
TO BAPTIST

Frank Kendall

I grew up in Tuscaloosa, Alabama, during the 1940s and 1950s. Although religion was not significant in life, I joined First Baptist Church of Tuscaloosa when I was about thirteen years old and always attended Sunday school. I learned the stories, but never understood the real message they conveyed.

I had a number of experiences during that period regarding black people that were shaping my life, even though I did not realize it then. When I was ten years old, my mother told me that I could no longer play with my black friend who lived in the alley behind our apartment building. It seemed wrong, but I accepted it because "that's the way it was." When I was twelve, I sold two tickets to an Alabama football game to Mr. Abe, the shoeshine "boy" who worked in the barbershop across the street. My father told me I had to get them back from him because he was black and the tickets were in the whites-only section. It seemed wrong, but I accepted it because "that's the way it was." I watched black children in Livingston, Alabama, walking several miles to their school while white children could just go to a neighborhood school. It seemed wrong, but I accepted it because "that's the way it was."

After college, Patsy (my wife), our two daughters, and I moved to Baytown, Texas, where we joined First Baptist Church. When I began studying the Gospel of Mark in Bob Norris's Sunday school class, I found things I never knew existed—things that brought to me a sense of excitement and commitment, things that convinced me that much of what I had been taught at home in Tuscaloosa was a lie. Ironically, my knowledge and understanding of the Bible expanded greatly during that time, as I went home after church each week to study the biblical text for that Sunday. I often found that my understanding of the text was quite different from what had been preached from the pulpit.

In the summer of 1962, the Married Young People's Department of First Baptist of Baytown held a retreat at LaNell Stuart's bay house. The speaker was a young black minister from Houston named Bill Lawson. As people arrived, they were introduced to Reverend Lawson, shook his hand, and talked to him. Having just moved from Alabama and a lifetime of being taught that blacks were inferior people, I could not bring myself to meet him and shake his hand. I had never been in a place with blacks unless they were in a subservient role. That night I heard an articulate, intelligent, and inspiring person speak of things that were new and enlightening to me. After he finished speaking, I finally worked up the courage to go up to him and shake his hand. Such an insignificant act, but such a monumental step in my journey.

I became convinced that, at that particular time in history (1963), God was calling his people to do something about segregation. I realized that segregation seemed wrong, and I could no longer accept something that seemed wrong simply because "that's the way it was." I became active in the civil rights struggle, including working to bring about open housing in Baytown, serving on the board of the Harris County Poverty Program, and striving to make quality public education available to children. I did not see Southern Baptists answering, or even hearing, God's call. Instead, I saw them opposing it. To me, it was reminiscent of the basic reason the Southern Baptist Convention was originally formed: to support the continuation of slavery.

During that period, a young white couple asked to join our church. They had been baptized in a denomination for the exact same reason and in the exact same method (immersion) as were Baptists. They were told that they would have to be rebaptized by a Baptist preacher. I could not abide such an action and led a campaign to eliminate the requirement that the hands of a Baptist preacher must baptize all members. It was an interesting fight in which we compiled two pages of scriptures that did not support this narrow Baptist interpretation. The opposition basically responded,

"If we change this one part of church polity, where will it end?" On the Wednesday night when the church voted, 268 people attended (several times the normal attendance), many of whom I had never heard and one of whom arrived in an ambulance to "defend the faith" by voting against the motion.

Needless to say, the proposed change was resoundingly defeated, although the 82 people who supported it represented the spiritual leadership of the church. I was aware of other Baptist practices that disenfranchised people, such as not allowing women to serve as either deacons or ordained ministers. I decided that if something as insignificant and as scripturally clear as the baptism issue would not be accepted by Southern Baptists, then nothing of real consequence, such as civil rights, would be accepted either.

So we left that church for one in Houston that was dually aligned with Southern Baptists and the United Church of Christ. The local Southern Baptist group later kicked that church out of their fellowship after Patsy and two other women were elected as the first female deacons in a Texas Baptist church. (I thank God that many Texas Baptist churches have progressed greatly since then.)

Upon moving to Summit, New Jersey, and then to Greensboro, North Carolina, we belonged to (and were active in) churches of other denominations. Imagine our surprise when, twenty-eight years after saying we would never again belong to a Southern Baptist church, we joined a group of people in a Southern Baptist church in Greensboro who, we felt, were true to the original precepts of Baptists. You will not be surprised that this church was in the process of withdrawing from the Southern Baptist Convention, which had turned even further toward the far-right fringe beginning in 1979. Our new church, College Park Baptist Church, has women deacons, women ministers, members of every color and kind whose commonality is to confess Jesus as Lord, serious study of the Bible with nondogmatic interpretations of it, and the conviction that our response to God's unfathomable love and grace is to try to further the kingdom of God—right here and now.

Maybe College Park will someday drop the name Baptist, which carries with it so much negative baggage. For now, however, Patsy and I marvel at the irony of our pilgrimage, which has led us from Baptist to Baptist.

FRANK KENDALL

NO MORE KNOCKIN'

Rachel Smith Childress

I grew up as a Southern Baptist. I have said that I grew up at Southern Baptist Theological Seminary. I was born while my father was in school. My parents lived in a cramped apartment in Seminary Village. I went to nursery school on campus. My first friends were missionary kids on furlough. I liked to visit my friend Cheri at the library there. Cheri was a mummy, but I considered her my friend. I felt about the campus much the same as I sense that my children feel about Lexington Theological Seminary (where I now serve)—a sense of belonging, a sense of home, a sense of acceptance and connectedness—because of who I was and because of the family to whom I belonged.

When we talk about what has happened in the Southern Baptist Convention, it is very personal for me. The process of determining whether or not *my* congregation should leave the SBC grieves me. It has been grieving me for over twenty years. Others talk about what has happened to folks in the Convention. But I have lived the rejection, oppression, and disenfranchisement of those who have taught, nurtured, prayed for, and even given birth to me. I watched as my father was "retired" from the Sunday School Board much too early. I grieved for a dear female friend who was rejected for pastorate after pastorate because her "voice wasn't deep enough." I have listened to countless recollections of calls to ministry which were not answered for many years because the called one was told "she was mistaken." Words of ridicule and self-righteousness echo in my head. My parents meant it when they said I could be whatever God wanted. Someone forgot to tell others!

For many years, I anticipated the pendulum to swing back. I felt confident of reconciliation. I harbored the need to talk and discuss and even to fight. I held on past the point of many others, but I remember the day that I became consciously aware that my hope had disappeared and that I had been shut out too many times to knock at the door again. I had begun working at Lexington Theological Seminary, and someone from the Association of Theological Schools called to get my personal information for their directory. She asked me my denominational affiliation. I found I could no longer say the words "Southern Baptist." That day, I began calling myself a baptist with a little *b*. I hung up the phone and wept, bitterly.

The rationale for a break from the SBC has been called a political one. It is that, for I believe that the quest for power is at the core of much of what has happened. But for me, the basis for the break is theological in its foundation. Yes, the issue of women in ministry is very dear to me. But women in ministry is a symptom, an example of the core theological differences which are crucial for me—the priesthood of the believer and the autonomy of the local church. It is not true to the gospel as I understand it or to the breadth and depth and length and height of the God in whom I have entrusted my life for someone to tell me that God cannot and will not speak to me or to others who do not fit in a specific, human-constructed box.

I have watched this church strive to be true to what I believe it means to be "baptist with a little *b*." I believe that God has multiple missions in mind for our church. I believe we can best seek out and follow the desires of God for us by directing our energies and our resources away from a group who would deny us the opportunity to listen for God's voice.

Our Southern Baptist heritage is a rich one. It should be a source of pride. We need not, however, continue to support or perpetuate what it has become. It is too late to fight. Those doors are closed. We need not bloody our knuckles with continued knocking. Let us move on. God will open others.

NOTE

1. This article is based on remarks made at an open forum at Central Baptist Church in Lexington, Kentucky, in the fall of 2000. In October 2000, the church voted to withdraw from the SBC and KBC.

GETTING MY HEAD ON STRAIGHT

Cecil E. Sherman

It's been a long time since 1980. I realize the fight for control of the Southern Baptist Convention began in 1979, but it took me awhile to take in what was happening. My part in "the wars" began in 1980. My wife and I went to St. Louis in June 1980 for the annual meeting of SBC. Adrian Rogers was the new president, the first who bought into a plan to remake the Convention. The meeting was different. The rhetoric from the platform was more like a political convention than a Baptist convention. My wife listened awhile, then leaned over and said, "Did we come to the wrong meeting? This sounds more like a political convention than the Southern Baptist Convention." And she was right.

Several couples sat together in that meeting. We talked of what was happening. We tried to figure out what "those people" were up to. One thing was for sure: They were organized. A tight group clustered near the platform. They cheered, encouraged the president. They voted in mass and with enthusiasm. They set the tone in the hall. And when issues were put to a vote, they won. There were more of them than there were of "us." And most important of all: they were together. Those who opposed the new leadership were without any leadership.

In September 1980, three months after that St. Louis meeting, Paul Pressler made a speech at a church in Lynchburg, Virginia. He lined out the strategy "those people" had for taking over the SBC. That speech was reported first in the *Religious Herald*, weekly newspaper of the General Association of Virginia. When I read that report, it came clear to me. "Those people" have a plan. That plan will work. If people who disagree with them do not get together, "those people" will win.

I wrote to twenty-five pastors. I asked them to come to Gatlinburg, Tennessee, on a Thursday through Saturday in late September 1980. Seventeen came. I laid out to them what all of us had observed, what Paul Pressler had said, and what I thought was going to happen. "Those people" would possess the SBC unless some of us got together and created a political resistance to political fundamentalism in our Convention. The group bought into what I proposed. We became the political group that came to be called moderates. We ran candidates. We always lost. But contrary to the cynical comments of some, we were not politically naïve. We explained to thousands the consequences of a fundamentalist takeover. We gathered thousands to the annual meetings of the SBC. Our percentage of the vote grew from about 40 percent in 1981 to just over 48 percent in 1988. We alerted the house. We did what we could, and we lost.

By 1990, it was obvious that the fundamentalists (for that is what "those people" turned out to be) had won. Moderates were dropping out. Fundamentalists were getting on board. It was time to go. I've had people say, "If you people had not quit, you could have won." I think those people are mistaken. Fundamentalists do politics "as unto the Lord." Moderates feel dirty when they do denominational politics; they have no heart for it.

A brief autobiographical word: I am of the Southern Baptist Convention. My parents were deep into church life. My education was by way of Southern Baptist (Baylor University and Southwestern Baptist Theological Seminary). I worked within the SBC system. I was not a leader in the Convention. I had a bit part. But my heart was with Southern Baptists, my money was there, and I bent my churches to invest in the denomination. A good part of my personal identity came from the Southern Baptist Convention. Since I was a Baptist preacher, my professional links were of the denomination. Then when I was in my fifties, after years of investing time, money, and influence, I was out (fundamentalists take no prisoners; if you are not for them, you are a nonperson). How do you handle that? And what do you do when it happens? Here's the way I've handled it.

I'M NOT MISERABLE AND WALLOWING IN "WHAT IFS"

I have friends who are damaged goods. They just can't get over it. One of the brightest retreated from nearly all religious activity except in his own church. When he spoke of the denomination, it was through clenched teeth. A previously cheerful disposition gave way to a good bit of bitterness. What happened really changed his life—and for the worse. Another friend meets me on Wednesday nights at our church dinner. With surprising regularity he says, "Cecil, how do you get over this SBC mess? I can't seem to get it off my mind." About 1990, I asked Winifred Moore to come to Broadway Church in Fort Worth and tell of his experiences in "the wars." Winifred said, "I can't do that, Cecil. I'm still mad about it." I suspect Winifred has moved a good ways from anger now. But he was having a hard time getting through and getting over the fight.

I have a feeling for people who can't get over it—when you invest the first fifty-five years of your life in something, then that something changes the rules and writes you out. If you are not careful, you will wind up a Confederate veteran; mad at the world for the rest of your life. When I resigned from the Peace Committee (October 1986), I came back to my church in Forth Worth. I was beat up from fighting "those people." I was angry with "those people." But most of all, I was angry with moderates. On the Peace Committee there were people who could have helped but wouldn't. They just couldn't believe "those people" were really going to make over the SBC. Or, they didn't agree that moderates needed to get together: "That's not the Christian thing to do." Or they had a kind of pietistic rationale: "If we could just have a prayer meeting, this would be resolved and we would all live happily ever after." And most often of all, "Cecil, if you will just stand down, be quiet, this will all work out. The pendulum will swing." I've no doubt moderates could have won the SBC wars if moderates had been able to get together. How do you live with that idea? The "what if . . ."

I have a pretty good grasp of the obvious. We lost. I can either be angry about losing, or I can get over it. The choice is mine. It took me about two years to work through, and that was that. The Christian religion has a built-in system to help people get past the failures and the disappointments, the breakdowns and frustrations of life. I reached for that system of religious forgetting. I've turned my mind to other things. When asked to reminisce, I can feel some of the passion. But I don't turn those pages unless there is good reason. It brings out a side of me that needs to stay buried. This article walks near the edge for me.

I SPEND LITTLE TIME FOLLOWING THE SBC

There was a time when I read eight Baptist state papers. I was pretty well informed about what was going on in the SBC. Now I get three, and I confess I read them quickly. There's too much about the SBC for my tastes. I know few of the people who lead the SBC. They come from the new leadership, and I never was connected to that set of people.

A digression may help: Before there was a controversy, before the wars, the SBC had two main groups. There was a group into evangelism, and this group tended to be very conservative theologically. And there was a group clustered around missions and the denomination. I was in this second group. We were theologically conservative by any reasonable standard (like when compared to Methodists, Presbyterians, Episcopalians), but we were open to ethical issues and usually came down on the progressive side of those issues. Race, hunger, ecology, women—these issues found us voting a Democratic ticket and pushing for social change. We saw these as justice issues and appropriate to Christian concern. These two groups were almost exclusive. If you were in one, you were not in the other. I invited people to preach and teach in my church. I never invited one of the right wing to my church. Their gospel was different from mine. They went about doing church differently from the way I did. They read the Bible differently from me. My side of the SBC was very large. Their side of the SBC was very large. The SBC house was so big until half the house was still a large company. They did not know me, and I did not know them. Now their side runs the SBC. I don't know them. I didn't know them. I disagreed with them a long time ago. I still disagree with them. They run the SBC world. I'm out of the loop.

Does this bother me? It did, but with the passing of time it doesn't. Sometimes I read about foolish things done by the SBC, like trying to impose a ban on Southern Baptists attending Disney entertainment. I think what they did was silly, inappropriate, and ineffective. But I am not a Southern Baptist anymore. I'm not only an exile, I'm out and not trying to get back in. It's not my company; I don't follow them.

I AM NOT CYNICAL ABOUT DENOMINATION

One of the major consequences of the wars is a sort of pulling back from denomination. One pastor told me, "I used to have heart for a denomination; I got burned. Now I'm through with denomination." As my pastor, Jim Slatton, says, "That Baptist pulled back into its polity." That means a Baptist doesn't have to take denomination seriously unless he/she wants to. That's not where I have settled in my journey away from SBC.

There are three things most churches need some help doing:

(1) We can't do what the New Testament says about missions without a missions delivery system. How can a local church do Matthew 28:18–20 without some help?

(2) We can't have a good educational program for ministers without some kind of cooperation. Serious theological libraries and faculties do not assemble without serious money.

(3) We can't have a program of Christian education without somebody to write the curriculum. Not many churches can turn out the literature for children, youths, singles, and adults by themselves.

If a church is to participate in missions, have an educated pastor, and have excellence in religious education, some kind of system has to be put together to make these things happen. We call that "some kind of system" a denomination. Then we get to the real question: what kind of denomination? This is the sixty-four-dollar question.

We can have a denomination that sets boundaries in theology and practice for the churches. This denomination gives the churches theology and a way to do church.

Or, we can have a denomination that carefully limits herself. The churches are free. They will interpret the Bible differently on some points. They will order their own priorities. The denomination will stand aside, let the local congregations make decisions. The denomination does not do theology for the churches. It is not a top-down system; that is bottom-up.

In 1992, I went to work for the Cooperative Baptist Fellowship. I had to sort out my mind. Is CBF a denomination? (CBF has refused to say she is.) Does CBF do the things a denomination should do for a Baptist church? I think the answer is yes. I wish CBF had declared herself a denomination a long time ago. If a Baptist church wishes to be in SBC, ABC, CBF—and all at the same time—it is none of anybody's business. This is Baptist polity. But that church needs help doing those three essential things. I'm not cynical about denomination, and I wish moderates would come together and make a larger (not necessarily stronger) denomination.

I HAVE A HEART FOR MODERATE BAPTIST CAUSES

Lost on most people is the amazing creativity of moderate Baptists *after* the wars. We did not go off and pout. The 1990 New Orleans SBC was the end. We knew it.

In the hotel at Dallas–Fort Worth airport in July, about fifteen of us met. Daniel Vestal presided. Any additional politic to possess the SBC was a dead issue. What now? We didn't know, but we knew there was still life in moderates. We called a meeting for Atlanta. About three thousand people assembled on short notice. We came in August to the Inforum in Atlanta. It was the most spiritual meeting I've ever attended in my life. It had life, vigor, heart. Some wanted to rehash the past, but the mood of the majority was to pitch it forward. Where do we go from here? What can we do? I did not say one public word at that meeting, but that meeting would change my life.

CBF was conceived in August 1990 in Atlanta. The official birth would be May 1991, also in Atlanta. The group wanted a coordinator to pull them together, gather funds, and set an agenda. Dot and I were asked to take the job. We began April 1, 1992. For more than four years I traveled the country pulling people toward CBF. Sometimes I failed, but most of the time it was exciting, energizing work. I met great people. We had to re-think Baptist ideas (one of the extras that has come of the wars has been a rediscovery of Baptist polity). Too many people were just caught up in the Baptist mission; now they had to think Baptist ideas. Walter Shurden has guided our thinking in this ongoing study. Not many churches have had the backbone to pull out of the SBC, but several thousand churches have reexamined Baptist polity. Though these churches have not pulled out of the SBC, they have pulled back from her. They divide their money with CBF and other good causes. They have come out of the Baptist cocoon; they are more likely to cooperate in interdenominational causes. These churches have put denomination in her place. The SBC had become too dear to us. It had become big, rich, and very powerful. We worshiped her.

It was an idolatry, and we will not do that again. But we still need the services of some kind of denomination.

So out of thin air there came a multitude of small, new organizations. Theological schools were being born at the rate of almost one a year. There was Truett Theological Seminary at Baylor; Baptist Theological Seminary at Richmond; Gardener Webb University began a divinity school; Mercer opened McAfee School of Theology; Campbell University; Wake Forest; and John Leland School of Theology in Northern Virginia. The people at Hardin Simmons University in Abilene, Texas, began Logsden School of Theology. We've connected with established divinity schools and opened Baptist houses at Duke and Emory. An old link with American Baptists has been reestablished through Central Baptist Seminary in Kansas City, Kansas. Most are growing. And don't forget Associated Baptist Press, Smyth & Helwys, groups that specialized in ethics, and the list runs long. There is going to be a moderate voice in this century. The fundamentalist victory in the SBC wars did not silence us. We are teaching, redefining ourselves, and stirring a next generation of moderate Baptist leadership.

I am an adjunct teacher at Baptist Theological Seminary at Richmond. Close up I get to see the nearly three hundred students who are enrolled. They are great people. For six years I've watched them. They do good in the churches they serve. They do not diminish them. They are not liberal (with a few exceptions). They love the Lord and go forth to serve the churches. A dollar invested in this school is a dollar well spent. Dot and I tithe our salary to BTSR. We believe in BTSR.

So, are Dot and I just sitting around licking our wounds from the SBC wars? Not at all. I've spent the last twelve years investing myself in a future for Baptist ideas. I preach revivals, teach young ministers (male and female), write commentaries for lay Bible teachers, do interim work for churches seeking a pastor. And I enjoy every minute of it. I'm outside the SBC, but I find I am not alone. I'm in good company.

Have I gotten over the SBC wars? No and yes. No means that conflict is ever with me. It defined me and many others. We lost; it hurt. We were run out of our own house. That event is always "back there" in my mind. But I suppose it is a little like a World War II veteran who had some horrible experiences in battle. Does he come home and dwell on them, turn them in the mind, keep handling them? Or does he move on with his life, have a family, get a job, get into his church, and do life? You know the answer to my questions. And I've tried to live by that answer.

CECIL E. SHERMAN

The yes side of me is the activity since 1990. That life has been filled with good people, good causes, and great hope. I like what I did in the wars; in fact, I'm proud of that time in my life. Better still is where we are and what we are doing now. I am grateful to a good and gracious God for letting me live in such a time, and the road rises before me.

STILL A BAPTIST WOMAN

Gladys S. Lewis

The planners for this Oklahoma Conference on Baptist Women invited me to be the banquet speaker and address the subject, "Why I am still a Baptist." They said, "We want you to tell your story." I will give you three reasons and tell you three stories to satisfy that assignment.

I am a Baptist because of my captivity, my exodus, and my pilgrimage. My captivity status helps me understand being human and defines me; my exodus experience helps me recognize the divine and shapes me; and my pilgrimage formation helps me synthesize the human and the divine and identifies me. Being Baptist puts those interpretive strategies in my power because of basic Baptist adherence to soul liberty and soul competency in the captivity, individual freedom in Bible study and prayer in the Exodus, and priesthood of the believer and church autonomy in the pilgrimage. Because we connect with each other most thoroughly through our stories, I will tell you a story about each of those areas and explain it through my

Originally presented as "Gathering for Connection and Collegiality" at the Oklahoma Conference on Baptist Women at First Baptist Church, Oklahoma City, March 2, 2001. Reprinted with permission. First published in *Christian Ethics Today,* a journal available free of charge and accessible at www.christianethicstoday.com, and printed as a chapter in *Putting Women in Their Place: The Baptist Debate Over Female Equality,* ed. Audra E. and Joe E. Trull (Macon, GA: Smyth & Helwys, 2003). The book may be ordered from http://www.helwys.com or 1-800-747-3016.

assimilation of its meaning in my life in the three areas I will address and interpret as I tell you why I am still a Baptist.

CAPTIVITY

Captivity is our basic human orientation. It describes our natural condition and provides a way to understand and define our life condition. The Old Testament overflows with allusions to being carried away captive, taking captives, and becoming captives. Bondage is a principal preoccupation. The overarching captivity analogy in accounts of the literal physical bondage of Israel in Egypt grants a bedrock for understanding Old and New Testament worlds. We are also captive in other ways. Paul writes about captivity: "But I see another law in my members, warring against the law of my mind, and bringing me into captivity to the law of sin which is in my members" (Romans 7:23). In spite of all the varieties of bondage, there is a positive side to captivity, which elevates our dismal condition. We meet it first in Isaiah 61:1 and again in the experience of Jesus when he goes to the synagogue and reads from the scroll (Luke 4:18) after his captivity-shattering encounter with Satan on temptation mount: "The Spirit of the Lord God is upon me; because the Lord has anointed me to preach good tidings unto the meek (poor); he has sent me to bind up (heal) the brokenhearted, to proclaim (preach) liberty to the captives, (and recovering sight to the blind), and the opening of the prison (set at liberty) to them that are bound (bruised)." We are not just a herd of cattle in a pen. We are individuals so worthy of saving that a living God engages himself in our redemption.

That kind of importance defines us spiritually. That kind of individual worth also defines us culturally, a nation of individualists from our beginning. The first prolonged collision the New England colonists suffered with the Indians occurred in the spring of 1675. King Phillip's War, as the two-year guerrilla battles were known, ended a half-century of cordial co-existence between the English settlers and the Algonquin tribes of southern New England. Metacomet, the Wampanoag chief, dubbed Phillip by the colonists, hated the colonists and resented their high-handed ways and incursion on tribal lands.

In February 1676, a group of Narragansetts raided Lancaster, Massachusetts, a frontier community with about fifty families. Many were killed and others taken captive for ransom. Among the captives was Mary White Rowlandson (c. 1635–c. 1678), a daughter of one of the town's founders and wife of its clergyman. Eleven weeks later, just before the war ended, she was ransomed and reunited with her husband and two remaining children after twenty stages of flight, or "removes," as the Indians moved through Massachusetts into Vermont, New Hampshire, and back. During those weeks, she endured unimaginable suffering.

A couple of years later, Rowlandson recorded her "narrative of her captivity," and it became immensely popular because it served her readers on so many literary, spiritual, and psychological levels. It was a lay sermon by a woman, a spiritual autobiography, and an amazing adventure tale. Her narrative does what captivity tales always do. The captive defines self in contrast to the captivity culture, and, if redeemed, returns to the prior community to share what was learned. We receive rich imagery from the Puritans in the concept of a mission into the wilderness and identity with the land. The promised land which the Israelites in exile sought, by transference in the Puritan colonial's mind, became the New Israel in the New World. The Bible reinforced their experience of boundaries, wilderness, land, captivity, exile, and return. Mary Rowlandson's captivity narrative birthed a principal literary genre in American writing which comes straight from a biblical model. But captivity is far more than a literary genre which serves as a communication device. Captivity provides a metaphoric construct for our individual and group experience in that we learn from our suffering, or we are destroyed by it.

And there is more. Culturally, women have been captives of patriarchal institutions. Captivity is not new to our horizons. We have a grammar of capacity in our past, our present, and our future. The fundamentalists and their overt program of exclusion are debilitating and embarrassing, but it is not new. In many ways, it is more honest in the present than that captivity we have known in the past. But we can turn all of it to our advantage. We will never be free from the captivity which surrounds and threatens, but we can make it more negotiable, more pragmatically useful if we learn from marginal experience and teach our communities.

Current rules and dicta don't affect us as Baptists moving in *soul liberty* and *soul competency*. A conscience-free Baptist can survive the wilderness captivity. I am still Baptist because soul competency allows me to work out my own faith positions when life gives me conditions not covered by doctrine. We are all Catholics pragmatically. We want someone to make the rules, tell us how to live in them, bless us when we succeed, and correct us with assignments for extra credit when we fail. In Baptist circles right now, we call that fundamentalism, but it is a Catholic position by ecclesiology, which would be decried by Baptists, and it is fascist politically, in its denial of liberty. The trouble with that kind of rigidity comes when life dishes up a serving of something without rules for solutions. I live on a plane daily where nothing of faith markers has been mapped. Soul liberty and competency allow me to be my own cartographer without losing my way on the journey. I learn from my captivity about my humanity. Engagement with my soul in the experience defines my humanity.

EXODUS

My exodus experience helps me recognize the divine and shapes me. When God set Israel free, the people needed forty years to become free before they could go on into their promise. In the removes, or stages, of the exodus, they learned of God's reality and presence to take the form he intended for them. Usually, we read the exodus from the point of view of Moses, or the people, or the text writers. In Isaiah 51 and 52, we have God's account: "Hearken unto me, my people . . . for a law shall proceed from me. . . . The captive exile hastens that he may be loosed. . . . But I am the Lord thy God, that divided the sea, whose waves roared. . . . And I have put my words in your mouth, and I have covered you in the shadow of my hand, that I may . . . say . . . You are my people. . . . I have taken out of your hand the cup of trembling. . . . You shall no more drink it again. . . . Shake yourself from the dust. . . . Loose yourself from the bands of your neck. . . . Break forth into joy . . . for the Lord has comforted his people."

The New Testament position on our exile condition as Gentiles outside grace beckons us from Ephesians 2:12 and 19: Remember, Paul says, "At that time you were without Christ, being aliens from the commonwealth of Israel and strangers from the covenants of promise, having no hope, and without God. . . . Now . . . you are no strangers and foreigners, but fellow citizens with the saints, and of the household of God." My exodus experience helps me recognize the divine, and it shapes me.

For many years, our family went to Copper Mountain, Colorado, to ski during the interim between Christmas and New Year's when the Physicians' Winter Retreat, sponsored by the University of Oklahoma Health Sciences Center, features a continuing medical education forum. In 1993, my surgeon husband, Wilbur, and I arrived two days before Christmas with our children: Karen and her husband, Howard; David, his wife, Sadako, and baby, Jason; Leanne and her husband, Carey; and Cristen. Wilbur, an excellent skier, was coming down B slope at Copper Mountain, on Monday, December 27, a bit after 12:30 p.m., with Leanne, Carey, and David. The day was somewhat snowy and overcast, so there were no shadows to indicate ridges or other elevations in the terrain or flags to alert skiers. Leanne, in front of the pack, went right and took off her skis to go in to lunch. Wilbur followed her, but turned to the left. Just a few steps from the door to the inn was a drainage ditch with a culvert into it, making a slight elevation which did not create a shadow. Because it was not flagged, Wilbur did not note its presence. He was not going fast, because he was headed toward a snow bank to remove his skis. As he skied over the area, the tips of his skis caught in the elevation and he fell full-face forward into the ground. The impact caused a ring fracture of his first cervical vertebra and shattered the second one. His injury was the kind often associated with those which divers receive. (It is exactly the injury of actor Christopher Reeve.) Because that area of the spinal cord services autonomic systems of the body, such as breathing, he was immediately without the ability to breathe. Carey saw the entire scenario and rushed to him, calling for help. David, last in the group, came just after the fall, hurried to help with resuscitation, but watched in panic as he saw his father turning blue. Leanne ran to Wilbur, and he mouthed, "Get help! Get help!" Attending our same conference were a cardiologist and his physician assistant wife who immediately began CPR. The ski patrol came quickly with oxygen and carried Wilbur to the nearby clinic. After emergency attention, he was evacuated to Denver to St. Anthony Central, a trauma center, placed on a ventilator, and diagnosed as quadriplegic: paralyzed from the neck down. His condition was so grave that he was not expected to live through the night. However, when his vital signs and mental condition improved by Tuesday morning, his orthopedist, neurologist, and general surgeon operated.

After his surgeries and several interchanges between his mouthed questions and our carefully explained narratives, he knew exactly his condition and what we faced. Wilbur is a ventilator-dependent quadriplegic, a bleak, grim, dismal reality. We have learned our exodus expulsion was not at the Red Sea; it was at the base of a ski slope in the Colorado Rockies. At that instant around noon, December 27, 1993, our lives were shot into another orbit forever as long as we live—an existence of exodus where we live on a plane somewhere between life and death, neither totally one or the other. Not a day goes by when he does not face death in life, nor I face life in death. We are neither where we were, nor where we are going on the existence level we have been awarded where we try to marshal our exodus. We go to sleep and wake with Death's arm about our shoulders. We fight

GLADYS S. LEWIS

on two fronts; his is despair and mine is cynicism. His comes from living on the brink of death. Mine comes from facing the threats to our survival each day, knowing as soon as I solve one set of problems, another will take its place. We have two sides of the same problem: time. He cannot do one thing, and is oppressed by time. I must do everything, and am oppressed by time.

So we beg for manna to have nourishment for our paralyzed wanderings. Food comes with prayer and Bible study, but not the kind of devotional exercise I had known in the past. Set-apart rituals of spiritual enhancement require time, and I have none. None. For many months, I existed on one to three hours of sleep in twenty-four as I cared for Wilbur, kept my job, and supervised closing his office, managing caregivers, and struggling with financial survival at the hands of people who should have been helping us.

In learning from the exodus, we discover we all have different experiences of grace. One of my grace gifts came the day I realized I could be a spiritual person on the hoof. I could "read" the Bible in my mind and hear God's voice. I could "speak" my thoughts and ideas to him at red lights, and it counted as prayer. My discipline with language helps me at this point. I have so many words in me, good investments I have made of great artists. At any given moment, I can "read" Shakespeare's sonnets, Fitzgerald's *Great Gatsby*, God's New Testament, or my husband's love letters, none of which any of them will ever write again. I love words. I can roll around in them, pull them over my head as a blanket, and be renewed. When I am locked in linguistic combat with a laboratory, I "read" Shakespeare's, "A man can smile and smile and be a villain"; when I recall the days of our other life, I "read" Fitzgerald's benediction on Gatsby that he drove on to that vision not knowing his dream was behind him; when I think of what I face each day, I "read" Jesus in the Gospels, "Take up my yoke and learn of me"; when I finally reach the end of my day, I "read" Wilbur's "To my loving wife." In the process, I have read through a window on all of life experience, and I pray, "Thank you."

What do we learn in our captivity margins of exile and exodus? Wilbur is a captive of his poor, diminished, suffering, petrified body. And so am I. The alienated American cultural subject is the soul we recognize as our own in our particular captivities. Anthropologist Victor Turner's work in studies of people in liminal landscapes examines what happens to groups and individuals with a retreat or forced exile into the marginal, into an existence where the boundary is removed, the exile position. We should feel at home as Baptists in our culture if we understand the secular expression to be fruition of an ancient *correlation* between Old Israel and New Israel as our founders compared themselves. We go into the wilderness for testing and growth. We must look to this current alienation as opportunity for expansion of self, group, and context. When colonial captives were redeemed from captivity, they returned with stories of lessons learned which would benefit the group. Our task as human beings and Baptist women? Learn our stories well and teach them ethically as we learn in the exodus how the divine and human interact to shape us.

Baptists are uniquely equipped to deal with the marginal experience and proving of exodus living because of our historic emphasis on *Bible study and prayer.* Two weeks ago, I read again Ralph Waldo Emerson's essay, "Self-Reliance," because I had assigned it to a class. I have read that essay a dozen times, but his comments on prayer grasped my mind as never before. He said, "Prayer looks abroad and asks for some foreign addition to come through some foreign virtue, and loses itself in endless mazes of natural and supernatural. . . . Prayer that craves a particular commodity— anything less than all good, is vicious. Prayer is the contemplation of the facts of life from the highest point of view. It is the soliloquy of a beholding and jubilant soul. It is the spirit of God, pronouncing His works good. But prayer as a means to effect a private end, is theft and meanness. . . . As soon as [we] are at one with God, [we] will not beg. [We] will see prayer in all action." An exodus lesson? Prayer is not selfish, not an insurance policy for what we want.

Wilbur suffers especially at night when real darkness joins the other shadows on life. He wrestles with Jacob's night angel. And so do I. Because I have wrestled with the angel, I have had to learn how to renegotiate previous patterns, because I can't walk the same way. We do get the blessing, Wilbur and I, but blessings come at a price. We are crippled. Coming to grips with the disintegration of my life as the wife of my husband and the shift in my position in my family with my husband's injury sabotages these ridiculous rules which say I must wait on my husband for direction and authority. My husband is paralyzed and ventilator-dependent. I am our wage-earner, business manager, and linchpin. What nonsense to pose as weak and dependent. I wrestle with the angel in an ambiguous stranglehold. Jacob never saw the angel's face; we have never seen our angel's face, but we know him. Wilbur wrestles with the Angel of Death; I wrestle with the Angel of Life—and they are both God. We are equally blessed, but we remain horribly wounded. And I am independently wounded with my own pain.

I am woman; I love God; he loves me. In the words of C. S. Lewis, my "pain is his megaphone." I will not let others define me as an intrusion before that which I know exists between myself and the one I worship and move in day by day. *I . . . will . . . not.* That was a struggle I faced long before the arrival of the current set of silly sibilant sayings some sources set before us as sacred. The contemporary crowd of creed makers is a bunch of children piping in the market, using Jesus' words about immaturity in serious spiritual issues. Baptist women have a history of facing sophisticated obstacles. This current language is helpful, in fact. We shrug, smile, and reengage in lives where that mindset has absolutely no connection and certainly no collegiality.

In our exodus, I have gained a new attitude and understanding about Bible study. I am glad I spent all those years on the six-point record system and study courses and Bible study in Sunday school. But in my current exodus, I am reading the Bible by the way I live. Remember the vacation Bible school memorization programs? My two are: "Thy word have I hid in my heart that I might not sin against thee" and the watchword: "I will do the best I can with what I have for Jesus's sake today." The two go together and must be present for us to survive in the exodus. From my wilderness vantage, I have noticed people do two things with Bible study. They make it a substitute for practical ministry or a substitute for belief. What else can be deduced when people drive miles to a Bible study but won't go across the street to help someone? What else can be deduced when so much language extols its precise merits but not a word offers its spirit?

The Bible is a collection of narratives of violence: murder, betrayal, brokenness; in our connections with it through the collegiality of our own brokenness, we find meaning for our narratives—inspiration from the violence done to us *and* from those which we perpetrate on others. To make it a totem, an object of worship, or a lucky charm violates its spirit and diminishes its force for healing. It is a road map for our journey, a diary for our reflection, and a compass for our direction: a text with many voices, many narrators, many themes, many interpretations.

We learn a great deal by reading the Bible about Jesus which affirms us spiritually and culturally. Especially as women. Especially Jesus and non-Jewish women. He first announced his ministry to one: the woman at the well. Jesus never got entangled with doctrine; he lived it, and while living it, told stories and took care of people. I think this is the edge women have with Jesus. He announced he was the Messiah to a non-Jewish woman. That event came out in a practical ministry setting and conversation; he wanted a drink of water. Of course, the emphasis we get is on his knowing she was a woman with a bad reputation and being kind to her anyway—chalk one up for male rhetoric.

The Syro-Phoenician woman helped Jesus clarify his ministry by using his language against him. Does the jingoism and ethnic chauvinism of Jesus in that passage bother you? After he had fed the multitudes, she came asking him to heal her daughter. He said, "I can't take the children's bread and throw it before dogs." He called her a dog, and I don't think it was because she was not cute. She said, "Dogs eat crumbs under the children's table. I would take those." Jesus checks himself. I am helped enormously by thinking of Jesus as a teacher. I think Jesus had just restated the syllabus to fifteen freshmen and this Syro-Phoenician woman graduate student walked up with a real question, and Jesus responded in a tone he wanted to use for the freshmen. But she, knowing how to use language and metaphor, turned it on him. Submissiveness? Bah! Balderdash! My exodus experience helps me recognize the divine, and it shapes me.

PILGRIMAGE

My pilgrimage formation helps me synthesize the human and the divine and identifies me. My pilgrimage comes from my salvation story, which rises from my being my own priest in spiritual matters. The altar stone in our cherished belief in *the priesthood of the believer* as Baptists is John 3:16. "For God so loved the world [in its captivity, its exodus, and its pilgrimage] he gave his only begotten Son that whosoever [every single individual] believes in him should not perish but have everlasting life."

My salvation story and my service stories all have Baptist bindings. As a seventeen-year-old, I converted to Christianity at the Exchange Avenue Baptist Church in south Oklahoma City in one of those youth-led revivals when OBU student at the time, Milton Ferguson, former president of Midwestern Seminary before the purge, was the preacher. Very soon afterward, I became a mission volunteer and prepared myself as a nurse. I met Wilbur. We fell in love. (I did. He sort of eased into it, but I knew I had him. I could tell by the little things.) We finished our education, had two babies, spent two terms on the mission field at the Baptist Hospital in Asuncion, Paraguay, had two more babies there, and had to leave because of political shifts in the government which surfaced in the Public Health Ministry, the license-granting authority for us. We have lived in the Oklahoma City area since 1970. Wilbur developed a prominent private surgical practice, was one of the seven original founders of the Baptist Medical-Dental Fellowship, and gave his total means in service to others from the Grace Rescue Mission clinic locally to mission hospitals in South America and East Asia. I moved into a role I call my professional Baptist era, and gave my time, energy, and talent to Baptist churches, Woman's Missionary Union, and Southern Baptist Convention boards. We went all over the world in service capacities through medicine and Baptists. I was on the Committee on Order of Business the year the fundamentalist take-over occurred. I sat in meetings and listened and knew my days as a woman Baptist in the circles I have been traveling in had ended. By that time, I also knew that volunteerism, satisfying as it was, could not substitute for professional engagement in a work. So I returned to study, earned a master of arts in English and Creative Writing, and found my niche in academia. I went on to earn a Ph.D. in American and British Literature and have been an English professor at the University of Central Oklahoma since 1990. All of that had finished, and I had been at my post two years when our accident happened. My work forms a backdrop for our lives and provides the financial means I must have to care for Wilbur as well as maintain my own sense of reality and contribution beyond myself.

"Tell your story." "Why are you still a Baptist?" I am still a Baptist because that is who I am. I was a Baptist long before the current epidemic of theological soul-eating bacteria infected us. Baptist is my name. My life orientation and soul habits have always emanated from that name which identifies me. I suppose I could move into another room in Father's house and live in the Presbyterian room or the Methodist room or some other. But I am more comfortable with the furniture in the Baptist room. I became a Baptist by choice, and I remain one by choice. That is not to say I have not considered rearranging the furniture or engaging in some more radical activity within those walls, but Baptist I remain, because those parameters help me define my faith system in the most practical manner. In response to being my own priest in salvation matters and being in a church that is autonomous under the will and direction of God, I move forward in my pilgrimage and sharpen my identity. I was born and given a name. When I converted, I chose a name. When I married, I took another name. All of those names constitute who I am. I will not change; I cannot change. We have Baptist connections, Wilbur and I, and we continue to enjoy a sustaining collegiality with people who share our history.

I am my own agent in salvation matters because we cling to our belief in the priesthood of the believer. I work it out with God, who has provided the way through Christ. We must not allow current language of disenfranchisement to rob us of our history of the struggle; the good old days were good because we had years of experience in subversive success. We knew how to work within the system to make our contributions, fuel our personal sense of mission. When women began to move out of those parameters, you will recall that we were not met with resistance. We should do now what we did then: continue to respond to the free-moving Spirit in our hearts, talents, and sensitivity to God's claim on our gifts to respond to him in soul liberty.

I am still a Baptist, because I am part of an *autonomous church*. The emphasis and the New Testament imagery of church always fixes on individuals and their metaphoric analogy as body and body parts to underscore the necessity of cooperative action in our individual reality. Under God, we are free-gifted individuals voluntarily participating in the Body of Christ, his church, to do his will and honor him. Romans 12:4–5 ("For as we have many members in one body, and all members have not the same office; So we, being many, are one body in Christ, and every one members one of another") and 1 Corinthians 10:17 sketch this portrait for us ("For we being many are one bread and one body; for we are all partakers of that one bread"). But this community of service never supplants individual worth before God. Galatians 3:26 stresses that fact ("For you are all the children of God by faith in Christ Jesus"). An individual moves out of freed, experienced exiles, helping other strangers bring order to their pilgrimages.

A major problem exists with the current SBC regime's dictating to churches and getting away with it. I am not shocked by the patriarchy in recent SBC resolutions. But I am surprised that Southern Baptist churches have gone along with the trickle-down theology that becomes polarizing in the congregational context. Some of our shameful present comes from religious people's basic insecurity with women, because they are insecure about their own identity and cast that doubt in religious robes. It has always been that way. My generation was taught Roger Williams was the great pioneer in soul liberty—the first Baptist-founder of Rhode Island, the historians tell us. And he was, but he was taught by a woman, Anne Hutchinson, who challenged the group control of the early Puritan ministers over individual biblical interpretation. So Mistress Hutchinson held weekly Bible studies in her home and retaught the Bible lessons from the Sunday sermons. Roger Williams was a member of her Monday school class. I did not learn that in a church or seminary context. I had to go to one of those secular humanist institutions and get a degree in Early American literature to get the skinny on Mistress Anne. Her story parallels the demonizing of Women's Missionary Union promoted by, of all groups, the Foreign Mission Board, now the International Mission Board. Her movement, the Anti-nomian Crisis, meaning against authority, or freedom within authority, is WMU's history. They gave us credit for being witches, but not for being principal actors and causative agents in the creation of church history. My pilgrimage formation helps me synthesize the human and the divine and identifies me.

I am a Baptist because of my captivity, my exodus, and my pilgrimage. My captivity status helps me understand being human and defines me; my exodus experience helps me recognize the divine and shapes me; and my pilgrimage formation helps me synthesize the human and the divine and identifies me. Being Baptist grants me those interpretative strategies because of basic Baptist adherence to soul liberty and soul competency in the captivity, individual freedom in Bible study and prayer in the exodus, and priesthood of the believer and church autonomy in the pilgrimage. Because we connect with each other most thoroughly through our stories, I have told you mine, proclaiming as I do, I am still a Baptist woman.

MY DEPARTURE FROM THE SUNDAY SCHOOL BOARD

Alan G. Jolly

I did not want to write this article. The period of time was so stressful that I have deliberately forgotten times, and to avoid potential harm to others, I will not use names.

I felt the Lord calling me closer to his work. I left General Electric Major Appliance Division, Louisville, Kentucky, to join an advertising firm that was sold to one of the top-ten advertising agencies. My work included account supervisor, media relations, senior vice-president, and director of the agency. The Lord led me to establish my own marketing, advertising, and public relations agency, where we handled mass media for "Good News, Americans, God loves you." Subsequently, my wife and I went to Kenya to assist in "Good News, Kenyans, God loves you." A short time later, we were invited to join the Baptist Sunday School Board where we served for about seven years.

We joined a church in Nashville, Tennessee. The church was widely known for mission work in this country and throughout the world. When the conservatives assumed control of the 30 million–member Southern Baptist Convention and the Sunday School Board, I was told that "you belong to the wrong church." When the comment was made, there were some twenty-six members who worked at the Board. Gradually, that number dwindled until I was one of only two left. The others resigned, were asked to leave, or retired.

The Board saw most of its senior officers walk the same road as our twenty-six church members. When the president left, that sent shockwaves throughout the Board. As more senior management left, the waves got bigger and the stress level increased. Some were asked to leave while on trips. Others got the news by being "called in" by the new senior management.

Gradually, it became apparent that my days were numbered. God has always blessed my wife, me, and our family, even in troubled times, so that faith kept me going. In fact, I prepared a manual of operation for my position, including recommendations for future actions to assure the continued success of that mission. I presented that to senior management after my position was eliminated. I have been delighted to see that several of those suggestions were implemented.

I began to hear stories about monitoring our e-mail and telephone. I asked persons not directly associated with the Board business to stop calling, because I didn't want them to become entangled in the political situation.

I worked daily as usual, but was invited to fewer and fewer meetings. I attended chapel services, and noticed that speakers were all from the churches where the new leaders attended. At breaks and luncheons fewer people that I knew were still around. Most of the conversation centered around who had left that week and who was scheduled to "depart" in the weeks to come. I wanted, for some strange reason, to stay. Deep down, I knew I wouldn't. This was one of those transitions in life which led me closer to the Lord. I spoke to all with all the happiness I had come to choose in my life. If people didn't return my greeting, I felt it was their problem— not mine. People in my Sunday school class tried to help, and the fellowship was truly his Love. I turned the whole situation over to the Lord.

Finally, the ax found me. I was called in to a senior vice-president's office, and discovered a member of the human resources department was there. This was a clear signal that my time had come. After a brief "Hello, how are you," the meeting opened with their announcement that my position had been eliminated. The senior vice-president stated that this was no reflection on my work, but I was no longer needed. An outplacement firm would assist me in securing another job. There would be three months' severance pay and no medical benefits. That hit hard. I took copious notes, which I have since discarded. I remembered saying, "At my age, who's going to hire me?" The senior VP said, "You don't tell them how old you are." I responded, "With asthma?" The response was, "Don't tell them about that either." "You wouldn't want me to lie, would you?" I then explained that this was not acceptable to me. I worked in a basement environment for years at the Board when I was diagnosed with asthma. I needed the health benefits, I explained. And, if I received those, I would tell the world that they had treated me fairly. The meeting ended with no hope on their part. Several weeks later, I received a phone call at home from Human Resources, and this person said, "Are you sitting down?"

"Yes," I replied.

"You should be," the person added. "We found a little-known policy which states, 'If you've been in position for a certain number of years,' which you have, 'and if your position is eliminated,' as is the case with you— 'then you are entitled to full medical benefits plus a pension!'"

"Praise the Lord," I said, "and thanks for the good news." My wife and I began singing, "God is so good. . . ." We still are. What Satan intended for evil, God turned to good, thanks to the Board policy.

"Now Glory be to God Who by His mighty power at work within us is able to do far more than we would ever dare to ask or even dream of—infinitely beyond our highest prayers, desires, thoughts or hopes" (Ephesians 3:20).

STRANGERS IN MY HOUSE

S. L. Harris

A number of years had elapsed between my last attendance at a Glorieta conference (New Mexico) and the one at hand. Fond memories of inspiring worship, challenging messages, enlightening Bible study, informative content sessions, and wonderful fellowship with others of "like mind and spirit" made the trip of several hours through the New Mexico plains seem short. My wife and I were excited at the prospect of a week of spiritual rejuvenation like we had known before. Our expectations were short-lived.

Aside from the absence of familiar names and faces on the program roster (although many former well-known presenters were still on the speaking "circuit"), and being heard of arrogance in a single "right" position in matters formerly open to interpretation now became a critical attitude toward differing viewpoints. The principal speaker for the week was heralded as a "young and rising star" in the Convention. He embodied all of the characteristics above in both his personal and program demeanor. The supporting cast for the week was, with some notable exceptions, of the same ilk.

When we left at the end of the week, disappointed and somewhat dejected, we tried to analyze our experience on the long ride back home. What had happened in the years we were away? Was what we had seen and heard only the natural change that comes with the passing of time? Were our observations simply reflections of our nostalgia confronting new worship styles? After lengthy analysis, we both agreed, "Strangers have moved into house and taken over while we were away."

The identity of the strangers was not difficult to determine. By their demeanor, proclamation, and overt behavior, they were the fundamentalists who had been at work ruthlessly attacking and attempting to discredit friends and acquaintances in places of leadership in the Southern Baptist Convention. We had observed, read, and heard firsthand reports of their goal to gain control of the presidency and knew of their blatant "get out the vote bus-ins" to the annual meetings, but the Glorieta event was our first face-to-face encounter with major players. What we had suspected in contemplation was confirmed: "These aren't our kind of Baptists."

We were blessed with a pastor who was informed, alert to the dangers inherent in the movement, and bold enough to enlighten the membership as to what was happening. On one occasion he invited Cecil Sherman, one of the early voices crying in the wilderness, to meet with interested members for a question-and-answer time. Cecil carefully described the goals and methodology of the fundamentalists, relating experiences along the way to validate his assertions. He concluded by saying, "What you need to realize, folks, is that these people don't believe like we do." Subsequent events, culminating in the reconstruction of the Baptist Faith and Message, have verified his assessment.

Not long after, during a discussion time in the Wednesday night prayer meeting, I voiced my opinion as to what the process of the takeover would be like. I said that upon their successful seizure of power at the national level, the fundamentalists would restructure the governing boards of the various convention institutions and agencies to reflect their viewpoint only. We could say good-bye to the seminaries as we knew them, and the boards and agencies as they had existed. The next step, I predicted, would be a concentrated effort to gain control of the state conventions, followed by associational control. Ultimately, I said, every church, including ours, would have to decide whether or not they would be Southern Baptist. I suggested that the church appoint a denominational relations committee to study and keep the church apprised of developments along the way, and to make recommendations when deemed advisable. My suggestion met with favor, and soon the committee was in place.

The appointment of the denominational relations committee was apparently the action that smoked out the clandestine fundamentalist elements in the membership. While never claiming more than a handful of sympathizers, their leader, a young deacon, was vocal and vociferous. Fed by his cohorts at the national level and employing the same tactics as they, he engaged in scurrilous personal attacks on the pastor, criticizing his preaching, his theology, and his pastoral ministry. By innuendo and out-right falsehood he attempted to undermine the pastor's standing with the congregation, all the while encouraged by the tiny minority who followed him. When confronted by the deacon body, he first denied any ill motive and agreed to stop his destructive behavior, only to engage in the same kind of activity again in a matter of days. The pastor's personal attempts at reconciliation were met with same deceitful response. Finally, after repeated efforts by the deacon body and others to quench the brushfires he contin-ually set, he was advised that his tactics weren't going to succeed and that he would be wise to find fellowship elsewhere. His departure, and that of his cohorts, finally brought peace to the church.

As unpleasant as it was, the experience was the defining moment for the church. In those difficult times, the church discovered its true identity, and my wife and I learned once and for all time that we were no longer Southern Baptists. The denomination of our birth was on the way to the graveyard, and we wanted no part of the burial. We moved from that com-munity upon retirement, and in two relocations have been blessed to find churches that embrace true Baptist beliefs and polity. We have not thought of ourselves as Southern Baptists, nor been inclined to support any of their endeavors, since confirming what we had suspected: strangers moved into our house and took over.

YESTERDAY'S DREAMS, TODAY'S REALITIES

Lavonn D. Brown

In the greater part of my ministry I would have been considered a denominational loyalist. I followed a familiar path not unlike hundreds of Southern Baptist ministers.

I grew up in a non-Baptist home. Became a Christian while in high school. Sensed God's call to ministry. Graduated from a Baptist university. Received the Th.D. degree from a Southern Baptist seminary. For a number of years, I pastored churches in Texas and Oklahoma. In 1991, I retired from the pastorate of FBC in Norman, Oklahoma, after twenty-nine years of service.

On the Convention level, I had opportunities to speak at Ridgecrest and Glorieta, gave lectures at preaching conferences across the country, wrote books for the Convention and Broadman Press, and had articles published in Convention magazines. On the state level, I was president of the state Convention, on the Board of Directors for the state, spoke at our youth assembly, and served on numerous committees. Also, I was active on the associational level.

Through the years, First Baptist Church, Norman, has been a traditional, mainstream Southern Baptist church. If anything we had learned our lessons too well. We were giving 17 percent of our income to the Cooperative Program. If we had an overage at the end of the year, we took a "thirteenth check" to the state office for mission causes. Our church had a strong WMU program and excellent missionary education. Over the years, more than sixty missionaries claimed FBC as their home church. In fact, twenty-three retired missionaries presently are members of our church.

Because my seminary degree was in homiletics and pastoral care, I had been approached by four of our six seminaries about teaching. My plans for the future included the possibility of teaching and certainly visions of service to the denomination after retirement. All that began to change in the late 1970s.

I was aware of tension between fundamentalist and moderate conservatives in the Convention. I did not know how serious it was until I read about a group being organized to "go after the jugular" of the Southern Baptist Convention. Those words sounded harsh to a freedom-loving, faithful Baptist.

In 1980, I was invited to a meeting of moderate-conservative pastors who took the Pressler challenge seriously. We met in Gatlinburg. We discussed what could be done to save the SBC from a takeover by fundamentalism. In some ways, this was the birth of the Moderate Movement. My decision to attend was a point of no return. I would pay a price within my state and on the national level.

The reaction was almost immediate. It became obvious that my services would no longer be needed on the state and on the national level. I could no longer be trusted. Requested articles I had been asked to write for Convention periodicals were returned to me. I had taken my stand against the conservative resurgence and would suffer the consequences. This response was to be expected.

The result was that I began seeking fellowship with those in the Moderate Movement. They understood some of the pressures and the isolation we were all having to endure. I attended the Cooperative Baptist Fellowship convocation held in Atlanta in May 1991. Daniel Vestal, who had been defeated as president of the SBC the year before New Orleans, was presiding. My involvement with the CBF, especially my service for a number of years on the Coordinating Council, resulted in my being elected moderator in 1996–97. This made bad matters worse as far as the SBC and state conventions were concerned.

The strategies of the takeover movement have been well documented. Some were behind the scenes and, therefore, not widely known. My eyes were opened in the annual meeting of the Southern Baptist Convention held in Kansas City in June 1984. I was asked to give a nominating speech for a moderate-conservative candidate for vice-president. I arrived at the platform early. I was met at the steps to the platform by one who asked my purpose. After telling him, I was asked to remain at the bottom of the steps and told I would be called for at the appropriate time. As others arrived for the same purpose, I told them about the instructions. A line formed on the floor level.

When time came for the nominating speeches, we were invited to the platform level. On approaching the microphone I noticed there was a person in front of me. I asked him his purpose. He was making a nomination speech. I asked where he had been waiting, and he said he had been seated on the platform. I said, "Look, we both know what is going on here. I dare you to let me speak first." He responded, "I can't do that," and walked to the microphone. He nominated a person acceptable to the conservative resurgence. The democratic approach would not be tolerated at this convention.

The response was the same on the state convention level. In 1989, our church celebrated her centennial. We decided to invite the annual meeting of the Baptist General Convention of Oklahoma to meet with us to celebrate our hundredth year. I wrote a letter of request one year ahead of time. Our church facilities were adequate to house the state convention. We had just completed a city block of new parking space. A month before the decision was to be made, I called the state office to be sure that our letter was in the file. It was.

The time for the decision came and went. We did not hear a word. A few weeks later I saw the state executive director and his associate and asked them about it. The response was simply, "1989 was our year to meet in Tulsa." On the one hand, state leadership insisted that the local church is autonomous and that Convention decisions were not binding on local congregations. On the other hand, when local congregations did, in fact, practice autonomy and make local decisions which differed from the ones handed down from the top, there was a price to be paid.

The following results were predictable:

(1) The pastor would become a persona non grata and would be denied a leadership role and speaking opportunities on the state level.

(2) The members of that congregation would be denied leadership roles in the state and national agencies, trusteeships, and committees.

(3) The church would be ignored into nonexistence even though it continued to fund state and national programs.

(4) The church was considered to represent an "elitist liberal view," was misrepresented as "not believing the Bible," and people were advised not to join.

LAVONN D. BROWN

Increasing dissatisfaction caused by the above circumstances led to decisions made by the members of First Baptist that would deepen her problems with the state leadership.

In July 1993, after a diligent three-year study of appropriate Bible passages, ecclesiastical history, and Baptist history, our church voted that "all members of First Baptist Church, Norman, be considered eligible for any office of the church." Even though it was not mandatory, this opened the door to the ordination of women as deacons. In subsequent years, the names of excellent women were presented and elected by the church. This resulted in confrontation with, and attempted discipline by, associational leaders. Resolutions were passed, but no formal action was taken. On the state level, we became known as one of only two or three churches in Oklahoma that "ordained women deacons."

Also, in the early nineties, our church voted to make it possible for our members to designate their missions dollars "according to conscience." Each member could choose to give 100 percent to the Cooperative Program of the SBC, 100 percent to CBF Global Missions, or divide their gifts to the World Missions Offering at Christmas time.

These decisions were made by a local autonomous church. It seemed good to the Spirit and to us. But not to the association or to state leadership. The door shut tightly. All opportunities for service now came from the free and faithful Baptists within the Cooperative Baptist Fellowship.

It is difficult for me to comprehend the changes that have taken place in the past twenty years. I have been compelled to give up old dreams and dream new ones. Having reached retirement age, I have had to adjust to new realities. The most difficult of these realities is my limited role in kingdom service. I made a deliberate choice to cast my lot with the more moderate-conservative body of Baptists. In my part of the world, that is an unpopular choice. There are only twelve to fifteen churches in Oklahoma that would invite me to their pulpits.

Looking back over the past twenty years, I realize it could not have been otherwise. The leadership of the new Southern Baptist Convention has consistently moved away from the mainstream Baptist life. Conscience no longer permits any loyalty to the Convention I have loved and served for so many years.

ONE LAYMAN'S RELUCTANT JOURNEY TOWARD "HIGHER GROUND"

Wayne C. Bartee

Leaving the local church I had attended most of my life and the denominational organizations with which it was affiliated never entered my mind before my sixtieth year. My reluctant journey away from familiar places and preconceptions grew out of my interest in Baptist history and developed in the course of my involvement in church and denominational affairs. The immediate issues usually concerned policy questions, but I came to realize there is a striking difference in the basic conception of God between myself and those called "fundamental-conservatives."

Born into a devout Baptist family, I participated in church activities from childhood as a matter of course. My church, originally dually aligned with American Baptists and Southern Baptists in the Missouri tradition, chose to align only with the SBC when I was a boy. History always fascinated me and ultimately became my vocation; Baptist history, first learned in Training Union, held a particular magic, all the more after I discovered two of my ancestors were founders of the Missouri Baptist Convention in 1834. My college BSU experience included a summer's work at Ridgecrest Assembly, where I heard many SBC leaders. I recall being uncomfortable with SBC attitudes on race and later on women, but Foy Valentine, T. B.

Maston, and others offered hope that things were moving, if slowly, in the right direction. I began attending state and national conventions with my father and reading more about church institutions and programs.

History as an academic field became my profession, and three years of graduate school in New York City opened a broader understanding of other Christians and Baptists. Still, I felt most comfortable with Southern Baptists and joined SBC churches in New York, then Virginia and Oklahoma. My first teaching experience, a very pleasant one, was at Oklahoma Baptist University.

After returning later to teach at my alma mater in Springfield, my family and I settled into a busy academic schedule and into church life back at my home church: Sunday school teacher, deacon, chair of deacons, and so on. I recall my pastor returned from the SBC meeting in 1979 very upset by the messages and the presidential election. Encouraged by him, I interested myself in SBC affairs, attending several national conventions in the 1980s. In 1984, I heard Russell Dilday appeal eloquently for Southern Baptists to seek "Higher Ground" and to reconcile their differences. It was incomprehensible to me that the fundamental-conservatives should ignore such appeals and engage in "going for the jugular" of their supposed enemies, other sincere Baptists. I concluded they really held a different conception of God: harsh, judgmental, and unloving, based on parts of the Old Testament and alien to what I believed.

I was there when the moderate-conservatives lost their last, best chance in San Antonio in 1988 and began to distance myself from the SBC. My son and I joined a group that went to the SBC meeting in Las Vegas in 1989, witnessing again the triumphalism of the new leaders and the rudeness of many of the messengers. The defunding of the International Seminary in Ruschlikon in 1990 served as the last straw. My wife and I attended the first gathering in Missouri of what became the Cooperative Baptist Fellowship of Missouri. We persuaded the finance committee of our church to allow us to divert our missions gifts to the CBF; others in the church soon followed.

Events in my local church in the 1990s are even now painful to recall. For several years, I believed the church would be understanding enough to allow members to follow their consciences and choose between CBF and SBC as long as they loyally supported the church's own programs. The new pastor who came in 1992 was clearly a moderate. Our number grew slowly; one woman friend was elected to the CBF National Council, and my wife and I served on the CBF of Missouri council. Keith Parks was invited to speak for the church's missions week. However, it is clear in retrospect that 1994 was a watershed when SBC decided to reject all missions contributions from CBF. Although our pastor denounced this to the deacons as an act of arrogance, the group that dominated the offices of the church began to view CBF with alarm. I and those who designated gifts to CBF came under suspicion as disloyal and plotting to take over the church! "Friends" of a lifetime, themselves ignorant of events, easily came to accept such fantastic stories and politely disbelieved my explanations. The pastor chose to leave rather than struggle, and the dominant group picked an interim pastor who would lead in "cleaning up" the church. A friend and I were called in and told our CBF activity must stop or else. We refused. After three stormy town meetings, the congregation voted early in 1997 to exclude CBF from the premises. So I reached another step in my reluctant journey: My wife and I, my two grown sons, and my eighty-nine-year-old mother left the church to which she had belonged since 1934 and I nearly as long. More than two hundred others also left.

Fortunately for us, this departure from "Egypt" did not leave us in the wilderness, but quickly into a "Promised Land," a friendly, open church that respected the complete freedom of members to support SBC, American Baptists, or CBF, according to the dictates of their consciences. This church, University Heights Baptist in Springfield, remembers and follows historic Baptist principles: no creed but the Bible, priesthood of every believer, autonomy and democracy in the local congregation, separation of church and state. I grieve for friends in other places that have no such church to which to go. My family has found good fellowship and broadened further our interests in attending national meetings of both CBF and ABC.

I had hoped—naively it now appears—that Missouri Baptists would resist fundamentalist pressure to conform and chart their own course as have Texas Baptists. As a member of the MBC Historical Commission and convention nominating committee I struggled to that end, but with little success.

Outsiders have great difficulty comprehending our Baptist battles, and so do I. Inerrancy, creedal statements, and social issues have too often become clubs for attacking fellow Christians in the quest for power and control. My journey, in a sense a reluctant one, has been an effort to avoid sinking into the swamp of such issues and to try to follow my conscience in seeking to serve a loving God through the church in the Baptist way—

WAYNE C. BARTEE

the real Baptist way. Remembering the actions of former friends still occasionally hurts at a personal level, but my whole journey has broadened my understanding of being a Christian and of church life and has providentially put me in touch with wonderful, inspiring women and men, pastors and laypersons, whom I would otherwise never have met. The journey has brought my family and me to higher ground.

EXILED FROM THE SBC

June Brown

I was born into a Southern Baptist family, married in a Southern Baptist church, and assumed I would die as a member of a Southern Baptist church. My Christian heritage came through my father. In fact, he led my mother to the Lord, and she was baptized in a creek on their wedding day. Likewise, my father helped me find Christ at an early age. During an old-fashioned revival, I cried every night because my parents thought a five-year-old was too young to walk the aisle, but my persistence paid off. Later that week I surrendered my heart to Jesus while wrapped in Daddy's arms in our backyard.

My family attended a Southern Baptist church in the country where thirty-five people on Sunday was a crowd. Everyone in our community was poor, but no one knew it because we were rich in love. Sunday morning found us in church; often we were the first to arrive and the last to leave. My mother taught my primary and intermediate Sunday school classes. For Christmas, she gifted each child with a New Testament and signed her name; in mine she simply wrote, *From your Mother.* As I grew in my Christian faith, I cherished vacation Bible school, loved singing in the children's choir, and lived for summer camp. Like many others, I was thoroughly immersed in Southern Baptist life.

Throughout high school, I prayed for a Christian husband, and the Lord honored that request. In college, I met and married a Southern Baptist young man—grateful that his church background matched mine.

Saved and married in a Southern Baptist church! What could be more perfect? Of course we joined a Southern Baptist church immediately after our honeymoon. I thank the Lord for my Christian husband and his gift of discernment. Long before I understood what was happening to women in the Southern Baptist Convention, he was defending their call to ministry. Because of sermons I had heard on female submission, I mistrusted women pastors in the early days of our marriage. As a wife of a godly man, submission was not a concern for me. However, my husband convinced me that we were equal partners—submissive to God and to each other. He wanted Christ to be the spiritual head of our home. Eventually, I began to realize that fundamentalism was not about women graciously submitting to men, but rather about men wanting power and control.

As newlyweds, we joined a local SBC church each time we moved to a different community. In 1973, we completed our education, relocated to our current city, and, of course, joined an SBC church. We were enlisted to teach young couples in Sunday school. For more than thirty years we shared our time, talents, and tithes with that church. During the early 1980s, our pastor repeatedly warned the congregation of turmoil in the Southern Baptist Convention. By listening to his yearly convention reports, my husband and I realized that something had gone desperately wrong in the SBC.

As fundamentalism grew, we found a haven in the Cooperative Baptist Fellowship (CBF). In the summer of 1996, we attended our first national CBF conference and rediscovered our Baptist roots: the priesthood of the believer, the autonomy of the local church, the separation of church and state, and no creed but the Bible. We resolved to support CBF missions, but did not tell church members about our private decision. We met other CBF sympathizers in the community and occasionally met in homes for fellowship.

In retrospect, I believe the first storm warning was a secret deacons' gathering in the fall of 1996. The meeting's agenda was to destroy any CBF links, even though the church had approved the CBF designation of mission gifts the previous year. My husband was excluded from the meeting, but two CBF supporters were accidentally included and bravely defended the Fellowship. Confusion ensued, and the meeting broke up without any action.

When the whirlwind struck, I realized that two related events helped it form. First, the senior minister retired due to his age and poor health. Second, his replacement resigned after only a few years. Later we learned that when the younger pastor arrived, several church members began demanding that he "get rid of CBF." Therefore, I believe his resignation triggered the actions that followed. For when a church lacks leadership, someone will take control and assume power. Thus, a group of older deacons began to assert their authority over the congregation. Their first action was to hire an interim pastor—an older, retired minister who supported their agenda.

No one was prepared for the funnel cloud that resulted. The climate changed swiftly when some individuals with whom we had worshiped for over a quarter-century began making totally unfounded accusations to a few CBF associates. Even though we were not initially the target of these attacks, we saw the dark clouds forming. Our CBF friends were accused of supporting programs that were not true to the Southern Baptist way, starving SBC missionaries, taking money away from mission causes, trying to split the church, and not being real Christians.

In December, we were invited to a Christmas brunch where, much to our distress, we overheard a group of older deacons whispering about problems with CBF. Of course, our involvement in CBF was not known at that time. Accordingly, my husband dreaded the next deacons' meeting. As expected, CBF was the major item on the agenda, and my husband spoke up courageously. But how could he possibly describe his personal convictions to Christ and historic Baptist principles to men who had already decided that CBF was the enemy? Tears flowed freely that night as we mourned the loss of our church, for we knew exile was pending.

In the following weeks, a document was prepared to purge the church of CBF. Two business meetings were scheduled. The first was an informational town meeting, and then a second assembly to vote on the document. Due to negative climate, the first session seemed like a witch hunt. Scare tactics, similar to those at national SBC meetings, were used to alarm senior adults. Consequently, a large crowd of uninformed, unfriendly church members gathered. Electricity charged the sanctuary. Was it any wonder that few people braved the angry congregation to defend the Fellowship?

Shortly after that meeting, a younger deacon attempted in good faith to resolve the conflict by scheduling a compromise forum in his home. Possibly due to fear, only three CBF followers arrived to face a hostile environment of about fifteen deacons. As the only woman in attendance, I sat next to my husband. We endured intimidating remarks and antagonistic questions from men whom he had loved for decades, from men who had dined in our home, and from men whose children we taught in Sunday school. Later, we wept again out of sorrow, but also out of anger and frustration.

March 12, 1997, was the final business meeting and the last time we attended the church. (Even though these events occurred several years ago, tears push their way to the surface as I type these words.) Once again the large crowd contained frightened individuals—many of whom we did not know. CBF supporters, who were given three minutes to speak, were interrupted if they exceeded that time. However, the opposing side had no time limit, so one church member spoke for an hour. As a practicing attorney, he presented his case by mentioning my name in order to refute statements made at the previous debate. I felt as though my life was on trial, yet I could not offer a rebuttal because I had already used my three minutes earlier that evening. Again, the atmosphere was filled with negative comments and innuendos about CBF. Right before the vote, a woman wondered out loud why anyone would want to support an organization that favored "gay rights and abortion." Needless to say, the vote was overwhelmingly in favor of cutting any ties to CBF.

As I pen these thoughts, five years have passed. Last year, the Missouri Baptist Convention (MBC) fell under the control of fundamentalism. Again, I believe the real issue is *power*, not about sharing Christ with a lost world. Consequently, historic Baptist churches are disappearing in my state, although a few brave congregations have cut ties to the SBC. In spite of sorrow over the MBC, my story has a happy ending. I discovered a dually aligned American Baptist and Cooperative Baptist Church in my city. When you are exiled from your home church, you leave memories and precious relationships behind; thus, I grieved for weeks as if a death had occurred. Yet, God surprised me with a treasured family reunion of more than one hundred Christians from my former church who joined our new congregation. So instead of feeling like a Baptist orphan, I now worship with family members from earlier years. Together, we celebrate God's grace with a free and faithful pastor and a loving congregation. We have never been happier in a church! We are truly blessed!

In conclusion, I was born and married in a Southern Baptist church, but I do not think I will die as a member in one. Sadly, fundamentalists have shaped a new type of church in the Southern Baptist Convention—completely different from the ones I knew as a child. Still, like many others, I am a Baptist by conviction and not Convention. In essence, I have not changed, but the SBC has. I did not leave the SBC; it left me. Furthermore, I prefer Christ-centered, grace-oriented, mission-minded, and spirit-filled congregations to legalism. Therefore, I am a happy exile in a new and wonderful land. Upon reflection, I compare my experiences to those of Joseph with his brothers—what at first seemed evil, God used to bless me beyond my wildest dreams. Thanks be to God!

FREEDOM HAS NEVER BEEN SO PRECIOUS!

Michael K. Olmsted

At seventeen, I came to Christ and found the freedom of God's grace. My heart was changed and my life began to change while living in the state of Virginia, where our Baptist forefathers and foremothers fought the battle for religious freedom. But I knew nothing of Baptists, only that my heart needed a church where it would find love and nurture in the scriptures, so the search began. Over the next two years, I visited many different churches with high school friends, examining each in the light of personal Bible study, but without satisfaction. Because of my dad's military career, I ended up in Texas and there found Southern Baptists. For almost a year I studied, visited churches and the Baptist Student Union, and asked questions. What I found was a fellowship of churches that shared a solid biblical faith, were committed to missions, respected the freedom of the individual believer, and did not organize itself on the secular model of authority from the top. My circuitous two-year search ended in November 1961, when I was baptized in a small rural Oklahoma church.

During those college years, I grew in faith and found my preaching voice. The more I learned, the more I celebrated Southern Baptists. On a state campus I found opportunities to share my faith and impact the secular community. Southwestern Seminary challenged and broadened my

theology and prepared me for ministry. I met and married a Southern
Baptist girl from Fort Worth. For the next twenty-seven years, there was
joy as I celebrated faith and involved myself in mission causes through the
SBC. I became zealous for the Southern Baptist cause: no one could do
missions like the SBC, alien immersion is unacceptable, Southern Baptists
are closer to scripture than anyone else. As I continued to study scripture,
some of my ideas were exposed as denominational culturalism. My denomination did not have a claim to the seat at the right hand of Christ! There
resulted a healthier perspective and the freedom to fellowship with Christians who bore different labels, but the same love for Christ.

In 1981, the storm that was to overwhelm the SBC appeared on the
horizon of my safe, comfortable denominational world. There had been
news reports and overheard conversations at state and national conventions. Some seminary professors spoke of a "group" who wanted to take
control of the Convention. I had met W. A. Criswell when I served a
church in southeast Dallas, but Paige Patterson was unknown to me until
1981. I wrote a letter to the *California Southern Baptist*, expressing opposition to this movement that was being led by Paige Patterson and Paul
Pressler. On January 21, 1981, I received a letter from Dr. Paige Patterson,
president of Criswell Center for Biblical Studies, in which he wrote: "I find
it incredible that you are able to judge (1) that our concern is political
rather than theological, (2) that we have made irresponsible accusations,
and (3) that we are encompassed with 'petty Jealousies.'"

Patterson went on to say: "Now, my brother, please know that the real
purpose of my letter is simply to try to call attention to the fact that if we
do find a way to have real understanding and real unity in our Convention,
we must speak of issues and not indulge in motivational judgments which
are the sphere only of the Lord."

Sadly, my concerns were verified. The next several years were marked
by "motivational judgments," brutal political maneuvering, slander, and
deception. The only unity and understanding that fundamentalists know
is for everyone to submit to their authority and control. I was in Dallas
when the lie was circulated that Billy Graham supported Charles Stanley
in his bid for the SBC presidency. I was in San Antonio when "they" locked
us out of the convention hall to be sure the bussed-in messengers had
seats. I kept thinking, "Southern Baptists are too smart to let this happen."
At the St. Louis convention, I was interviewed by a national network news
team and told them, "Southern Baptists will never agree on everything,
but Southern Baptists will stay together and work together in the cause of

missions." That same day Herschel Hobbs was booed from the convention floor, and I knew it was over.

Because of long-standing friendships with people in Nashville, in several state Convention offices, and in some of the SBC seminaries, accounts of ruthless fundamentalist tactics were relayed to me. When the trustees of the Foreign Mission Board were publicly stating that Dr. Parks was respected and would not be forced out, a friend in California called to tell me that the chairman of FMB trustees had just told him that Keith Parks would be gone within a month. When the prediction came true, I could no longer restrain myself. My faith and principles would not allow me to remain silent. From the beginning it was obvious that this "conservative resurgence" had nothing to do with saving the SBC from "liberalism" and everything to do with control and a legalistic approach to religion. How could these men call us back to the Bible when they were operating as though they were ignorant of its teaching? I was serving as a trustee of one of our Baptist colleges and watched the controversy divide the board and create stress for the administration and faculty. Fine people were destroyed by false accusations.

I went to my deacons and told them that I intended to address the takeover of the SBC on a Sunday morning. They were concerned about negative fallout but supportive. The sermon was announced a week in advance so those who wished to avoid the topic could be absent. On that Sunday, the crowd was large and focused. At the conclusion, I called on the church to take a stand, and to my amazement, the congregation stood and applauded. A denominational relations committee was formed, and we began to designate our gifts to the SBC mission boards. Today, the only funds that go to the SBC are designated gifts from a handful of members. Likewise, our giving to the Missouri Baptist Convention is all designated and subject to revision as the fundamentalists take control of various agencies.

University Heights Baptist Church began in 1945 as a dually aligned church. The founders believed then, and the attitude today is that Christians should be able to work together for the cause of Christ. The church struggled to be included in the state convention and the local association, because of our insistence that we be affiliated with the American Baptist Churches—USA. This congregation has a stronger sense of historic Baptist distinctive than most SBC churches. There has always been a sense of joy in sharing missions with two great denominations. Although my doctrine did not change when I became pastor of UHBC, in the eyes of some, suddenly I became a "liberal." Occasionally, an outsider would ask, "When are you going to get the church to sever its ties with ABC?" My response was either "Why?" or "Never!" Today, University Heights is dually aligned with the American Baptists and the Cooperative Baptist Fellowship. Members are allowed to designate their gifts outside the church, so there is only the thinnest connection to the SBC. Fundamentalists are duplicating their SBC takeover in Missouri, so that connection is dwindling rapidly.

The heritage of Baptists has been largely lost in the SBC. Men like Al Mohler, Paige Patterson, and Morris Chapman are rewriting history to support their theology of control. The 2000 Baptist Faith and Message is no longer a simple statement of shared beliefs: it is now a position pamphlet for the Christian far right and a test of fundamentalist orthodoxy. The Southern Baptist Convention today is a different denomination than the fellowship of believers I found in 1961. "Baptist" should be removed from their title. Their corporate structure comes from the world, not the example or words of Christ.

Like Baptists from our earliest days, the Word of God is my guide for faith and practice. I treasure as distinctive principles the priesthood of every believer, autonomy of the local church, and the separation of church and state. For years I struggled to keep those ideas alive in the SBC, and I fought to stop the legalism and judgmental spirit of fundamentalism. But when the votes continued to support the takeover, I realized there was no point in fighting for those who did not want to be free.

Several years ago, in another state, a woman came to talk to me about the abuse she was suffering. Her husband had never hit her, but she was constantly afraid that he would one day. The verbal/psychological abuse had begun about six months after the wedding. He criticized her housekeeping, complained about her cooking, suggested she was dumb, and repeated the idea that "You're lucky I would have you, because most men would never take a second look!" When their baby was born, the husband began almost immediately telling his wife she was a "crummy" mother. At the same time, he professed to love her, reminding her that he would make the right decisions, think for her, and make sure their son would grow up to marry someone better than his mother. Years had passed, and she had been so emotionally and spiritually beaten down that she had no strength, no will to break free. The husband laughed at the idea of counseling. She resigned herself to an oppressive, negative life. That woman reminds me of what has happened in the life of a denomination that once afforded me joy and opportunities for ministry.

There is no freedom like that found in Christ. Through so many of the years of struggle in the SBC, I kept working and praying that we could save our denomination. But there came a day when it was clear that people would prefer to live under the negative, oppressive bondage of fundamentalists than be free. Southern Baptists did not save me. They could not bring God's grace into my life when I failed as a Christian. When I stand before my Savior, a denominational label will mean nothing. Their seal of approval does not validate God's calling in my life. The CEO and Executive Committee of the SBC are unimportant when I read the Word of God and listen for his voice. Ever since that midnight in Hampton, Virginia, when I quietly asked Christ to forgive me and take up residence in my life, I have been free. Thank God! Freedom has never been so precious!

A LOT LIKE DYING

Gregory L. Hancock

Being exiled must be a lot like dying. While it is happening, you feel pretty bad about it. After you've gone through it, you realize how good it is to be with God! That is my experience, in a nutshell.

The following remarks are spoken in my opinion and from where I stand. God meets people where they are, and I am prepared to accept that he has met others somewhere else.

I became involved in the counter-takeover movement in the SBC somewhere around 1980. I was a pastor in Kentucky at the time, but my background was in communications and journalism. I was asked by some other pastors, seminary educators, and denominational servants to serve as managing editor for a moderate tabloid named *The Call*. After the first edition, we began to add a tag to the masthead that indicated where the next annual meeting would be conducted, that is, *The Call: Dallas '85*. We believed this moderate voice would counter the negative influence of the fundamentalist tabloid, *SBC Today*, and would awaken mainstream Southern Baptists to the threat of what was going on. Larry Dipboye, pastor of another Kentucky church, was to be the editor.

Only three or four editions of *The Call* were published. I cannot recall the specific content of any one of them except that they voiced the

moderate perspective and encouraged people to attend the annual meeting and vote against the takeover. I wrote some of the copy, Dipboye wrote
some of the copy, and there were a few "cameo" contributors and some
stuff that "appeared" from a source Dipboye trusted and I did not question. I always suspected it came from people who were employed by the
SBC in one capacity or another and were afraid to let their names be published lest their jobs be in danger. It was poor journalism to allow that to
happen and I regret it today. As it turned out, most moderate employees
of the SBC either lost their jobs or retired anyway.

Back then, however, many of us who were close to the Southern Baptist denomination believed that the takeover could be stopped. We believed
it to be the product of shallow, unchristian thinking, and we believed God
would not let it happen. I distinctly recall sitting in a prayer meeting with
others of the moderate persuasion and hearing a prayer voiced that God
would "assert his will and allow the right to win out." How were any of
us to know God was a literalist?

In retrospect, I see that prayer as the beginning of my pilgrimage into
exile. I prayed a paraphrase of that prayer in my every encounter with Father.
I knew others were praying it, and we all believed in prayer. Nevertheless,
the fundamentalist movement was winning victory after victory. Were we
being sent a message?

I began to examine my beliefs in light of fundamentalism. I prayed for
a spirit of humility that would allow me to accept a perspective different
from my own and, if where I stood at that time was wrong, to embrace the
new perspective. I was under conviction, struggling, and ready to approach
the throne of Grace in an entirely new paradigm.

Ultimately, I came to several conclusions. I concluded I had no cause
to doubt my relationship with Jesus Christ. My personal redemption was
the work of God through Jesus and the product was—pardon the expression—infallible.

I concluded my experience with Jesus Christ through the Holy Spirit
was genuine. God proves himself not through empirical science but through
revelation, and there were numerous instances in my life where God had
revealed himself to me.

I concluded that if fundamentalism were correct in its theology and
expression, I would just as soon go to hell. People of integrity and Christian intent may have populated the fundamentalist movement, but people
of mean spirit and selfish motivation characterized its leadership. When I

sought the Holy Spirit in the actions of fundamentalist leadership, I found—and still find—the spirit of Satan.

That much resolved, in my thinking, a more objective problem demanded solution: if we were praying for the right side to win and the fundamentalists were wrong, but they were winning, was it possible that God was out of control? My personal theology would not allow me to accept that.

The truth came to me in a revelation that was as stunning as it was personally painful: Whenever humankind has created structures and resources that rival God in their strength and authority, God has allowed the intervention of unpredictable events to take those structures and resources out of existence. The Southern Baptist Convention had created a political and financial realm that was so strong no power on earth could prevail against it. Even Satan himself could not find a significant foothold. Since the SBC could not be negated from without, God was allowing it to negate itself from within. To stand in the way was, quite simply, to obstruct the will of God.

I left Baptist denominational work in 1990. I moved into the secular workplace, adjusted, and found myself comfortable with God and conscience. Since then, I have served several interim pastorates, followed a calling comfortably removed from denominational involvement, and enjoyed membership in a local church where I conduct a senior adult Bible study. Moreover, I have found what I believe to be a valid and dynamic ministry in and through corporate America.

I still oppose the entire concept of religious fundamentalism. In my opinion, the SBC takeover effectively prevented the word of God from reaching the lost world in our lifetime. I have come to grips with that, however, and believe there is a divine reason for it.

To be sure, some structure remains to the organism that once was the SBC, but it is a rather pitiful derelict of a once-impressive instrument. From the wreck, however, we may be seeing a revival of a local, unaffiliated, community church that conducts its ministry on faith. That church does not need to own property or exert material influence. It merely needs to lift up the Christ.

THE TEXAS TWO-STEP

Rick McClatchy

My mind was liberated by the work of a small Texas Baptist university. I enrolled there to study for the ministry. The professors introduced me to a broader world of thought and instilled in me a desire for continued exploration. They permanently enriched my life and faith. I will forever be in their debt.

Several years later while working on my dissertation at seminary, I started teaching as an adjunct at my old alma mater. Soon I was teaching two to three classes with about 90 to 120 students each semester. The religion faculty and several trustees told me that they were impressed by my work and believed I had a future teaching at the university. They even offered me a one-year contract to teach full-time, but it would have required my dropping out of my Ph.D. studies for a year, which I did not think best to do. Therefore, I declined the offer and continued to teach as an adjunct, rushing to finish my work so I could begin teaching full-time.

There was only one cloud on the horizon. It was the late 1980s and the fundamentalists' takeover was in full force. Moderates were against the ropes and reeling. At the 1990 SBC meeting in New Orleans, moderates threw in the towel. A few months later, I attended the meeting in Atlanta that gave birth to the CBF.

Meanwhile, in Texas, the battle was not over. What would become of the Baptist General Convention of Texas? Would it follow the lead of the SBC and bring about radical changes in the state Convention? Many of us in Texas did not want the fundamentalists to succeed in our state, so we threw our hearts and lives into the work of Texas Baptist Committed (TBC). We believed we could save our state Convention. David Currie set up a statewide structure to get out the moderate vote for the state Convention meeting. I worked one of the zones to help get out the vote.

My colleagues at the university watched our efforts closely, with good reason. If the state Convention fell to the fundamentalists, then the gagging and purges which occurred among the SBC's seminaries' faculties would occur in the state Convention's universities. A spirit of apprehension filled the air. My faculty colleagues were adamantly opposed to the fundamentalists and within a safe, limited circle let their feelings be known. However, they stayed beyond the political activities. They supported my involvement and wanted to know what was happening though. Likewise, the administration opposed the fundamentalists and quietly supported the efforts of TBC. Once, after a heated state Convention meeting in which moderates prevailed, the president of the university told me that it had been a good day and that he appreciated my work with TBC.

It was good to know that one's efforts were appreciated, but more important was the preservation of our universities' academic freedom. Without this freedom our universities cannot liberate the minds of students. This was a battle worth fighting because so much was at stake. I was happy to make small, behind-the-scenes contributions to this effort. However, as events unfolded my efforts did not remain entirely behind the scenes.

Moderates and fundamentalists were soon announcing slates of candidates and campaigning for them prior to the state Convention meeting. One year, the fundamentalists announced their slate of candidates, and two of their nominees were serving as trustees for my alma mater, which goes to show that fundamentalists were never denied representation as they alleged. TBC sponsored public forums across the state that year to discuss what was at stake. I organized a public forum in my zone at a church across from the campus. Several of the religious faculty attended, but none of the administration did. They were in a difficult position. They did not want the fundamentalists to win, but they had to act as if they were beyond being concerned about or involved in the election, especially since two of the fundamentalists' candidates were sitting on their board of trustees.

The fundamentalists lost the election that year. However, unknown to me at the time, I also lost my future at the university.

The following semesters the number of classes that I had been teaching was cut back. Also, I began to get messages that they were not sure that they were going to have any openings in the religion department as they had anticipated. About halfway through one semester, I picked up the listing of the next semester's classes only to discover that I was not listed as teaching a single class. No one had notified me of this decision. Feeling grief and anger, I continued about my work. Several of the religion faculty, seeing my hurt, went out of their way to be my friend in the few remaining weeks I had. I will always appreciate their kindness at this time.

Meanwhile, I hastily looked for other teaching positions or pastorates since I had a family to feed. It was at this time circumstance led me to hope not all was over. One of the religion faculty resigned. I applied for the position and had several trustees make contacts on my behalf. However, they informed me that the administration had other plans. Clearly, my teaching future was over at the university, and so I continued to search for employment.

It was my friends at TBC, David Currie and Bill Bruster, who came to my assistance and helped me find a new church to serve at this time. Through their contacts a church in Oklahoma began visiting with me, and soon a date was set up for me to make a visit to the church in view of a call. About a week before my visit to the church, the university president wrote me a letter offering me a part-time job at the university working with international students. I declined the offer and went to serve a church in Oklahoma.

Later I found out the university had hired an adjunct to teach in the religion department. He was an open fundamentalist from the largest church in the area. In a short while, he was publicly accusing several of the religion faculty of being liberals. Thankfully he moved to a new church out of the area and ceased teaching and attacking the university.

As I have looked back on the events that transpired, I have reached two conclusions. I am fully convinced that universities are a gift to the church and play a vital role in its future. However, the church is seldom a gift to higher education and frequently plays a detrimental role.

Administrators and faculty of denominational universities must walk a difficult road. The institutions they serve were created by churches to help the development and training of church leaders, lay and clergy.

Denominational universities want to produce people with sharp, analytical, and creative minds with a high degree of spiritual sensitivity. Frequently such leaders are not well received in Baptist churches, especially those prone toward fundamentalism, as most Baptist churches are. Therefore, Baptist churches distrust the universities and their work. The consequence of such a situation is that people working in universities get hurt if they attract the ire of the churches, as I did.

My experience is not unique, and others have been treated much worse than I was. Nonetheless, my experience is illustrative of what others have had to endure. I violated the basic requirement for survival at a denominational university. I had become an object of fundamentalist attention and concern. My efforts in TBC—or more specifically, challenging the suitability of two fundamentalist trustees to lead the state convention—were, I'm sure, a serious dilemma for the university administration. In their heart they knew I was right, and they knew someone had to lead the resistance to fundamentalists, but I'm sure they would have preferred it not be someone so close to the university.

At this point, denominational universities have difficulty. Those who are their most ardent defenders are from their own ranks and not those on the outside. Consequently, many people inside or very close to the institution get used to defending the institution and then being tossed aside once their usefulness is done. Sometimes I wonder if I would not have been better off if I had kept my mouth shut and maintained a low profile. Certainly, my possibilities for a teaching career would have been better, but I'm not sure in the bigger picture that things would have been better for the kingdom of God.

At the time I became involved in TBC, it looked like the fundamentalist machine could not be stopped. There was legitimate reason to believe that Texas would be the next major target of the fundamentalists. Not many, especially pastors, were willing to put it all on the line to oppose the fundamentalists for fear of ruining their career. If a few key leaders had not acted immediately to organize hundreds of Baptist laity, all might have been lost. I'm glad today that my old alma mater has a higher degree of academic freedom than it would have had the fundamentalists won the day, and I know that students' minds are still being liberated. I like to think that I played a small part in preserving that for future generations.

Those who decided to remove me from the teaching picture do not deserve harsh condemnation. They are good people who really meant no personal harm to me. They were caught in a situation where the institution was under attack from the fundamentalists, and the most expedient thing to do was to remove me from visibility and get a new fundamentalist adjunct. Their effort to give me a position less visible with international students was an effort to try saving me some financial hardship.

The key to the Baptist future is going to be finding leaders who have analytical and creative minds with a high degree of spiritual sensitivity. Universities will have a key part to play in the formation of these types of leaders. Will Baptist churches allow universities to do this? My hope is that churches and denominational universities can find a more healthy way of relating to each other. If not, then others in the universities will have to be willing to come forward at the appropriate time to defend academic freedom. I wish them the best and urge them to do so even if the cost is great.

A LIBERAL BAPTIST'S STORY OF EXILE FROM THE SBC

C. Fred Werhan

Back in the early 1980s, right after the election of the first few conservative presidents of the SBC, a time when moderate Baptists were still in charge of most of the SBC functions, Monday mornings at the weekly Buncombe Baptist Pastor's Conference in Asheville, North Carolina, frequently found me off on the side before or after the formal meeting, debating with Cecil Sherman about appropriate strategies for countering the fundamentalists' takeover efforts. Cecil, of course, was a key leader of the moderate cause, while at the same time a conservative Southern Baptist. I, on the other hand, was, in fact, one of those liberals about whom fundamentalist Southern Baptists were raging. I was not a part of the inner circle of moderate leaders, but simply a pastor of a small rural Southern Baptist church that was a strong advocate of traditional Baptist distinctive, such as religious freedom, church and individual autonomy, priesthood of the believer, and so on.

Being a liberal (M.Div. and D.Min. from Vanderbilt Divinity School) who had come out of an ultra-fundamentalist background, and being a Baptist who cherished our traditional distinctive, led me to a position of seeking parity for all reflections of Southern Baptists' diverse theology. What I was hearing, in the beginning of the controversy, was a concern being expressed by very conservative, and fundamentalist, Baptists that they were not being given fair representation by the leadership at the time in the SBC. They were not being invited to teach in our seminaries nor write for our literature. Having been a fundamentalist, I understood their concern, though I no longer identified with their theology.

I believed that being Baptist meant that we must allow a broad diversity of theology and practice among our churches and convention membership. I personally wanted the freedom as a liberal Baptist to express the faith, and it was my contention, at the time, that on the other end of that continuum, the fundamentalist Baptist should have the same freedom. I understood that fundamentalists believed that they held the only right positions, and those who disagreed with them were wrong. But for me to deny them a fair place at the SBC table was for me to assume a similar position. Though they did not understand, nor practice, the Baptist principle that guided my thinking, in my mind it was still my responsibility to that principle to practice it in relation to them.

In a letter to my neighbor pastor, Cecil Sherman, just prior to the 1982 SBC convention in New Orleans, when moderates were trying to formulate an agenda and a strategy in response to the fundamentalist resurgence, I outlined my position and suggestions as follows:

> If we are going to advocate a broad-based Convention, then it seems to me we have to be active advocates for some of the following:
>
> (1) An inerrancy line of literature published by our Sunday School Board, along with the other lines now provided.
>
> (2) Faculty members and teachers in our seminaries who represent *all* theological views held by Baptists, including inerrancy.
>
> (3) Places of leadership and service for our various Convention agencies and programs for persons who hold an inerrancy position.
>
> (4) Efforts to define our Convention as "both/and" rather than "either/or" theological "left/right."

I soon discovered that Cecil Sherman and those who set the moderate agenda were not in favor of any of those suggestions. I was told it was stupid to think that you can include, and work with, fundamentalists. (I already knew that; I had been a rigid fundamentalist in the past with whom more moderate Baptists could not work! I knew that mindset.) I was told that letting fundamentalists teach in our seminaries was like letting a witch doctor teach in a medical school. (That, to me, was as arrogant as the fundamentalists' condemnation of liberals teaching in our seminaries.) It became obvious to me that those who were setting the moderate agenda had little tolerance or acceptance of those with whom they disagreed.

Based on a belief that the great majority of Southern Baptists were neither fundamentalists nor liberals, but somewhere in a broad middle, I went home from the New Orleans convention and wrote a paper entitled "Some Strategy for the Southern Baptist Middle" and conducted a survey among the ninety Baptist church pastors in the Buncombe Baptist Association, the results of which, along with some of my thoughts on agenda and strategy, were published in the very first issue of *SBC Today* in April 1983.

In the paper, I offered this analysis to the ninety church pastors:

> It is obvious from our last two annual sessions (L.A. and N.O.) that our Southern Baptist Convention is divided into two camps, loosely called Conservative and Moderate. Each camp links the other with an extreme group. The Conservatives are linked with the Fundamentalists and the Moderates are linked with the Liberals. The fact is, most Southern Baptist Conservatives are not Fundamentalists and most of the Moderates are not Liberals.
>
> Conservatives and Moderates have more in common with each other than either of them has with the Fundamentalists or the Liberals. The great majority of Southern Baptists form a broad middle. Most of these probably do not wish to identify with either of the two camps into which Southern Baptists are now divided. But as long as there are only two camps, then those in the middle have to join the side with which they are most comfortable.
>
> The great majority of Southern Baptists are being forced to support positions and methods on one side or the other, that are neither of their making nor to their liking. Most Southern Baptists are being used to fight the battle of a few, and the great majority of Southern Baptists won't be the winners, but the losers, in this fight. As long as we are divided into two camps, each seeking control, pulling up apart, tearing us at the seams, the faith held by Southern Baptists and the mission we support together will always be in disarray. Somewhere we must find the leaders and the strategy to bring back in the middle, and leave the fighters out on the fringes.

I asked the pastors to identify where they considered themselves by marking only one of the following seven choices:

Fundamentalist
Fundamentalist/Conservative
Conservative

Moderate/Conservative
Moderate
Moderate/Liberal
Liberal

Everyone who responded marked themselves as somewhere between the extremes. No one claimed to be a Fundamentalist or a Liberal.

With this analysis, I then asked the pastors to either "agree" or "disagree" with the following strategies (simply listed here, though more thoroughly elaborated in the paper):

(1) The strategy of the middle must be inclusive, not exclusive.

(2) The strategy of the middle must include a commitment to work just as hard for the other person's right to be represented as we do for our own.

(3) The strategy of the middle must be to admit openly our differences, rather than insisting that we all be alike.

(4) The strategy of the middle must give priority to missions.

(5) The strategy of the middle must be to find and elect leadership representative of all Southern Baptists.

Ninety percent of the respondents expressed agreement with all of the strategies. (This was not a scientific poll; those who disagreed may not have responded, I don't know.)

This survey and dialogue took place only in the Buncombe Baptist Association, not the entire Southern Baptist Convention. However, Cecil Sherman, a key leader in shaping the moderate agenda, was a part of that association and a part of that dialogue, and thus the moderate leadership had access to these ideas and positions. Other moderate Baptists had access to these ideas and positions through the article in *SBC Today*.

There was no rally to take up these positions for which I had lobbied in these early years of the controversy. Therefore, I and the church I pastored supported the moderate position, being one of the first churches to join the Baptist Alliance, and later, one of the first churches to support the CBF. We always took a full complement of messengers to the SBC right up through 1989. Then in 1990, we began taking our people to the CBF gatherings.

Looking back, we all now know that the fundamentalist takeover of the SBC is complete and that moderate Baptists are moving on with other structures for carrying out their mission. At first, there was a strong sense of loss, felt by members of our church and me, but we soon got beyond that. Shortly after I retired in 1995 after serving as pastor for twenty-three years, under the leadership of its new pastor, the Hominy Baptist Church in the Buncombe Baptist Association disassociated itself from the SBC in 2000 and identified as a CBF church. All is well, and Baptists of all positions are moving on.

Could it have been different? I surely am not suggesting that following the strategies I proposed would have changed anything, or that the Southern Baptist Convention would have survived as the diverse Baptist entity for which I had lobbied.

What I do know is that the strategies of those who led the moderate cause did in fact fail, and we who identified as moderates, and worked for the moderate cause, lost the SBC and our place in it, along with its seminaries, mission boards, and other benevolent agencies. The strategy of the moderate leadership was not a winning way! It was a losing way! Given the fundamentalist opposition, perhaps there was no winning way. But I still wonder.

I admire and commend Cecil Sherman and the many others who sought to provide leadership during the days of struggle for the SBC. I know they gave it their best effort, sometimes at great cost and sacrifice to themselves. But the fact is, they, and we, lost. And out of that loss, it is my hope that we might learn lessons that will help us as Baptists in our future struggles with one another, whether it be in the CBF, the Baptist Alliance, our Baptist state Conventions, or other groups of Baptists with whom we may identify. And there will be future struggles.

Being Baptist is not easy. Being a liberal Baptist is even more difficult. May we find ways to let our actions in relation to one another genuinely reflect those Baptist distinctive we cherish and proclaim.

EXILED:
SOUTH CAROLINA–STYLE

E. C. Watson

In the northern part of rural Robeson County, North Carolina, where I was born in 1923, Ten Mile Baptist Church was the center of our religious and social life. When we moved to Ingold in Sampson County in 1937, some forty miles away, again church and home were the centers around which life for our family revolved. The call to the ministry came for me at age seventeen. In the area where we lived, a Baptist prepared for the ministry in Campbell and Wake Forest colleges and Southern Baptist Theological Seminary. Each of these schools, of course, was supported in part with Cooperative Program funds. One year, while a student at Wake Forest College, a state Convention scholarship paid about a fourth of the total cost of my education.

In pastorates, before and after graduation, support for and promotion of the Cooperative Program was taken for granted. When a career change took me into associational missions, this support and promotion became an even larger part of the role I filled. As an employee of the North Carolina Convention's Sunday School Department and as Consultation on Associational Administration for the Home Missions Board, the relationship changed and my salary and support came from the Cooperative Program and other missions gifts. The same was true for my twenty years on the staff of the South Carolina Baptist Convention. By this time, state Conventions, SBC, and the Cooperative Program were so much a part of me that I could hardly imagine life without them.

The year 1990 was one to remember. The major event of that year for me was retirement from the South Carolina Baptist Convention. Storm clouds of fundamentalism were gathering in the Southern Baptist Convention, but so far they kept their distance from South Carolina. One responsibility as executive assistant to the executive secretary was to assist the Convention's Christian Life and Public Affairs Committee. Supporters of the Right to Life movement attended committee meetings uninvited. The Convention had not taken a stand against abortion and on some other issues on the right-to-life agenda that were satisfactory to this group. The Education Committee of the state House of Representatives held a hearing on teaching sex education in public schools. Two Baptist laymen and I spoke. They were not pleased with my report of Convention actions, which were different from the position they took. I received angry letters from both. The next year, the Convention elected one of these laymen to the committee. At the first meeting of the Christian Life and Public Affairs Committee which he attended, he apologized to me privately for the tone of the letter. But conservative positions now had a foothold in the committee. This was only the first salvo in a battle that followed. That year, my wife Mary Anne and I attended the Southern Baptist Convention Annual Meeting. Mary Anne majored in music in college and in church music at Southern Seminary. My preparation for leading worship left much to be desired, but I learned much from her. There were elements in SBC in periods designated for worship that to us were abrasive and even obnoxious. This was no more the Convention we had known and loved. The division we felt among the people, even in the worship services, left us feeling more distant from God and others rather than drawn together in God. It was the last national we attended.

Soon afterwards, retirement came. Dinner, speeches, gifts, and honors expressed love and appreciation for fifty years of ministry. The presence of some three hundred persons, including pastors, denominational workers, representatives of other denominations, African Americans as well as Caucasians, bishops, and political officials, was an affirming experience.

From the euphoria of that experience, we moved back into the real world. A letter from a pastor asked for my permission for him to nominate me for Convention president. After thought, prayer, and discussion with trusted friends, I agreed. My identification with moderates was well known. But after serving twenty years' service on the Convention staff, there were friends in every part of the theological spectrum. Conservatives offered as their candidate a layman with limited Convention exposure. What followed was the largest attendance ever at an Annual Meeting of the South Carolina Baptist Convention—5,086 messengers and 106 visitors. The 1981 convention registered 2,087 messengers, and there were 3,118 in 1989. The layman won by 216 votes. Probably the losing candidate received more votes than the winner ever received in past years. This election demonstrated the determination of the conservatives (as they were called then) to control the Convention. The conservatives had won the war in South Carolina.

Friendly relationships prevailed, I still felt, between most of the people of the Convention and me. A count of those I considered hostile would be quite small. There were others who seemed to say that they felt no relationship, and preferred that it stay that way. All of the convention staffers were friends. Some expressed appreciation for what we were doing in the Fellowship. There was no effort to exclude me completely from Convention affairs. The executive director brought me back on board for two weeks to help in the Convention's battle against video poker. However, the relationships and atmosphere were so different I felt there was little positive contribution I could make.

The 1991 Convention elected me as a trustee of Anderson College for a five-year term. Only in the last year was the influence of fundamentalism beginning to be felt in trustee affairs.

When moderates met in Atlanta and set in motion the organization of the national Cooperative Baptist Fellowship, we were there. Steps were taken to follow up with something similar in South Carolina. A meeting of persons from South Carolina named an interim steering committee, which planned a state meeting for October 1991. At the request of the committee, letters of invitation were sent out in their behalf over my name. They also requested that I moderate. Attendance was estimated at five hundred persons. Officers were elected, and plans made for a continuing organization, using the national CBF group as a model. A. Harold Cole, retired Convention executive secretary, and I were asked to serve as advisors to the state CBF Coordinating Council, a relationship that continues today.

Fortunately, while taking a stand as a moderate firmly and early on, the harsh and ugly attitudes and actions that reports indicated were present in some places were never something that I experienced. But that does not mean that the exile is not a reality nor that the pain is less real. Before retirement, invitations to preach kept me in the pulpit almost every Sunday. After retirement, invitations were few and far between. When two invitations were withdrawn, I suspected it was because of my moderate stance. Later, one invitation was reissued. This said to me that there were pastors unwilling to risk their standing in a fundamentalist-controlled Convention by having a known moderate as pulpit guest.

In one instance, a leader of the movement told me that he had been asked to help remove me as an Anderson College trustee. His answer, he said, was, "E.C. is my friend. He has always helped me when I asked him. Let him serve out his term like everybody else." I felt that statement was both affirming and loaded with information!

Actions of the Southern Baptist Convention have been disappointing and embarrassing. Mary Anne and I soon realized that we could no longer identify ourselves as Southern Baptists. We are embarrassed that being part of a church and association that relates to SBC implies that we are also connected.

Probably my worst disappointments were these: First, after my defeat in the bid for the Convention presidency, I wrote a letter to a friend who was not fundamentalist in theology or spirit. I told him that he was one of three persons in the Convention at that time who could be most influential in keeping us together; he, because he moved to amend a recommendation of the General Board, which was interpreted as "protecting" the Cooperative Program; second, the newly elected president; and third, the one who nominated the new president. I urged all three to take steps to help preserve unity and cooperation in the Convention. Copies of the letter went to all three men. No response was received from any.

The second disappointment had to do with visits to and conversations with the Convention executive director. We were long-time acquaintances. We had been coworkers at the Home Mission Board. We worked together in developing cooperative relationships between the state Convention and the Board. On my retirement, he succeeded me as executive assistant. I told him of my desire for a small, carefully selected group of leaders from either side of the growing controversy to dialogue and pray about unity and cooperation among South Carolina Baptists. His answer, "I don't know anybody who would be interested in that." I don't question the truth of what he said. My disappointment was that there probably were no interested persons, and that I sensed no concern to see it happen.

Why have bitter battles not been fought in South Carolina as they have in some other states? Why did moderates not stand up and fight? Why can movements like Mainstream Baptists not get a foothold in South Carolina? Let me address this as an immigrant to the state.

Two state Conventions have given me opportunity for full involvement: North Carolina and South Carolina. When attending my first Convention session in South Carolina, I felt a different atmosphere from what I had known in my native state. The word that best describes it for me is civility. While North Carolina had frequent disagreements on the convention floor, a good spirit prevailed. Some went away disappointed, but I can't remember sensing lingering anger or hostility. South Carolina is a smaller state, and Convention staff can stay in close contact with persons across the state. Many differences, I believe, were resolved outside Convention sessions and off the convention floor. That is the heritage I felt. There is a distinct dislike for "preacher fights." Many pastors prefer to go their own way and do their own thing in the churches they serve, understanding that Baptist doctrine includes freedom of the individual and autonomy of Baptist bodies. In 1993, when moderates again made a political effort to continue as partners in Convention affairs, it is reported that moderates left the meeting hall in droves headed for the exhibit area. The moderates lost by twice as many votes as in 1990, and with a much smaller number of messengers present. They were sick of so-called Convention politics. Since that time, many moderates have withdrawn from participation in Convention sessions. Or, those moderates who remain active prefer to switch rather than fight. Consequently, there were soon no officers, committee members, or trustees who were moderates and voted moderate convictions. Most pastors honor the perceived wishes of their members by sending support to state and national Conventions.

But I sense no longing among moderates either for the "good old days" or for institutions and agencies that have been lost to fundamentalism. What I hear is that there is no desire to get back either the Conventions or their agencies. In the freedom of the Fellowship, these are seen as things of the past. They have given way to a new philosophy and approach that sees their ownership as excess baggage and their ministries provided in other ways.

Make no mistake. Exile is still exile. We exiles know that no matter how much money a church sends to the current Convention, there is no place for the person, if the person does not adhere to the party line. We miss the fellowship we knew when we were accepted for ourselves. But we see the

E. C. WATSON

pleasure of participation and fellowship replaced in other ways more acceptable to moderate convictions. Disdain for moderates is expressed by such actions as refusing to include in the *Baptist Courier*, journal of the South Carolina Baptist Convention, either advance stories or paid advertising about forthcoming CBF events. And no longer do we hear "they are our people too."

Like Jimmy Carter, we too have found a home in the Fellowship. We have no interest in being part of the new SBC or the new state Convention. There is too much in both that is offensive to my understanding of the Baptist faith and Christian practice. And the feeling of integrity is great! My exile is not because of actions of some other person. It is a choice I make because today's Conventions have become something I cannot. However, my wish for dialogue still stands, because I believe it is the Christian thing to do.

A SEPARATE PEACE

Ronald D. Sisk

Everybody who has been marginalized and excluded by the resurgence of Southern Baptist fundamentalism has responded differently. Some have left the church. Some have left the Baptists. Some have suffered silently within the ranks. Some have spoken out loudly and long. My story, like that of many an exile in more violent wars, is a story of living in a refugee camp for over a decade till the time came for me to choose a new home.

As a 1982 ethics and church history graduate of the Southern Baptist Theological Seminary, I realized early on that the fundamentalist challenge was serious. But like most SBC loyalists in those days, I didn't realize how very serious it was. In early 1982, I went on staff at the SBC Christian Life Commission as director of program development. As the ethics agency for the SBC in those days, the CLC was responsible for speaking to Baptists on controversial issues such as abortion and peace.

Allowing for the possibility of abortion in cases of rape, incest, and to protect the life of the mother, the CLC position in those days represented a relatively conservative treatment of the topic, but it wasn't nearly conservative enough for the fundamentalists. By 1983 they were appointing right-to-life trustees to the CLC board. One I particularly remember had been Baptist for only about eighteen months when he became a CLC trustee. From a Roman Catholic background, he set out to change the Commission's position on abortion to conform to his own essentially Catholic understanding.

My wife Sheryl and I realized that my own areas of responsibility, alcohol and drug education, peace with justice, and women's rights, would soon come under pressure as well. We no longer felt safe trusting the welfare of our family to a trustee board selected by the fundamentalists. I chose to reenter the pastorate, and, since my wife is a westerner, we went to a church in California, Tiburon Baptist Church, the church that served as the primary congregation for students and faculty at Golden Gate Baptist Seminary.

As a pastor, I got involved in the seminary in an adjunct way, helping with the supervised ministry program. The selection of a fundamentalist president to run that institution, however, made participation there more and more uncomfortable for me. At the same time, I became active in the moderate effort to regain the Convention presidency. At the historic Dallas SBC meeting in 1985, I was one of the moderates who got to the microphone to challenge the legitimacy of the fundamentalist nominees. All our challenges failed, of course. The moderates never were able to muster the kind of organizational unity or the simplistic but compelling rhetoric that the fundamentalists brought to bear.

By 1990, I was ready to join with those disaffected moderates who became the Cooperative Baptist Fellowship. I served as West Cluster representative on the first Coordinating Council. That action, though, caused me trouble in my church. Faculty members feared that my activism would endanger their jobs at Golden Gate. They said as much in church business meetings. And they continually argued that the SBC troubles didn't really apply to California. We soon realized that we needed to be in more friendly moderate territory.

In 1991, we moved to the Western Hills Baptist Church in Fort Worth, Texas. The church had a historic connection with Southwestern Seminary, which by then was coming under serious fundamentalist pressure. President Dilday was soon fired. And we watched yet another seminary fall.

In 1994, we moved back to Louisville, and I took the senior pastorate of Crescent Hill Baptist Church, the congregation historically most closely affiliated with Southern Seminary. Al Mohler was already moving to place a fundamentalist stamp on Southern. From 1990 to 1997, Crescent Hill lost about 35 faculty and staff families and went from about 150 students a week in attendance to zero.

The church had already taken a firm moderate stand before I arrived. We were active in the Cooperative Baptist Fellowship. We soon went even further, adding an alignment with American Baptists. In that process, something happened to me that I had not really expected. I realized, first of all, that the old SBC, the family that had nurtured and called and educated me, no longer existed in any recognizable form.

I also realized that the CBF, despite the fact that I support it and love and feel comfortable with its people, was content to continue what seemed to me to be a kind of shadow existence, as sort of SBC in exile—a kinder, gentler SBC, if you will. They were unwilling to declare themselves a separate denomination. And despite their talk of diversity, they seemed content to remain a white, middle-class, southern group. I discovered that I could no longer be content with that kind of truncated vision of Christianity.

As a result, in 1996, I had my ordination recognized by the American Baptist Churches, and I began to attend their meetings and learn about the ABC family. I quickly realized that they believe what I was taught to believe in the old SBC. Their meetings and power structure are intentionally diverse. Women are fully equal participants. A concern for justice is part of the fabric of their common life. With them, I didn't have to live in a psychological and spiritual refugee camp any longer. I could come home. And so I have.

Unlike many of my colleagues and mentors and friends, who continue to fight the same battles but on the state convention level, I have made a separate peace. In effect, I've gone back to the tradition from which the SBC split when it took its wrong turn on slavery in 1845. And for me there is something deeply satisfying in reorienting my identity. In some ways, I'll always be a southerner, of course. We can do nothing about our cultural background. And I'll continue both to be active in and to support the Cooperative Baptist Fellowship, hoping to move it toward the day when it will be willing to leave regionalism behind. I'll always be a Southern Baptist. But I no longer think of myself as a Southern Baptist. That's become an identity foreign to me. I am an American Baptist. And that feels very good indeed.

RONALD D. SISK

EXODUS FROM THE SOUTHERN BAPTIST CONVENTION

Michael R. Duncan

The seeds of my exodus from the Southern Baptist Convention were sown by my mother. In my parents' home, church attendance and Bible study were not options; they were part of the weekly routine. The small, rural church that we attended had been heavily influenced by the Landmark tradition, and our pastors' preaching reflected such. I cannot recall my mother ever criticizing any of our pastors. I do recall her often repeating something our pastor had said, then adding, "But, you know, I think. . . ." By giving me an alternative view to consider, she taught me that authentic faith flowed from honest inquiry and open relationships. From such early childhood experiences, I learned to think critically about my faith, about scripture, and about the church. Little did I know then that a lesson learned at my mother's knee would lead to my leaving the Southern Baptist Convention.

When the messengers to the 1970 SBC annual meeting voted to require Volume One of the *Broadman Bible Commentary* to be rewritten, I rushed to my college bookstore and bought the entire set. The controversy that ensued over issues related to this commentary series gave me my first inclination that I was not totally at ease within the denomination. The kind of scholarship that was being attacked was the very scholarship that was opening the Bible to me and bringing alive both my faith and my sense of calling to ministry. My experience in college (Union University, Jackson, Tennessee, 1967–71) and seminary (Southern Baptist Theological Seminary, Louisville, Kentucky, 1973–76) deepened both my faith and commitment to ministry. By the time the SBC takeover had begun in 1979, both of my alma maters were under attack and branded as "liberal." Neither of them survived the takeover unscathed.

While the changes in the institutions from which I had received my higher education saddened me, it was not enough to drive me out of the denomination. It was enough to push me toward the edge. I continued to attend SBC annual meetings through the 1991 meeting. That was my last SBC meeting. I knew by that time that I no longer had a place in the denomination, but I did not know where or how to move beyond that knowledge.

The exodus seeds sown in my childhood sprouted and produced new life early in the so-called SBC holy war. That new life reached full growth on Sunday, June 14, 1998. On that Sunday morning, I stepped to the pulpit of the Southern Baptist church of which I had been pastor for eighteen years to announce, in words reportedly uttered by Will Campbell, that I would be Baptist until I died but that I would no longer be a Southern Baptist. The politicizing of the Convention, the power grabbing, and the denigrating of professors and seminaries had all served to push me to the edge of Southern Baptist life. The action of messengers to the 1998 SBC annual meeting that resulted in an amendment to the 1963 Baptist Faith and Message Statement article on the family was the final straw. Our church was already on record as supporting and welcoming women as both ministers and deacons. For this Baptist preacher, it was time to act.

As I spoke to the congregation that morning, I reminded them that for eight years I had sought to live out my faith and ministry in two houses, the Southern Baptist Convention and the Cooperative Baptist Fellowship. During the last five of those years, the church had divided its mission giving between these two bodies. I fully believed that I, and I hoped the church, had come to a fork in the denominational road. Forward momentum would carry us past the fork. There would be no option for making camp. Our only choice was which fork we would follow.

> One road is broad and paved with manicured right-of-ways. The other is narrow and unpaved, and its right-of-ways will not be pictured in travel brochures. One leads to the destruction of all I hold dear as a Christian and a Baptist. The other holds promise for an opportunity to link heart, mind, and body with other freedom-loving Baptists.

Like Abraham of old, I do not know what lies before me, but I do know who it is who beckons me to travel a new way. Having committed my life to Jesus Christ, there is no longer a choice to make. I will follow where I understand the footsteps of Jesus to lead. For me, his footsteps lead down the narrow road which separates me from the denomination of my heritage. They take me to a promised land where a free and faithful Baptist is still allowed to live out his commitment to Christ as he, under the leadership of the Holy Spirit, understands it.

No matter what the cost, I am committed to a new way. I would make this decision public today even if I thought it would lead to your asking me to resign as your pastor. For me, this is a matter of conscience. I cannot do other than I am doing.[1]

By action, I chose to leave the Southern Baptist Convention. In reality, I was left without any other choice. I could not have remained a Southern Baptist and been at peace with myself. I am saddened that the denomination, in which I was birthed to faith, called into ministry, and educated, no longer had room for me. As I look back, I am surprised that the anger, which I occasionally experienced, did not persist. Anger was not even the most prominent emotion that I felt. Far more prominent were emotions of sadness, disappointment, abandonment, and grief, all flowing from a growing sense of homelessness. For me, all these emotions are mostly in the past. I have entered a promised land and am discovering that there is more than enough here to occupy my energies. The so-called Baptist holy war is over for me; and, yet. . . .

The leaving of place is never over! There are those moments when the words of the slaves from Egypt rise up in my heart and mind. "If only we had died in the land of Egypt, when we sat by the fleshpots and ate our fill of bread; for you have brought us out into this wilderness to kill this whole assembly with hunger" (Exodus 16:3, NRSV). While fleshpots and bread from the past are better in memory than they were in reality, when the memory is combined with the harsh reality that promised lands are always demanding lands, one does discover that the leaving is an ongoing process.

Have I second-guessed my choice to leave? Not once have I done so. Would I return were the SBC to change? No, I would not. In new relationships within state and national Cooperative Baptist Fellowship groups, I have found a new home. Those with whom I share this new home are as

1. Michael R. Duncan, "The Hijacking of the SBC Is Complete," unpublished sermon prepared for and preached to the Eminence Baptist Church, Eminence, KY, June 14, 1998.

MICHAEL R. DUNCAN

varied in their theology and methods of doing church as are those who have remained in the SBC. The difference that I find in my new home is that everyone's beliefs and understandings get a hearing at the table of faith. With others, I am embracing the challenging ventures of forming new partnerships, establishing new seminaries, and seeing the call to missions in a new light. My new home is not a paradise, but it is a land of promise.

That which seemed so devastating a few years ago has become a source of new life and new hope.

FINDING A VOICE IN EXILE

Paul D. Simmons

The Dalai Lama and I are both in exile. He travels the world outside of Tibet from which he had to flee with the invasion and occupation by Chinese military forces. He is in exile because of a radical shift in the political situation in his home country. So am I. The Southern Baptist Convention had been my home and base of operations until the takeover by forces hostile to most everything I stand for as a Baptist professor of Christian ethics. Reading the Dalai Lama's autobiography[1] has been a disturbing reminder of the parallels—while recognizing the significant differences—between his situation and mine.

Freedom is a central concern and commitment for both of us. He went into exile to escape Chinese oppression and be free to speak out as the religious leader of Tibetans. I see freedom as a central theme in Christian ethics and vital to being a Baptist. An emphasis on responsible freedom is therefore basic to all I do as an ethicist. Both the Dalai Lama and I wound up in exile precisely on that issue. The Chinese are repressive; they insist on conformity to a Communist political ideology. The Dalai can only be free to express his religious and political points of view outside the land of his birth and national identity.

---

1. Tenzin Gyatso, *Freedom in Exile: The Autobiography of the Dalai Lama* (New York: HarperSanFrancisco, 1990).

The evangelicals who have come to dominate the Southern Baptist Convention are also repressive and controlling.[2] Freedom to disagree with or challenge the basic tenets of fundamentalist theology and their sociopolitical agenda is simply not tolerated. Southern Baptists had birthed me, nourished me, encouraged me in theological and educational endeavors, and ordained me. But fundamentalists made it impossible for authentic Baptists to live out their calling, emphasizing the freedoms of faith and grace that are so basic to the Christian biblical message. I am by no means alone.

There are many Baptists who, like me, have either chosen to go or been driven into exile. Many went quietly without any attention being drawn to their situation. The dramatic shift in emphases and directions in the Convention and the extensive alterations of individual life-plans caught the attention of the secular as well as religious media covering the carnage. Carnage is not too strong a word. The ideological bent of fundamentalism has as sharp an edge and nonnegotiable spirit as Communism. They use different weapons, but their spirit and oppressive tactics have notable similarities.

BEING PERSONAL ABOUT EXILE

My going into exile was the result of the politicization of academia among Southern Baptists. I had been educated among Baptists from a one-room church in rural west Tennessee, through large urban churches. I had attended Baptist colleges and seminaries. I am a Baptist to the core of my being, believing in personal conversion, individual soul competence, direct responsibility to God, and freedom of conscience. These lead directly, it seems to me, to commitments to integrity in scholarship, respect for differences among people, and religious liberty for all people in matters of public policy.[3]

Such personal commitments led to an increasing tension between my approach to moral and social issues and the right-wing views held by the leadership of the Southern Baptist Convention. My teaching and writings were fully consistent with Baptist beliefs from Roger Williams to E. Y.

2. I use the terms "fundamentalist" and "evangelical" interchangeably, though important differences can be discerned historically. Southern Baptist leadership insists on being called "evangelicals." But there are good reasons to argue that their characteristic styles of leadership and the doctrinal and ethical beliefs are more typically those of fundamentalism. There may be distinctive differences, but they are so intertwined among Southern Baptists that they cannot be separated.

3. See Paul D. Simmons, *Freedom of Conscience: A Baptist Humanist Dialogue* (Amherst, NY: Prometheus, 2000).

Mullins. My 1983 book, *Birth and Death*,[4] was thoroughly biblical, Christocentric, and committed to such notions as voluntarism in religious faith, the immediacy of the leadership of the Holy Spirit, the priesthood of the believer, and religious liberty. The issues dealt with were abortion, biotechnical parenting, elective death, and genetic engineering. Data drawn from science and law, as well as personal and community experiences, were brought together in a way that led to certain conclusions concerning options and alternatives when believers face these complex issues.

In each area, the believer is the responsible moral agent who must decide in faith how to resolve the questions posed by a particular problem. Whether it is a problem pregnancy, or an ugly, prolonged death, or how to proceed with various options to overcome infertility, people are faced with decisions that both test and reflect their faith. No one else should stand between the believer and God. The burden of decision making belongs to being human, to being created in the image of God.

The Bible gives no definitive prohibitions or requirements on these or any other complex issue. Sufficient information and professional guidance are available, however, that make a decision in faith fully possible. God provides guidance in the form of biblical teaching and principles, the wisdom of the Christian community, the insights of trusted pastors or friends, and the discernment of the Holy Spirit.

Resolutions passed at the Southern Baptist Convention, on the other hand, harshly condemned certain options and called for absolute legal solutions. SBC resolutions condemn all elective abortions and support a law to prohibit any except those to save the life of the woman.[5] Convention leadership rationalized the extremist approach to abortion and elective death as a matter of "the sanctity of human life." Not only is the notion of the sanctity of human life nowhere taught in scripture, it results in an abstraction from concrete cases that begins to prefer protections for embryos to that of actual people, namely, women. The Bible begins the story of personal human life before God with the portrait of Adam and Eve. They are portrayed as persons who are born; they have birth and breath (Genesis 2:7). They are not embryos, much less isolated sperm and ova. They are living, breathing, responding-in-faith (or unfaith) creatures directly responsible to God.

4. Paul D. Simmons, *Birth and Death: Bioethical Decision Making* (Philadelphia: Westminster, 1983).
5. *Annual of the Southern Baptist Convention* (Nashville: SBC Executive Committee, 2000), Resolution 4, p. 80.

PAUL D. SIMMONS

How one resolves questions pertaining to procreation and contraception should be a matter of personal faith, not of imperial decisions made by powerful persons untouched by the pathos of the particular problems being confronted.

Not only were Convention resolutions increasingly harsh and absolutist, they were also removed from any careful attention to what the Bible actually teaches. No room was given for scholarly differences of opinion, nor was any challenge on logical or ethical grounds tolerated. Seminary professors were regarded as employees of the Convention who should teach as Convention authorities dictated, not as scholars who had opinions informed by biblical, historical, and theological research.

The final insult to scholarship was registered when a pastor declared that "if a resolution says that pickles have souls, seminary professors are to teach that pickles have souls." He was not just any pastor; he had also been president of the Convention and a lead drummer in the march to the right. The implications and directions of that declaration were simply horrendous. Despite the justifiable derision that greeted the statement in academic circles, it became a working principle for Convention policies. Baptists had embraced an approach that resolved complex problems simply by a majority vote. What was right became a matter of what a resolution declared. This extremist brand of right-wing evangelicalism has now imposed rigid controls on the seminaries and their leaders.

The evangelical/fundamentalist approach signaled the end of theological education that could claim neither intellectual nor ethical integrity. The seminaries had lost their soul because the Convention power realities had assumed all authority for settling thorny moral questions. Academic freedom was scuttled in the interests of conformity and uniformity in doctrinal and moral perspectives. The first step toward control was to stack the Boards of Trustees of all Convention agencies and commissions with like-minded persons, that is, trustees who would carry out the sociopolitical agenda of the religious right.

FACING THE BAN

My exile began with a conversation mandated by the administration between the chair (and vice-president) of the Board of Trustees at Southern Baptist Theological Seminary and me. The seminary president and provost were also in attendance. Just the five of us met for a face-to-face. Trustee chair Wayne Allen and I did most all the talking. He wanted me to take two years' severance and walk away quietly. I insisted I had every right to be there and felt no call from God to leave. I emphasized the damage they were doing to a major theological institution. The vice-president, Chris White, was a graduate of the seminary and knew of its outstanding credentials. But he had joined the effort to force me out. It was a straightforward confrontation between people who represented divergent and irreconcilable perspectives.

After this meeting, the only questions were just how and when I would be sent into exile. The trustees were determined to have me removed, I was determined to stay as long as possible, and the administration was caught in between. The confrontation deepened with a resolution passed by the trustees in April 1990, which threatened my dismissal if I did not curtail my speaking and writing in favor of legalized abortion. I was given three options as communicated through the president and provost: (1) teach it their way—that is, adopt the extremist point of view against the legal availability of abortion (and other issues); (2) hold my opinions in silence and not teach contrary to positions taken by the Convention and/or the trustees; or (3) leave Southern. The first two were out of the question. To teach a position as my own that I regarded as intellectually unsupportable and unethical to the core would be a fundamental violation of my sense of being and integrity as an academician. Academics have a moral mandate to expose and oppose poor scholarship. Critical thinking requires that the intellectual supportability of any argument or position be openly examined. I believe the extremist antiabortion approach to be unsupportable ethically, biblically, or logically.

I refused to accept any of the three options put forward by the trustees. I insisted, to the contrary, that I would not accept a point of view I found offensive nor would I be silent about the issue. Contractually, faculty were assured protection for academic freedom. The Faculty and Staff Manual of the seminary declares that: "So long as the professor remains within the accepted charter and confessional basis of this seminary he or she shall be free to teach, carry on research, and to publish, subject to the adequate performance of academic duties as agreed upon with the school. . . . The curriculum of the seminary shall be determined by the faculty and each professor shall have the freedom in the classroom to discuss the subject in which he or she has competence and may claim to be a specialist without harassment or limitations" (Sec. E-16.2, 3, p. 196).

No faculty could expect a more generous institutional commitment to academic freedom. Southern Seminary had cultivated the development of scholars in every field of theological education and had attempted to provide an environment in which any issue could be responsibly explored. The assumption was that scholars would disagree strongly on certain issues. We might all agree on the inspiration and authority of scripture, for instance, but might disagree on issues from the nature of inspiration to the question of the security of the believer. We were not expected to agree on all matters in theology and ethics; we were expected to be responsible and to hold one another to high standards of scholarship.

I thus sought to maintain my teaching post at Southern *and* to insist on my right to contend for the truth as I understood it. I believed I was well within the bounds of contractual obligations and of Baptist theology and ethics. I represented far more of a consensus of scholarly opinion among Baptists regarding reproductive issues than did the trustees. Every professor of Christian ethics at Southern Baptist seminaries had signed the "Call to Concern" circulated by the Religious Coalition for Reproductive Rights in 1979. The statement affirmed that legalized abortion was supportable on grounds of women's reproductive rights and the protections of religious liberty. It was supported by thousands of ministers, priests, and rabbis nationally.

Every Southern Baptist professor or denominational employee who signed the Call was targeted for removal. Many retracted their signatures. But some staunchly maintained the commitment and suffered accordingly.[6]

My resistance to the effort to remove me from my teaching post took several forms. One was to hire an attorney. He provided enormous comfort and courage in the face of the misrepresentations and constant harassment I endured. There was even hope for some legal grounds for a suit against the seminary for wrongful termination, if it came to that. At a minimum, the strategy proved helpful in slowing the process.

Bellicose trustees were nonetheless determined to have me removed. They met a total of five times for special called meetings to deal specifically with "the Simmons issue." An enormous amount of money was spent to pay the trustee expenses to travel to places like Atlanta for such a narrow agenda. Each meeting cost a minimum of fifty thousand dollars. No resolution of the question ever came from that dysfunctional group.

The trustees probed every avenue of leverage against me. Three times they had their attorney examine my record to see whether there was not a violation of contract on my part that would warrant my termination. Each time the attorney (two different attorneys) returned with the finding that

6. *Western Recorder* (Middletown: Kentucky Baptist Convention, March 21, 1995), 7.

I was fully in accord with my contractual duties. I met classes faithfully, I dealt with issues responsibly, and I was not in any way guilty of insubordination. They had absolutely no legal case against me.

Meanwhile, just remaining on the faculty meant that I was a thorn in the side of the administration. I attempted to remain low-key, but did maintain my commitment to academic freedom. Just pressing the issue made life more difficult for President Honeycutt and Provost McSwain who had to listen to belligerent trustees berate them repeatedly for not getting rid of me. It would have been easier for them had I simply stepped aside. McSwain said on numerous occasions that he would take a buyout in a minute, which he encouraged me to do. I was not interested.

But the trustees were pushing hard for the administration to force me out. Honeycutt had already announced his early retirement, and trustees wanted him to resolve "the Simmons issue" before the next president was installed. They had already moved Honeycutt's retirement date to June 30, the end of the fiscal year in 1993, instead of his announced date of December 31, 1993. A lot was at stake in his dealings with me. The generosity or lack thereof with regard to his retirement package would undoubtedly be determined to a great degree by the way he handled critical issues in his closing months.

Two events coincided to determine the final outcome. One was the opinion of the Sixth Circuit Court of Appeals regarding a suit for wrongful termination by a Seventh-Day Adventist minister. The court ruled that if a minister were terminated by the highest judicatory body in a religious organization, the court would not intervene, even if they did not follow their own rules and guidelines.[7] The decision reflected religious liberty protections, that is, the separation of church and state. No (secular) court could intervene in a religious matter. My legal case was dead. That was in November.

The second event took place in the closing days of the semester. The administration used my showing a video in a class on human sexuality as an excuse to impose sanctions against me. The film had been used in other classes without any hint of interference or criticism from the administration. The controversy surrounding me became the critical factor in why the administration chose to impose penalties on me, under the guise of "protecting me" from the trustees, which was disingenuous. They used

---

7. *Joseph P. Lewis: Julia A. Lewis v. Seventh Day Adventists Lake Region Conference*, No. 92-1085, US Ct Appeals, 6th Circuit, November 4, 1992.

the flimsy excuse that students had complained. Actually only four students complained; ninety-six were enrolled in the course. I know of only one student from the class in that group of four. The brownshirts were active on campus.

The final insult had been imposed. Administrators came through for the trustees. The sanctions to be imposed ranged from a letter of apology to withdrawal from undergraduate classes. I felt betrayed by administrators who pretended both support and friendship. As a friend had warned me, it will not be your enemies but your friends who get you. I submitted my resignation to protest the action.[8] The official date was December 31, 1992, though the actions and paper signing took place in 1993, and I had faculty responsibilities through the spring term, so did not leave campus until June.

EXILE: DEALING WITH DISENFRANCHISED LOSS

Going into exile was painful. I felt devastated. The stress of a three-year full-court press by trustees, the constant cajoling from administrators, the impending death of my father-in-law, and dealing with an adult child with major health problems were all part of the mix. Disillusionment and near despair followed. The disappointment I felt with the cynical display of power by the administration was a major part of that hurt. In short, I was faced with another of the major challenges confronting those in exile: how to deal with disenfranchised losses.

The pain of being in exile is sharp and profound. Ostracism and isolation are hard to bear. The absence of a sense of place that had been so solid for years now contributed to insecurity and anxiety. Self-identity is related to the social role one plays. The task is to know oneself well enough to survive in spite of the emotional and spiritual burden such a major life change creates. One can become emotionally and professionally paralyzed by the desire to return to the place of origins. That place is no longer my home of spiritual nourishment, but of bondage. The task is to recognize it for what it has become, not remember it for what it was.

The biblical wisdom was an enormous help. The secret of the Israelites' victory over despair in exile was their acceptance of new realities and their determination to make the most of it. Jeremiah's advice was that they

---

8. The letter was one of resignation. It was changed to "early retirement" for purposes of the final documents.

settle down in the land, build houses and live in them, plant gardens and enjoy their produce, and intermarry and have children. They were to seek the welfare of the country and pray for the people (Jeremiah 29:5–7). In short, they were to make a new life for themselves, not live with bitterness and resentment, constantly longing for the way things were or to return to the previous life. They have a new home and a new people to call their own.

That does not mean the transition is easy. Exile is painful under any circumstance. Wayne Oates had it right in saying it was like an amputation, which was an apt analogy. But medical amputations are done with anesthetics. Executions carried out with a guillotine are swift and clean. Religious warriors seem to prefer to inflict as much pain as possible. They use a dull ax, not a sharp sword. Grief from forced exile involves anger, disappointment, disillusionment, disgust, and moments on the edge of despair. The poet William Aytoun put it strongly: "They bore within their breasts the grief / That fame can never heal / The deep, unutterable woe / Which none save exiles feel."[9]

Jeremiah's advice to the Israelites in exile was to remind them of God's larger plan for their life. They were not to live with fantasies or futile dreams of getting back to the homeland. Home was a new place with a new purpose. They were still God's people and were to keep their sense of identity for God's future purposes.

I had the good feeling that I had not compromised on principle with either the trustees or the administration. I had refused to sell my right to speak freely or to fall silent in order to appease belligerent trustees. Looking back, I would probably have been better off personally had I accepted defeat during the 1990 conversation with trustees and administrators. I lost valuable time that could have been used for less stressful pursuits. I was fighting a losing cause. I would not have wanted to remain in the seminary that emerged from the controversy. And I was, in any case, destined for defeat. In religious circles, administrators never lose in their battles with faculty over such things as academic freedom, classroom prerogatives, or other sources of conflict. They have an enormous arsenal of weapons and strategies, none of which is available to faculty.

Exile has been a time of reflection and transition for me. The transition has been one of accepting my alienation and isolation from the tradition of my rearing. But I have found a new home among people that share values

9. William E. Aytoun, *The Island of the Scots*, stanza xii (1849), www.visitdunkeld.com/scottish-quotations.htm.

PAUL D. SIMMONS

I had earlier learned among Baptists. They have now embraced what they once despised. But what they have forsaken, others embrace. The experience has been illuminating and inspiring. I have been reminded again that church is where you find it. When the institutional church ceases to live out its calling, the "church" is still there to be experienced, perhaps among people once thought to be hostile or indifferent to religion itself. But they seem to grasp the meaning of community and what love requires in personal relationships and what commitments are necessary to seek goals that bless the common good.

Even so, a profound and multifaceted grief remains. A beloved seminary has fallen into disrepute and academic mediocrity. The foundation and building blocks of a great school had been demolished. And a people who had borne witness to individual responsibility and personal faith had taken up the banner for dogmatic faith and managed religion. Christians who once thought the first order of business was loving one another and joining hands in mission had become an angry, belligerent people intent on dominating the American culture with narrow sectarianism, rigid moralisms, and strident judgmentalism. I have seen friends humiliated by the fundamentalists to the point of tears. Families and professional lives have been disrupted. People have died prematurely from stroke or heart attack from the stress induced by constant acrimony and unfair accusations.

The disparity between the ethics of care and the belligerence of intolerance was felt in being treated like a pariah while being told I was loved. Such insults to the mind and spirit are hypocritical to the core. Even sadder was the awareness that so many Baptists turned a blind eye to the evils in their midst. Many local churches would not even allow discussions of the conflict, much less register opposition to the bloodletting.

Exile thus necessitates coming to terms with a profound and irresolvable grief much like that of losing a loved one suddenly to death. The grief of forced exile involves anger, disappointment, disillusionment, disgust, and moments spent on the edge of despair. Psychiatrist John Schneider says three things are necessary for one successfully to move beyond the pain: (1) discovering what's lost, (2) discovering what remains; and (3) discovering what's possible.[10]

What had been lost was considerable, if not inestimable, in my judgment. Southern Baptists had been strong champions of religious liberty

10. See J. M. Schneider, *Grief's Wisdom: Quotes That Validate the Transformative Process* (Traverse City, MI: Seasons Press, 2000).

and the separation of church and state. They have become what they once despised. They now are enemies of separation and seek political advantage so as to coerce others in their religious affections and commitments. They now embrace a type of civil religion that so blends Christian loyalties with American patriotism that the two can hardly be distinguished.

FINDING A VOICE IN EXILE

The final and perhaps greatest challenge facing those in exile is to find a voice. Silence is an enemy, perhaps evidence of a dread depression. Finding a voice in exile to a great degree means *keeping* one's voice; one cannot find what one never had. If one was vocal before the ban, one will likely be outspoken in exile. But, if one has sacrificed one's voice for the sake of "peace," likely one will never have a voice in exile.

One of the things I was most concerned about both while at Southern and in leaving the seminary was the freedom to speak against the injustices and hypocrisies I had observed and experienced. I was not silenced while I was on faculty, and I certainly would agree to no settlement that compromised my freedom to speak. I kept a poem on my office door that read:

> No one escapes when freedom fails;
> The best ones rot in filthy jails;
> While those who cried 'Appease! Appease!' .
> Were hung by those they sought to please. (Anonymous)

My voice was not for sale no matter the pressures from trustees, Convention leaders, or administrators. The image that haunted me was the tragic story of Maeyken Wens during the Inquisition. As Will Campbell tells the story, this Anabaptist mother of nine insisted on her right to preach and teach in spite of the threat of the Inquisition leaders to silence her. Finally, found guilty of heresy and insubordination, she was condemned to die at the pyre. On the way to the execution, her tongue was screwed to the top of her mouth in order to keep her from speaking.

That screw in the tongue has been a vivid mental image regarding efforts by Convention leaders to silence their opposition in Southern Baptist circles. Some accepted the screw without much resistance. Some emerged early on as strong voices against the fundamentalists, then fell silent and publicly withdrew from the fray under pressure. Some sold their birthright for a lucrative severance package or the promise of promotions within the denomination. But the price of "success" was either that of not telling what was known about the unethical practices that were so commonplace in the fundamentalist juggernaut, or never being able to reveal what was known even after going into exile. The screw in the tongue was a severe test of integrity. Few things were sadder than reading the statements of leaders forced out who could only mouth platitudes and defer to "the will of God" while admitting they would not be telling the inside or behind-the-scenes story. They went silently into the night, their tongues screwed securely in place.

To be sure, the fundamentalist movement took no prisoners. It was a fierce, no-holds-barred assault against the moderates in the Convention. They had the temperament for a fight to the finish, while moderates had no taste for the excesses involved in any political battle worth winning. Fundamentalists fought with the ferocity of a medieval crusader. They are "true believers" as described so well in the classic by Eric Hoffer.[11] They are intransigent, dogmatic, aggressive, domineering, controlling, and ideological. They are also motivated by fear—fear their goals will not be realized, fear their faith will falter, fear homosexuals will ruin the family, and that pluralism will dominate the country.

Such fears involve a paranoid style in political and social movements. Thus, angry invective is aimed at those who see the issues differently and do not support the goals of the movement. Women and those who are homosexual are especially at risk of having their rights denied. The School of Church Social Work at Southern Seminary was closed, but finally "sold," because accreditation standards required a nondiscrimination policy for admissions and placement. Southern Baptists have taken a strong stance against homosexuality, and insist on the right to discriminate against gays and lesbians.

I have great admiration for those who had spoken out or resisted before they were sent into exile. Some resigned because of the excesses they observed in the "purge." They could not maintain integrity and be part of such a problematic movement. Others resigned rather than carry out orders they felt were morally unjustified and contrary to the commitments basic to theological education. Many others chose the route of ducking their heads and trying to hide until the storm passed. But even those who did not speak out were exiled—that is, forced out of their place of ministry. Some of the most prominent persons during the fifteen-year period of realignment (1980–95) have never spoken out about what went on behind the scenes. Usually such silence was associated with a lucrative buy-

11. E. Hoffer, *The True Believer: Thoughts on the Nature of Mass Movements* (New York: Harper & Row, 1951).

out. At other times, the exiled were simply tempered in a way as not to enter the fray of controversy or were so exhausted they welcomed the tranquility of an earlier-than-expected retirement.

But voices have been heard from exile. There has been a remarkable amount of creative productivity on the part of those in exile. Six seminaries and a Baptist House of Studies have been established to assure the ongoing witness of traditional Baptist beliefs and commitments. Scholars have continued their writing and speaking from other schools or pastorates. Ironically, the more alienated and distant I have become from the Southern Baptist Convention and its excesses, the more I have been asked to write and speak about the troubles. Southern Baptists may not want to hear it, but there are those who do.

Many of us have felt that God was not through with us no matter how Southern Baptists tried to silence us or remove us from educational positions. Jeremiah's challenge to the Israelites in exile was that they would have a future and a hope (Jeremiah 29:11). Their task was to remain faithful and await the workings of God's patient providence. And they did. The exile was rather remarkable for its literary and prophetic activity. In many ways, Israel's core identity was shaped in exile, and from that emerged the authentic word of the people of God.

I can honestly say that I have no desire to return to Southern Baptist life in any formal sense. I seek no role in the Convention nor a place of leadership within any of its agencies. The air is sweeter and breath comes freer outside the circles in which thoughts and beliefs are dictated. Leonidas, a poet from Tarentum, Italy, was so devastated by being exiled that he seemed to lose all hope and meaning to life. "This is the worst of it—worse than death," he said. "An exile's life is no life." Pity poor Leonidas. He must have grieved himself to death.

I have found freedom in exile and have kept a voice. I have found a "home" at a secular university that is challenging and productive. I have found friends who profess no faith who are more committed to truth than those who talk so much about absolute truth and insist others adopt their faith, but mean their kind of dogma and intolerance. Life is both richer and fuller in exile than ever it could have been under the constraints of imperious administrators and opinionated but uninformed and powerful trustees. Who can be free when people in power insist upon conformity to ridiculous opinions as the price of employment? They make bigotry an article of faith and say they are being true to the Bible! When such arrogance is wed to deceit, the result is tyranny in the disguise of religious faith.

PAUL D. SIMMONS

THE HIJACKING OF THE SOUTHERN BAPTIST CONVENTION

W. H. Crouch

In my active ministry I witnessed the breakdown of the Southern Baptist Convention as my dad knew it. The takeover by the fundamentalists is complete now. It came as a surprise and shock for most of our people, for they were not expecting it to happen. Most of our laypeople are still in the dark and do not realize the changes made in the denomination. The disenfranchised have been the ones who built the institutions through the Cooperative Program. Perhaps the pride we developed over its success led to the downfall.

I served on the Sunday School Board during the debate over the Commentary and the book on Genesis. I witnessed the extreme views of some members and their determined efforts to control the issues and the decisions.

I also served later on the Foreign Mission Board and observed, firsthand, the attempts to control our mission work. Their emphasis was on evangelism of a sort and a lack of interest in theological training or social work. They were looking for certain phrases such as "inerrancy" in the interview process with new missionaries. They also were meeting in secret before regular board meetings to make decisions as a group.

So, when Dr. Cecil Sherman sent an invitation to a conference to be held at Gatlinburg, Tennessee, to discuss denominational issues, I joined a group with four other North Carolinians. We were unanimous in our concerns, but few in number. Later, we got dubbed the "Gatlinburg gang" by our opponents, but we were the first to oppose the political moves of the fundamentalists. There were only seventeen of us in attendance. We agreed on the danger facing the Convention and tried to organize opposition. I ended up representing North Carolina for several years (at my own expense) at the strategy sessions held over many locations. We were never able to arouse support. The bureaucrats thought the danger would go away and stayed neutral until it was too late. Our pastors were afraid to bring the issues before the churches. In North Carolina, we organized the "Friends of Missions" and were able to control our Convention until 1995.

I was also involved in the formation of the FORUM, which was an alternative to the Pastors' Conference. I served on the executive committee as the treasurer for four years. This was very popular and was well supported for several years.

At a meeting of the large-church pastors in Atlanta, a debate between Cecil Sherman and Adrian Rogers took place. In that debate, Adrian stated that the fundamentalists wanted to have parity in the seminaries, for the Sunday School Board to print their literature, and to be able not to contribute to the Cooperative Program and still be good boys. In truth, they finally took over all three completely. It was at this meeting that I understood that the Convention was being hijacked in reality.

In 1986, in Macon, Georgia, at the political caucus, a small group of us expressed that we were getting tired of a losing political situation. We felt that we were failing because of our inability to awaken average Baptists to the impending danger. We wanted to be positive and not negative in our approach. A small group began meeting in Raleigh and later in Charlotte emphasizing the concern for historic Baptist principles. So, on February 12, 1987, we went public as the Southern Baptist Alliance. We were not political and offered no candidate for office. On March 21, 1988, we reported twenty-one hundred members from thirty-eight states. Our biggest contribution was the starting of the Baptist Theological Seminary in Richmond, Virginia. This organization is now the Baptist Alliance located in Washington, D.C. I served as the first president of the Alliance. This organization helped in the formation of the Cooperative Baptist Fellowship, although it remains independent.

Dr. C. R. Daley, editor emeritus of the *Western Recorder* in Kentucky, wrote on November 5, 1987, "In years to come, many Southern Baptists will ask where were we when the Fundamentalists took over the Convention? We did not lift a finger when our beloved denomination was destroyed or replaced by another." I was there, and I did my best to keep it from happening!

INSIDE THE
GATLINBURG GANG

Edwin F. Perry

There were seventeen of us pastors and laymen in the late summer of 1979 who were coming together in Gatlinburg, Tennessee. Our mother denomination, the Southern Baptist Convention, was under siege, and we were gathering to confer with one another as to how we could work with the more aggressive pastors of so-called super churches. Each of these churches had a membership of ten to thirty thousand persons and had an annual budget of several million dollars each. They were more or less accustomed to having their own way. These pastors joined with two church politicians and adopted a motto of their takeover efforts of the largest non-Catholic group in America, the Southern Baptist Convention. Their publicly announced motto was, "We are going for the jugular." I wonder why no biblical reference was given. Democracy was the first casualty after the elitist group of super-church pastors took over.

I believe that ours was the first and perhaps the only organized group of the Southern Baptist Convention to oppose the takeover efforts. However, I understand there may also have been a group of Baptist men in Texas who organized later to oppose the takeover group.

In Gatlinburg, our group got down to business quickly. We chose Dr. Cecil Sherman as our chairperson. We agreed to ask for an individual conference with our newly elected Southern Baptist Convention president,

Dr. Jimmy Draper. He agreed to meet with us in Gatlinburg. Our group selected me to write our presentation to Dr. Draper and to present it to him at our upcoming meeting. This I did, and, for the record, I wish to include in this article the nature of our offer, as I recall it.

We wished to keep the lines of communication open, which we felt could be accomplished in several effective ways. One of the ways we agreed would be to broaden the membership base of the Committee on Committees. This, we believed, could be done by the inclusion of each cooperating Baptist state Convention president and also including the executive secretary of each cooperating state Convention. If this were done, the addition to the Committee on Committees would have been voted on by their respective state Conventions. This new approach would last for only a stated period of time, if the Convention desired.

When the conference had ended, Dr. Draper said, "I will come back three weeks from today and will give you my answer at that time." Three weeks later, Dr. Draper returned to Gatlinburg, and he was accompanied by Dr. John Sullivan. Following a prayer, I asked, "Are you ready, Dr. Draper, with your answer?" Dr. Draper responded, "I am. My answer is no, no, no," to which I replied, "That is not good enough to stand alone. What more can you tell us?" He replied that "They would not let me do it," to which I replied, "We asked you as our president and you tell us that *they* would not let you do this. Who are 'they'? Is your answer, 'I cannot or I will not'?" Dr. Draper replied, "It's a little bit of both."

As I recall, Dr. Cecil Sherman, our chair, addressed Dr. Draper, asking, "Who are 'they'? Who made this decision?" There was no direct reply. In a few minutes, our guest left the room. Our group sat back into our chairs to discuss what we had just experienced. My personal feeling was that with Dr. Draper's leaving the room and closing the door behind him, the Southern Baptist Convention as I had known it died. It was evident at that moment to all of us that there was no significant desire to reknit the torn fabric of our Convention.

We were aware that the real test of most enterprises is what was accomplished or what did you do? Where are the results? Did you make a difference? I take this opportunity to list some of the benefits that flowed from our work.

> (1) We bought time to allow others to prepare to meet the onslaught of the takeover group.
> (2) We provided early on leadership that resulted in the establishment of the Cooperative Baptist Fellowship some time later. As the evidence

of that fact, Dr. Cecil Sherman was the leader of our group and later became the first executive head of the Cooperative Baptist Fellowship.

(3) A national publication was begun, which later resulted in the present magazine entitled *Baptists Today.*

(4) We led several State Conventions in their instituting a thorough search and inquiry of their title to property and other major legal papers. This was especially true in Kentucky. Our suggestion was that all titles and deeds and covenant-binding relationships should be thoroughly examined and brought into alignment with Baptist state Convention requirements.

(5) My final act, as a retiring pastor, was to stop by the annual meeting of our Kentucky Baptist Convention to receive an award for the work we had initiated in clarification of our legal position. In addition, our group also acted with many churches, as well as some pastors and staff, in personnel placement and recommendations.

(6) Our group saw that an acceptable candidate was offered for each election. We also helped to get our supporters to come and to vote. I am told that our numbers never went below 42 percent. That 42 percent was a sizeable minority, made even more so by their giving.

(7) We learned from the opposition at the highest source that there was no significant interest in the takeover group for conciliatory progress. There was no word or proposal from the takeover group that expressed any conciliatory intention. Not a word of sorrow about what was happening. Following the 1979 Convention, the victors gathered at the very cafe where this entire conquest was conceived. They were now celebrating with their imported parliamentarian dancing on the tabletops.

(8) A former president of our Convention was asked if there were enough room in the tent for all Baptists. His answer was "no." That's too much room!

We also encouraged schools and colleges to enlarge their divinity schools and to start up seminary centers. One of the most important benefits of our becoming a pastoral group was helping to provide hope and consolation to those Baptists who were being abused and persecuted.

What was the biggest disappointment in the works of this group? My biggest personal disappointment was that our best efforts did not succeed. Unfortunately, there was a failure in leadership among our contemporary Baptist leaders almost without exception. There were, however, two notable exceptions. First, leadership failed us, and second, they missed the significance of the danger. They failed to take seriously the clearly stated intentions of the takeover group.

Some day, our second chance will arrive. Some day we will Judas-proof our eternal fellowship. That "some day" is sometimes called Heaven! We did what we could. To God be the glory, if any. The takeover group has succeeded. They are now in charge of the Southern Baptist Convention. They sought the jugular, and they found it!

The aggressive nature of those who hold to the ideology and methodology of fundamentalism has left a trail of victims, which I list below.

They attacked the Northern Baptist Convention with a desire to take it over before it became the American Baptist Churches. Next, they captured the Missouri Lutheran Synod power structure and proceeded to decimate their seminary with the mass firing of members of their faculty.

Later, they gained enough power in the Republican National Party to hold the veto power over the party's nominations. This is verified by Dr. Jerry Falwell, who said, upon discontinuing the Moral Majority, "The Republican Party now has a stronger group—the Southern Baptist Convention."

At this time the entire power apparatus of the Southern Baptist Convention is under the direction of the same ideological group of fundamentalists. The records of this power-hungry group have a list of successes in their conquest for more power. Now there remains one urgent question— "who's next"!

THE SKIRMISH OF FIRST BAPTIST CHURCH, JAMESTOWN, NORTH CAROLINA

Pascal L. Hovis

First Baptist Church, Jamestown, North Carolina, has a membership of some four hundred members with about half that number as resident members. At a regular business meeting in June 2000, the church moderator and deacon chair were authorized to appoint a committee to study our relationship with the Southern Baptist Convention. Denominational Relations Committee (DRC) was the title given the committee of four women and four men. Ages of committee members ranged from their late twenties to early seventies, and most organizations within the church were represented. I was elected chair. No organized effort had existed previously to influence the church away from or toward the SBC. Discussions in previous business meetings indicated it was time for the church to look into the relationship.

PROCEDURES PERFORMED BY COMMITTEE

Over the next seven months, the DRC

(1) met regularly and studied articles about actions taken by the SBC and other churches;

(2) established a suggestion box for church members to use;

(3) had the association director of missions discuss at two church-wide meetings our Baptist heritage, actions taken by the SBC, and the history of the Baptist Faith and Message;

(4) subdivided the DRC into smaller groups and invited church members on two separate occasions to come and discuss their feelings about the situation;

(5) had several church-wide meetings to discuss any questions and at one meeting had those present complete a questionnaire consisting of eight questions; and

(6) requested church members to meet with the committee for prayer each Sunday morning before the Sunday School hour.

RECOMMENDATIONS FROM COMMITTEE

Our recommendation was to remove the words "Southern Baptist Convention" from our church bylaws. On January 25, 2001, the following letter was mailed by the church moderator:

Dear Fellow Member(s) of First Baptist Church of Jamestown,

Enclosed you will find a notice from Terry Smith, Church Moderator, announcing a special meeting to vote on a recommendation from the Denominational Relations Committee (DRC). We would like to let you know why we are making this recommendation.

The DRC was appointed to examine the relationship First Baptist Church of Jamestown has with the Southern Baptist Convention (SBC), since recent actions taken by the SBC and the changes made in the 2000 Baptist Faith and Message have generated concern within the congregation.

The heritage of Baptists and the SBC rests soundly upon the belief in the priesthood of the believer and autonomy of the local church. Baptists have never been subject to a creed, but have had "statements of faith," as expressed by the Baptist Faith and Message. Recent changes in the Baptist Faith and Message have

(1) attempted to dictate what individuals within a Baptist church must believe,

(2) weakened the belief in soul competency/the priesthood of the believer and the ability of the individual to interpret the Bible him/herself,

(3) made the 2000 Baptist Faith and Message a creed,

(4) eliminated the practice of unity within diversity, and

(5) limited the opportunities for women to respond to God's calling.

Our committee has spent much time in prayer, attended many meetings, studied a number of articles, and listened to members of First Baptist Church of Jamestown. We have interpreted the results of a survey completed by members at a business meeting and reviewed a report from the stewardship committee describing the giving patterns as revealed by pledge cards. Our conclusion from the above analysis is that the majority of members of First Baptist Church of Jamestown no longer support affiliation with the SBC.

Our recommendation *does not* propose that we affiliate with any other Baptist organization of a national nature. It merely disassociates us from affiliation with the SBC. We will

(1) still be Baptists in the true meaning of the word,

(2) keep our membership in the Central Triad Baptist Association and the Baptist State Convention of North Carolina, and

(3) continue to allow members to choose one of the four giving plans adopted by the Baptist State Convention of North Carolina.

Respectfully yours, The Denominational Relations Committee

My own conclusion to disassociate from the SBC was greatly influenced by Dr. Herschel H. Hobbs in his book, *My Faith and Message* (Broadman and Holman Publishers, 1993), as well as the actions of the SBC since 1979. Quotations from Dr. Hobbs were also used in the meetings conducted by the DRC.

Dr. Hobbs—a man who preached *The Baptist Hour* for eighteen years, wrote "The Herschel Hobbs Commentary" for twenty-eight years, wrote "Baptists Beliefs" for Baptist state papers for thirty-four years, served as president of the SBC (1961–63), and served on the SBC Peace Committee (1985–87)—knew what had taken place in the SBC since 1979 and spoke as an "insider." He tried to reconcile the differences to no avail. Here are some of Dr. Hobbs's words from the chapter entitled *The Great Controversy*.

ORIGIN OF CONTROVERSY

How did the controversy begin? For years voices of protest were heard about what was being taught in our seminaries. Unfortunately, these were blanket protests. It was the "shotgun" method in which many innocent professors were hurt. In the midst of the controversy, Dr. Landrum Leavell, president of the New Orleans Baptist Theological Seminary, said to the Convention that if someone would name a person and present evidence supporting the charge, he would handle it. From experience in other cases, I feel certain that he spoke the sentiments of all the presidents (page 252).

But we failed to heed the protests, and this led to a political process. *Someone* or *some ones* found the "Achilles heel" of the Convention; namely the appointive powers of the president. Furthermore, the names "Conservatives" and "Moderates" were applied to the resultant contending groups in the Convention. Since neither adequately described the groups, the Baptist news media sought more adequate terms. However, I will use the original terms (pages 252–53).

PROBLEM IS POLITICS

In several subsequent meetings of the committee the discussions turned more to the political aspects of the problem. On one occasion I said to a leading Conservative, "You and I could write out our statements of faith and, except for eschatology, each could sign the other's statement." He agreed. "Yet," said I, "you call yourself a Conservative and by your standard I would be called a Moderate, even though you and I believe the same thing." (One's view on eschatology has never been a test of orthodoxy among Southern Baptists.) I continued, "So I must conclude that it is because I am not on your 'team.' Which tells me that these terms are not theological but political." He agreed (pages 256–57).

Because our concern had turned to politics, a subcommittee on politics was appointed. I was on that committee, whose chairman was Charles Pickering. We spent a full day in a Dallas/Fort Worth hotel interviewing those most closely identified with matters related to politics. I will relate only the two most outstanding ones (page 257).

We interviewed Paige Patterson and Judge Pressler. It was being rumored that Paige was one being considered for the presidency of Golden Gate Seminary. Someone asked, "Paige, if you were elected president of one of our seminaries with absolute power to act, would you get rid of all professors who do not believe as you do?" Immediately he replied, "NO! Through the process of attrition—death, retirement, or resignation—I would replace them with professors who believe as I do." Such would involve a long process, not an immediate academic blood bath. Since Judge Pressler did not reject what he said, I assume that he was in agreement (page 257).

RECOMMENDATIONS OF PEACE COMMITTEE

Two of the main recommendations in the Peace Committee report were (1) to appoint balanced committees and board members and (2) to end the politics and the use of inflammatory language. Frankly, I must admit that I do not know enough about the younger generation to make a personal judgment on this. But from information received from some who do know them, it appears that this has not been done. Had this recommendation been followed, I seriously doubt that the Cooperative Baptist Fellowship would have been formed (page 264).

HOBBS'S CONCLUSION

Upon their election, I said to three of the presidents during this time, "If you will appoint balanced committees you will have no problems." Each of these stated that as their purpose, but in the end it was not done. These are honest men. I believe the statement of their purpose. I cannot help but conclude that other influences were brought to bear on them (page 264).

RESULTS OF CHURCH VOTE

A majority of 89 percent voted in favor of the recommendation from the DRC. The church has continued the same as it was before the vote. Those who feel strongly toward the SBC and those who voted to eliminate the SBC from our bylaws continue to cooperate and work well together. Sunday school teachers can use literature from either the SBC or Smith & Helwys Publishing, Inc. The skirmish ended in a win-win situation at First Baptist Church, Jamestown, North Carolina.

I AM IN EXILE
I AM HOME

Tracy Dunn-Noland

WEDNESDAY MORNING, OCTOBER 30

Dropped the kids at daycare—Halloween is in the air! Stopped by the hospital for a quick visit—glad to see Mrs. Jones is doing better. Went to the office (home)—made three phone calls, started a load of laundry, wrote my weekly column for the newspaper, planned the order of worship, and wrote some notes for the Bible study. Went to lunch with a church member. Came back to the office/home—switched laundry loads, put the roast in the crock-pot for supper, finished up the Bible study, and started reading for Sunday's sermon. Took two more phone calls, then left to pick up the kids at daycare.

If this is exile, leave me here.

A woman pastoring a small congregation might not sound like "exile" to you, and most days it doesn't to me, either. On my one-year anniversary, I told the congregation I was preaching to them my fiftieth sermon of the year; this, from a woman who never dreamed she would preach fifty sermons in her lifetime. The blessings we have received from this congregation and our rural community have been so staggeringly abundant that we shout "Thanks be to God!" on a regular basis. The church allows me time to be their pastor and time to be a mother, and the two roles have found a very agreeable balance.

In the context of the SBC holy war, I am in exile. The church I serve has no denominational affiliation. I was raised a Southern Baptist. I was licensed and ordained in Southern Baptist churches. The last congregation I served as minister of children and education was dually aligned SBC and CBF. I have had incredible support from and several roles within the CBF. They have been my people in the past, and my husband and I still seek to maintain some ties with them. But there is a very real sense that we are on the outside, looking in. By every definition I can imagine, I am no longer a Baptist.

With that realization comes a loss. There are days I feel very alone in my ministry. I have no organizational system to use for resource or support. It is difficult to maintain anything more than a local perspective. I no longer have connections to a state or national or international religious group. I am very far away from what used to be my home.

With that realization also comes enormous freedom. I freely choose with whom I do ministry. I have been empowered to go to a plethora of sources for information and support. I am responsible for giving my congregation a perspective that grows outside of our community. We are free to choose our own connections. I am making a new home.

Shortly after we moved to this community, and before our subscription to *Baptist Today* expired, I read a brief article about the SBC once again explaining why a woman couldn't be a pastor. I closed the article and thought, "You say I can't—I say I already am." Those were battles I fought for a long time, conversations I had to delirium. No one questions anymore whether I should or shouldn't answer my call to be a pastor. They simply say, "This is my pastor."

I tell my story one more time in hopes that those whose ears are weary of hearing discouragement will perhaps hear this voice saying, "Listen to your heart. If God is calling you to pastor, that is all you need to know. God will be with you. Even in the exile."

 I am in exile. I am home.

"EXILE OF INNOCENCE"

Dawn Darwin Weaks and Tracy Dunn-Noland

Dawn Darwin Weaks and Tracy Dunn-Noland presented this antiphonal litany as a part of the evangelical tradition group's response to the topic of the 1994 National Conference of Christian and Jews Seminarians Interacting Conference, "Exile: Maintaining Hope in a Chaotic World." It is the story not of one woman, but of every woman called to a ministry of maintaining hope in the denomination where she is not welcome. Dawn and Tracy were students at Brite Divinity School, located on the campus of Texas Christian University. Dawn is currently senior pastor, First Christian Church (Disciples of Christ), Rowlett, Texas, and Tracy pastors Fellowship of Believers Church in Hereford, Texas.

The italic font indicates the antiphonal voice.

> Once upon a time,
> *long ago and still today,*
> a little girl danced down the aisles of her church,
> *and sang solos on special days,*
> and on Mother's Day, she even prayed in front of
> everyone, and they all said,
> *"How sweet!"*
> She immortalized Lottie Moon and Annie Armstrong,
> the great, adventurous missionaries.

She was treasured.
She was loved.
And on the night of the Christmas pageant, it was
she who held baby Jesus most tightly.
In her shone the image of God, and she memorized
Genesis 1:27 fervently.
"God created us in God's image; male and female
God created us."
Then she grew—
Womanly curves and a strong, gentle voice that
spoke freely the words she had been taught and believed.
She always knew in her heart that God had something
special in store for her.
One Sunday, after a summer youth camp, she
walked the aisle of her church to announce her call
into ministry.
Silence fell upon the congregation, and a cloud darkened her joy.
This was the beginning of her exile.
Home was home no longer, and the enemy was now
her pastor, family, friends and teachers.

She watched as her male friends, those less active
and involved than she, made decisions toward
ministry and were rejoiced over and welcomed into
the elite fold.
And invited to preach.
And she wrote her sermons on the backs of offering
envelopes and stuffed them into her pockets.
She did not know which was more painful—the
silence or the words of others.
She endured the lectures on the proper place of
women and the accusations against her own Christianity.
She awkwardly smiled at the spoken assumptions that
God's call to her as minister would naturally be
secondary to her role as wife and mother.
She cringed as people asked her husband what his
plans were, never acknowledging that she might
have plans of her own.
People stoned her with their words and crucified her
with their indifference.
And it was not her fault.
And it was not God's fault.

EXILE OF INNOCENCE

God wept . . . wrapped her in those divine motherly arms and pulled her into the heavenly bosom.
God whispered hope into her exile. For in exile is the hope that we can return to Eden, where we can be naked and unashamed; our sons and our daughters shall prophesy the dream of God made reality—the dream that we all come home.

DAWN DARWIN WEAKS AND TRACY DUNN-NOLAND

WITHDRAWAL AND EXCLUSION:
DOING THE RIGHT THING

J. R. Huddlestun

My first serious concerns with the Southern Baptist Convention began in the early 1960s. The Sunday School Board had published four thousand copies of Ralph Elliott's *The Message of Genesis*. I was then a pastor in the state of Kansas, doing graduate work at the University of Kansas in Lawrence. The Convention, in June 1962, passed a motion by K. Owen White, pastor of the First Baptist Church, Houston, Texas, which declared faith in the "historical accuracy" of the Bible and asked Convention institutions to change situations where views threatened "our historical position." The votes, indicating the number attending the convention, were over twice the number of copies of Elliot's book that had been published. I was concerned that messengers who had not had an opportunity to read and study a work could vote and would vote against it.

I was raised in a very conservative Baptist congregation, but one that did not often exert the worst fundamentalist spirit, which condemns all other viewpoints. I changed much of my attitude while a student at Southern Baptist Theological Seminary, but began my ministry in the state of Kansas where I continued graduate study. So I was familiar with the fundamentalist attitude, spirit, and method, and felt that moderates were very slow and inefficient in organizing opposition to the fundamentalist effort to take over the Southern Baptist Convention. The moderates are used to some form of cooperation, with both sides compromising on aims, actions, and attitudes. I knew the fundamentalists would not change any position in order to cooperate; they would continue to insist on their position until they gained every item they wished.

A particularly disillusioning element in my decision to withdraw from the Convention was the methods used to seize control. A few of these I observed personally. Others were related to me by officers and ministers in the Convention in the years that the takeover occurred. Past presidents of the Convention and often other messengers were allowed to sit on the speaker's platform and speak from the pulpit microphone. When the fundamentalists were elected president, this practice was stopped and the pulpit microphone controlled. Other microphones also were managed—especially women who said their audience microphones were turned off before they could speak or make a point. I asked why the fundamentalists seemed to sit on the main floor where TV cameras gave the appearance of overwhelming votes and was told that fundamentalist pastors and their congregations were allowed to enter the main seating area one hour before the doors were opened for the regular messengers. Some families registered children as young as five years to get voting ballots. The clerk informed us at one convention that up to ten thousand more votes were made on Thursday than the number present. (When buses were brought in on Tuesday and went home after the president was elected, the ballots were put in trunks of cars and voted by others. Later, the fundamentalists voted to do all the business on Tuesday so the convention was shortened for those who could be bussed in for one day of voting.)

These elements included hiring a parliamentarian from another denomination for the convention who made/verified all decisions of the fundamentalist officers. Previously, a knowledgeable pastor of our own Convention had been used as parliamentarian.

To my knowledge, the above items have never been publicized but are often discussed among moderate messengers. These elements made me (and apparently a great number of others) realize that we could never win by urging people to attend the Southern Baptist Convention and vote, even though some of the total votes were within 2 percent of each other. But many of us felt you can't win when the other side does not use fair methods and feels that the end justifies the means. So I gave up trying to "save" the Convention through votes for the president and began to propose a reduction in gifts to agencies of the Convention that were controlled by the fundamentalists. I served on a committee that also recommended we begin to use non-SBC Sunday school literature.

Proposals and resolutions adopted by the Southern Baptist Convention further excluded my congregation. The resolution to have the wife "submit herself graciously to the servant leadership of her husband" offended my wife, me, and my congregation. The statement (creed) on the scriptures does not permit interpretation of the written word with the living Word—the Lord Jesus. So, in 2002, our congregation voted to withdraw from both the Southern Baptist Convention and the Georgia Baptist Convention (since the state Convention also adopted the 2000 version of the Baptist Faith and Message). Actions by the national Convention and the state Convention since that time have reassured us that we made the right decision. Our larger relationships now involve the local association, the Cooperative Baptist Fellowship of Georgia, and the (national) Cooperative Baptist Fellowship.

PHOENIX RISING

Reba Cobb

One of the profound griefs of my life has been to leave the Southern Baptist Convention. I grew up in a family with a strong Baptist identity, attended a Baptist college, and a Baptist seminary. My life has been devoted to following Christ in a Baptist context. When the SBC was taken over and infiltrated by fundamentalists, I was left without a spiritual home, a faith context, and a place of belonging.

As the takeover plot began in 1979, I was oblivious to the political agenda afoot. But, I was not oblivious to the injustice being perpetrated on women in the SBC. The debate was raging over the issue of ordination of women as deacons and clergy. My anger and outrage over this injustice led me to spend the decade of the eighties being an advocate for women in ministry. The energy generated by my anger was used in helping organize Southern Baptist Women in Ministry and publish the quarterly newsletter for women in ministry, *FOLIO*. We were convinced that the voice of women needed to be heard in the Southern Baptist Convention, and further that Christian justice demanded that it be heard. We were daughters of the SBC and were rightfully claiming our prophetic role.

At the time I was advocating and affirming women called into ministry, meetings of the SBC were less and less comfortable to me because of the increased influence of fundamentalism. Women were being marginalized and even vilified, the role of lay leadership was being diminished by an increasing presence of authoritarian pastor types, and historic Baptist principles were being ignored in a cavalier manner. But it was at the 1990 SBC meeting in New Orleans when I knew that I could never go back. When the election for president was held that year, it was apparent that moderate Baptists would not ever take control of the convention. The fundamentalist takeover was complete. They had won, and we had lost. Philosophically, theologically, and sociologically, I knew that I no longer belonged.

The pain of it all was great for several reasons. First, our family unit was deeply invested in Southern Seminary. My husband and I, along with our two sons, lived in the shadow of the Southern Seminary. Our lives were intimately connected to the life of the seminary. The faculty and staff of the seminary were our friends and neighbors; the seminary students were in our Sunday school class and were frequent visitors to our home, as well as babysitters for our two boys! We were enmeshed in Southern Seminary.

Second, we attended Crescent Hill Baptist Church, the "seminary church," located on the opposite hill from the seminary. Membership at Crescent Hill included dozens of faculty and staff at the seminary, in addition to several hundred students, many of whom were in the Sunday school class my husband and I taught.

So the tragedy that followed was real to us as one by one our friends left the seminary, left Louisville, and left our lives. Crescent Hill Baptist lost forty seminary families over a ten-year period, leaving a huge hole in the congregation. Rapidly the student population at Southern changed, and we no longer related to any students and few faculty.

Our world had been altered. The grief has taken years to process. As late as ten years after the takeover of the SBC, I found myself lying in bed at night listening to the chimes of the clock tower at the seminary, my mind flooded with memories, and I cried.

The sweeping Machiavellian nature of the takeover of the SBC has left destruction in its path, but despite it all, the moderate Baptist movement, like a phoenix rising out of the ashes, has taken form and shape and in God's providence is a force for good.

The Cooperative Baptist Fellowship is now my context for Baptist life and identity. It is not a Convention, but a network of churches working together to be the presence of Christ in the world. That gives me hope and is, I believe, worthy of my life's energy.

POSES

Mark Fleming

My wife and I were born and raised Catholic, so becoming members of College Park Baptist Church five years ago represented a big change for us. A whole new world. One of the first discoveries I made was we hadn't joined just any Baptist church, but a Baptist church that's "an 'interesting' mix of enthusiastic, compassionate, and fun folks"—to quote our own PR— a "Progressive, Diverse, Ecumenical" body. All true, but what about the "Baptist" part? What about our roots?

Sounds like we meet in a warehouse thrown up on the outskirts of town, not in an established church soon to celebrate its centennial. Sounds like we're some kind of fly-by-night outfit, with no affiliation, no heritage. I would joke about McChurches that used such hip language to promote themselves; now we're one of them. To separate ourselves from the Southern Baptist Convention and what it represents—retrogression, white male chauvinism, dogmatic pronouncements—it seems we've had to perform some unusual contortions.

I was a beginner deacon when College Park dissolved its SBC ties, and I can tell you that as a church we were more than ready. At the time, though, I didn't fully understand what we were giving up. Yes, allegiance to those ridiculous dictums (no women head pastors, wives submit to your husbands, blah, blah, blah, etc.). But I never really considered the "history and tradition" factor, until recently.

Not long ago we had Dan, Mildred, and Linda over as part of a church program that randomly mingles members to share a meal. That evening I learned Dan and Mildred have belonged to College Park longer than I've been alive—forty-two years! They raised their children who raised their children in the church. What a legacy! I want my two children to experience the same.

On the other hand, Linda came to College Park after her small Baptist church, on the edge of explosive growth, instead mired in internal dispute. Nobody there seemed to know how to move forward. I think what her former church lacked was the foundation, built of believers with a shared past, to support a leap into the future.

Over pumpkin pie and coffee with these folks, I finally understood the cost of divorcing the SBC. We had to sacrifice a slice of our church history, of our identity. We wouldn't go back—no way!—but the way forward is a little less certain as we struggle to redefine ourselves in light of the fundamentalist takeover. And we've had to strike some interesting poses in the process.

EARLY RETIREMENT

Joe E. Trull

"Have you ever considered early retirement?" These opening words from our new seminary president caught me off-guard. The meeting with Dr. Charles Kelley and Dean Steve Lemke on February 26, 1998, was my final conference concerning sabbatical studies soon to begin in Austin, Texas. The academic dean later apologized, stating, "I had no idea the president was going to present this option or I would have told you!"

The offer stunned me. "Will my teaching career end now, five years before I had planned to retire?" I thought. After twenty-five years of pastoral ministry in Texas, Oklahoma, and Virginia, including First Baptist in El Paso (1980–84), I had felt led of God to make a major transition to teach Christian Ethics at New Orleans Baptist Theological Seminary. The seminary had been without an ethics teacher for ten years.

My mentor and major professor at Southwestern Seminary, T. B. Maston, often encouraged me to consider teaching when I served as his grader and teaching fellow during his final years in the classroom. His recommendation led me to accept a position teaching sociology at Carson Newman College in 1964, immediately after I completed my Th.D. in Christian ethics. I loved teaching, but the subject didn't fit. So, in 1965,

I returned to the pastorate. But Dr. Maston's challenge echoed in my heart, and I knew someday I would return to the classroom.

In 1985, I began fifteen exciting and rewarding years teaching seminary students in New Orleans. As the only professor of Christian ethics, I taught every student a basic introduction course and most students a second elective. I also taught D.Min. and Ph.D. students, as well as hundreds at our off-campus sites. (The ethics requirement for students has been reduced to one course; now, four years later, the position I held has not been filled.)

Of our fifty faculty members, I was one of the few who published textbooks in my teaching field, *Ministerial Ethics* (1993) and *Walking in the Way: An Introduction to Christian Ethics* (1997). The latter text contained discussions of "Authority and Submission in Marriage" and "Gender Equality," which were written just before the 1998 SBC Family Amendment and the 2000 Baptist Faith and Message. Although the text intentionally presented all points of view, my conclusions were not identical to those of the committee members who authored these two documents adopted by the SBC.

Remember also, our new president served on the BF&M Committee, and his sister, Dorothy Patterson, served on the Family Amendment Committee. When I spoke to him about the BF&M document, President Kelley confessed, "I told Paige (SBC president and his brother-in-law) not to appoint me to that committee because I was no theologian!" Yet, he did serve as one of fifteen who drafted major doctrinal changes.

During the presidency of Dr. Landrum P. Leavell (ret. 1996), I believe I was a valued faculty member who contributed to the excellence of our seminary. I contributed regularly to academic journals and denominational publications. Often I was invited to speak at Chaplains Institutes, medical ethics conferences, clergy ethics meetings, and students on foreign mission trips—once to Mexico City and once to Juarez, Mexico. I also taught Christian ethics at Baptist schools overseas.

In the pastorate I had been a "high-profile" denominational person, having served as a trustee on the Foreign Mission Board, the Baptist Standard, the Christian Life Commission (TX), and the Texas Executive Board, as well as on the Search Committee for Executive Directors of three of these agencies. Because of my pastoral experience and preaching ability, I served as interim pastor and supply preacher almost every Sunday of my years in New Orleans. At my retirement dinner, Dr. Leavell's personal words soothed my grieving heart: "Joe, bringing you to the seminary was one of the best things I did!" He did not know what had occasioned my early retirement until much later.

I share this capsule view of my teaching ministry at NOBTS, not to impress you with my credentials or accomplishments, but to verify that there was no good reason to encourage my early departure from the campus.

That is why I was stunned by President Kelley's opening words. In fact, I was so shocked that for one moment I became defensive, recounting my contributions to the seminary. Dr. Kelley's response brought me back to reality: "You are a hard worker!"

I couldn't believe it! The best compliment he could offer me was a word he could also give to Willie the yard man, who diligently trimmed the hedges outside. Suddenly, I realized the truth—the best the new president (who had been my colleague for the past twelve years) could say about my tenure of teaching and ministry was, "You are a hard worker!"

He was kind, but firm. "This is not an ultimatum," he assured me. "You can return after sabbatical, but. . . ." A pregnant pause followed. He continued, "This offer is unique—a rare door of opportunity that will soon close," he stated.

He tried to put a positive spin on the offer—the difficulty of commuting from Texas after sabbatical, the many opportunities I would have in my home state, etc., ad nauseam. I noted that we had several professors who commuted from Mississippi—a three-hour daily drive that involved many more hours than my Texas flight. No response.

His first offer was a free sabbatical—that is, I would not be required to return and teach for another two years, which was normally required. I noted that even with the free sabbatical, financially I would be unable to retire at this time. To get a pastorate after age sixty was very difficult.

"Let me talk to Audra," I responded. The whole matter was so unexpected. I remembered a conversation I had with Dean Lemke over coffee a few weeks earlier. He casually asked me then, "When do you plan to retire?" I considered it small talk, and just replied, "Oh, about five to eight years after my sabbatical, I guess." Evidently, this was a fishing expedition to see how long they might have me around.

I did some fishing myself over the next few weeks. I talked to a person whom I felt would be honest, an administrator at the highest level who was in on most major decisions. As I bared my soul, especially my hurt and disappointment at being "encouraged" to consider early retirement, he explained the reason: "Joe, because of your personal beliefs and your views as expressed in your books, the president is afraid of a confrontation with the trustees. If it came to that, he would not defend you or support you. It is probably better for you, as well as for the school, that you take early retirement." I believe he was the only one who told me the truth behind the offer.

Some faculty members didn't like the style of Landrum Leavell. I got along fine with our former president, perhaps because we both had pastored churches in Texas and shared many common friends and a common history.

However, President Leavell has one trait that the faculty loved. He often said to outsiders who were critical of some teachers, "You tell me the problem and I will take care of it. Don't try to go around me to get to my faculty. I will deal with them myself." We all knew that as long as we were moral and did not violate any major rules, Landrum would defend us. He was paternalistic, but sometimes it was comforting to have a Papa Bear guarding the cave from intruders.

The 1998 Family Amendment and the 2000 Baptist Faith and Message document focused on gender issues—the role of women in church and home. Though SBC leaders claim they only oppose women as pastors and support a "gracious submission" in the home, the reality is different. Taking their cue from these statements, Southern Baptist churches are reinforcing an attitude that women are somehow secondary to men. It is not uncommon for churches to prohibit female members from: (1) teaching men and boys; (2) serving as chair of church committees; (3) ushering; (4) serving as an associate minister; (5) serving as a deacon; (6) being ordained (even though our mission board appoints only ordained chaplains); and (7) leading music or even speaking from the pulpit.

For the last decade, I have done extensive research on this subject. Presently, I am coeditor and contributor (with my wife) of a book titled: *Putting Women in Their (Proper) Place: The Baptist Debate over Female Equality* (Smith & Helwys, 2003). Just as we did on the race issue in the nineteenth and twentieth centuries, so Baptists today are once again corrupted by our past culture and blind to the teachings of Jesus and the scriptures. I am convinced that my beliefs about biblical equality were a significant factor in my early retirement.

Eventually an agreement was worked out that gave me financial stability after my sabbatical, so that I could find a new ministry—for that I am grateful. Compared to many others who were forced to leave seminary positions, I was treated much more equitably. Nevertheless, my teaching career was brought to an abrupt halt several years early.

I have always believed, as the story of Joseph illustrates, that God often has a double agenda at work. Or to put it another way, when Plan A collapses, God always has a backup Plan B. Within a short time, I was asked to teach adjunctively by three seminaries and two Baptist CLCs on clergy sexual abuse, publishing four articles in *Broken Trust*, and holding several conferences on this subject.

I also was called to pastor a Baptist church, which was ready after meeting with our Methodist friends for ninety years, to begin again. In less than a year, our fifteen adults have grown to more than forty. We have baptized fourteen adults and youth, and acquired land for our first building.

And best of all, in 2000, Foy Valentine asked me to become the editor of *Christian Ethics Today*, the widely read journal he established in 1995.

My life is full of good and gracious opportunities. The Lord has allowed me to continue teaching, while filling my life with other joys—writing, pastoring and preaching, and editing a prophetic voice of Christian ethics.

I have come to feel toward those who desired that I no longer teach at New Orleans Baptist Seminary as Joseph did toward his brothers who had sold him into slavery: "But as for you, you meant evil against me; but God meant it for good" (Genesis 50:20).

What happened to me and to scores of other seminary professors was the beginning of a new era in SBC theological education. Open discussion of many controversial issues is now *verboten*! SBC leadership has established a new creed set in concrete, ideas based on debatable interpretations of scripture.

One of the serendipities of seminary life was the informal discussion times in the cafeteria. While we drank café au lait, faculty and students alike enjoyed debating the hot issues of the day. Often these moments were our best learning labs.

When I returned to the seminary for my official retirement in December 1999, I was amazed at the change of atmosphere. As I sat around a table with several faculty members, old and new, along with a few students, everyone seemed to guard their words. Later, a close colleague explained that professors can no longer discuss openly certain issues; for fear of jeopardizing their job, certain subjects were avoided.

That experience helped me realize I could no longer teach at an SBC seminary. What a sad day for Southern Baptists, when the graduate schools for ministers, missionaries, and church leaders no longer allow the official position of the SBC to be questioned. Hershel Hobbs must be turning over in his grave!

Former seminary professors may feel that we are exiled in Egypt, but God is not confined to Jerusalem or Nashville. And God's truth will never be bound by any human creed or convention. So let us "seek first the kingdom of God and his righteousness" (Matthew 6:33) and let the God of Moses and Miriam take care of the Egyptians in his own good time.

APPENDIX

COMPARISON OF 1925, 1963 AND 2000
BAPTIST FAITH AND MESSAGE

Preamble to the 1925 Baptist Faith and Message	Preamble to the 1963 Baptist Faith and Message	Preamble to the 2000 Baptist Faith and Message
The report of the Committee on Statement of Baptist Faith and Message was presented as follows by E. Y. Mullins, Kentucky:	Committee on Baptist Faith and Message

The 1962 session of the Southern Baptist Convention, meeting in San Francisco, California, adopted the following motion: | The 1999 session of the Southern Baptist Convention, meeting in Atlanta, Georgia, adopted the following motion addressed to the President of the Convention: |
REPORT OF THE COMMITTEE ON BAPTIST FAITH AND MESSAGE	"Since the report of the Committee on Statement of Baptist Faith and Message was adopted in 1925, there have been various statements from time to time which have been made, but no over-all statement which might be helpful at this time as suggested in Section 2 of that report, or introductory	"I move that in your capacity as Southern Baptist Convention chairman, you appoint a blue ribbon committee to review the Baptist Faith and Message statement with the responsibility to report and bring any recommendations to this meeting next June in Orlando."
Your committee beg leave to report as follows:		
Your committee recognize that they were appointed "to consider the advisability of issuing another statement of the Baptist Faith and Message, and report at the next Convention."		President Paige Patterson appointed the committee as

Preamble to the 1925 Baptist Faith and Message (cont'd)	Preamble to the 1963 Baptist Faith and Message (cont'd)	Preamble to the 2000 Baptist Faith and Message (cont'd)

In pursuance of the instructions of the Convention, and in consideration of the general denominational situation, your committee have decided to recommend the New Hampshire Confession of Faith, revised at certain points, and with some additional articles growing out of present needs, for approval by the Convention, in the event a statement of the Baptist faith and message is deemed necessary at this time.

The present occasion for a reaffirmation of Christian fundamentals is the prevalence of naturalism in the modern teaching and preaching of religion. Christianity is supernatural in its origin and history. We repudiate every theory of religion which denies the supernatural elements in our faith.

As introductory to the doctrinal articles, we recommend the adoption by the Convention of the following statement of the historic Baptist conception of the nature and function of confessions of faith in our religious and denominational life, believing that some such statement will clarify the atmosphere and remove some causes of misunderstanding, friction, and apprehension. Baptists approve and circulate confessions of faith with the following understanding, namely:

1. That they constitute a consensus of opinion of some Baptist body, large or small, for the general instruction

statement which might be used as an interpretation of the 1925 Statement."

"We recommend, therefore, that the president of this Convention be requested to call a meeting of the men now serving as presidents of the various state conventions that would quality as a member of the Southern Baptist Convention committee under Bylaw 18 to present to the Convention in Kansas City some similar statement which shall serve as information to the churches, and which may serve as guidelines to the various agencies of the Southern Baptist Convention. It is understood that any group or individuals may approach this committee to be of service. The expenses of this committee shall be borne by the Convention Operating Budget."

Your committee thus constituted begs leave to present its report as follows:

Throughout its work your committee has been conscious of the contribution made by the statement of "The Southern Baptist Faith and Message" adopted by the Southern Baptist Convention in 1925. It quotes with approval its affirmation that "Christianity is supernatural in its origin and history. We repudiate every theory of religion which denies the supernatural elements in our faith."

Furthermore, it concurs in the introductory "statement

follows: Max Barnett (OK), Steve Gaines (AL), Susie Hawkins (TX), Rudy A. Hernandez (TX), Charles S. Kelley, Jr. (LA), Heather King (IN), Richard D. Land (TN), Fred Luter (LA), R. Albert Mohler, Jr. (KY), T. C. Pinckney (VA), Nelson Price (GA), Adrian Rogers (TN), Roger Spradlin (CA), Simon Tsoi (AZ), Jerry Vines (FL). Adrian Rogers (TN) was appointed chairman.

Your committee thus constituted begs leave to present its report as follows:

Baptists are a people of deep beliefs and cherished doctrines. Throughout our history we have been a confessional people, adopting statements of faith as a witness to our beliefs and a pledge of our faithfulness to the doctrines revealed in Holy Scripture.

Our confessions of faith are rooted in historical precedent, as the church in every age has been called upon to define and defend its beliefs. Each generation of Christians bears the responsibility of guarding the treasury of truth that has been entrusted to us [2 Timothy 1:14]. Facing a new century, Southern Baptists must meet the demands and duties of the present hour.

New challenges to faith appear in every age. A pervasive antisupernaturalism in the culture was answered by Southern Baptists in 1925, when the Baptist Faith and

APPENDIX

and guidance of our own people and others concerning those articles of the Christian faith which are most surely conditions of salvation revealed in the New Testament, viz., repentance towards God and faith in Jesus Christ as Saviour and Lord.

2. That we do not regard them as complete statements of our faith, having any quality of finality or infallibility. As in the past so in the future Baptist should hold themselves free to revise their statements of faith as may seem to them wise and expedient at any time.

2. That any group of Baptists, large or small, have the inherent right to draw up for themselves and publish to the world a confession of their faith whenever they may think it advisable to do so.

4. That the sole authority for faith and practice among Baptists is the Scriptures of the Old and New Testaments. Confessions are only guides in interpretation, having no authority over the conscience.

5. That they are statements of religious convictions, drawn from the Scriptures, and are not to be used to hamper freedom of thought or investigation in other realms of life.

of the historic Baptist conception of the nature and function of confessions of faith in our religious and denominational life . . . ." It is, therefore, quoted in full as a part of this report to the Convention:

"(1) That they constitute a consensus of opinion of some Baptist body, large or small, for the general instruction and guidance of our own people and others concerning those articles of the Christian faith which are most surely held among us. They are not intended to add anything to the simple conditions of salvation revealed in the New Testament, viz., repentance towards God and faith in Jesus Christ as Savior and Lord.

"(2) That we do not regard them as complete statements of our faith, having any quality of finality or infallibility. As in the past so in the future, Baptists should hold themselves free to revise their statements of faith as may seem to them wise and expedient at any time.

"(3) That any group of Baptists, large or small, have the inherent right to draw up for themselves and publish to the world a confession of their faith whenever they may think it advisable to do so.

"(4) That the sole authority for faith and practice among Baptists is the Scriptures of the Old and New Testaments. Confessions are only guides in interpretation, having no authority over the conscience.

"(5) That they are statements of religious convictions, drawn

Message was first adopted by this Convention. In 1963, Southern Baptists responded to assaults upon the authority and truthfulness of the Bible by adopting revisions to the Baptist Faith and Message . The Convention added an article on "The Family" in 1998, thus answering cultural confusion with the clear teachings of Scripture. Now, faced with a culture hostile to the very notion of truth, this generation of Baptists must claim anew the eternal truths of the Christian faith.

Your committee respects and celebrates the heritage of the Baptist Faith and Message, and affirms the decision of the Convention in 1925 to adopt the New Hampshire Confession of Faith, "revised at certain points and with some additional articles growing out of certain needs . . . ." We also respect the important contributions of the 1925 and 1963 editions of the Baptist Faith and Message.

With the 1963 committee, we have been guided in our work by the 1925 "statement of the historic Baptist conception of the nature and function of confessions of faith in our religious and denominational life . . . ." It is, therefore, quoted in full as a part of this report to the Convention:

(1) That they constitute a consensus of opinion of some Baptist body, large or small, for the general instruction and guidance of our own people and others concerning those articles of the Christian faith which are most surely held among us. They are not

Preamble to the 1925 Baptist Faith and Message (cont'd)	Preamble to the 1963 Baptist Faith and Message (cont'd)	Preamble to the 2000 Baptist Faith and Message (cont'd)

from the Scriptures, and are not to be used to hamper freedom of thought or investigation in other realms of life."

The 1925 Statement recommended "the New Hampshire Confession of Faith, revised at certain points, and with some additional articles growing out of certain needs . . . ." Your present committee has adopted the same pattern. It has sought to build upon the structure of the 1925 Statement, keeping in mind the "certain needs" of our generation. At times it has reproduced sections of that Statement without change. In other instances it has substituted words for clarity or added sentences for emphasis. At certain points it has combined articles, with minor changes in wording, to endeavor to relate certain doctrines to each other. In still others — e. g., "God" and "Salvation" — it has sought to bring together certain truths contained throughout the 1925 Statement in order to relate them more clearly and concisely. In no case has it sought to delete from or to add to the basic contents of the 1925 Statement.

Baptists are a people who profess a living faith. This faith is rooted and grounded in Jesus Christ who is "the same yesterday, and today, and forever." Therefore, the sole authority for faith and practice among Baptists is Jesus Christ whose will is revealed in the Holy Scriptures.

intended to add anything to the simple conditions of salvation revealed in the New Testament, viz., repentance toward God and faith in Jesus Christ as Saviour and Lord.

(2) That we do not regard them as complete statements of our faith, having any quality of finality or infallibility. As in the past so in the future, Baptists should hold themselves free to revise their statements of faith as may seem to them wise and expedient at any time.

(3) That any group of Baptists, large or small, have the inherent right to draw up for themselves and publish to the world a confession of their faith whenever they may think it advisable to do so.

(4) That the sole authority for faith and practice among Baptists is the Scriptures of the Old and New Testaments. Confessions are only guides in interpretation, having no authority over the conscience.

(5) That they are statements of religious convictions, drawn from the Scriptures, and are not to be used to hamper freedom of thought or investigation in other realms of life.

Baptists cherish and defend religious liberty, and deny the right of any secular or religious authority to impose a confession of faith upon a church or body of churches. We honor the principles of soul competency and the priesthood of believers,

APPENDIX

A living faith must experience a growing understanding of truth and must be continually interpreted and related to the needs of each new generation. Throughout their history Baptist bodies, both large and small, have issued statements of faith which comprise a consensus of their beliefs. Such statements have never been regarded as complete, infallible statements of faith, nor as official creeds carrying andatory authority. Thus this generation of Southern Baptists is in historic succession of intent and purpose as it endeavors to state for its time and theological climate those articles of the Christian faith which are most surely held among us.

Baptists emphasize the soul's competency before God, freedom in religion, and the priesthood of the believer. However, this emphasis should not be interpreted to mean that there is an absence of certain definite doctrines that Baptists believe, cherish, and with which they have been and are now closely identified.

It is the purpose of this statement of faith and message to set forth certain teachings which we believe.

affirming together both our liberty in Christ and our accountability to each other under the Word of God.

Baptist churches, associations, and general bodies have adopted confessions of faith as a witness to the world, and as instruments of doctrinal accountability. We are not embarrassed to state before the world that these are doctrines we hold precious and as essential to the Baptist tradition of faith and practice.

As a committee, we have been charged to address the "certain needs" of our own generation. In an age increasingly hostile to Christian truth, our challenge is to express the truth as revealed in Scripture, and to bear witness to Jesus Christ, who is "*the Way, the Truth, and the Life.*"

The 1963 committee rightly sought to identify and affirm "certain definite doctrines that Baptists believe, cherish, and with which they have been and are now closely identified." Our living faith is established upon eternal truths. "Thus this generation of Southern Baptists is in historic succession of intent and purpose as it endeavors to state for its time and theological climate those articles of the Christian faith which are most surely held among us."

It is the purpose of this statement of faith and message to set forth certain teachings which we believe.

Respectfully Submitted,

The Baptist Faith and Message Study Committee Adrian Rogers, Chairman

1925 Baptist Faith and Message Statement	1963 Baptist Faith and Message Statement with 1998 Amendment	Current Baptist Faith and Message Statement
I. The Scriptures	**I. The Scriptures**	**I. The Scriptures**
We believe that the Holy Bible was written by men divinely inspired, and is a perfect treasure of heavenly instruction; that it has God for its author, salvation for its end, and truth, without any mixture of error, for its matter; that it reveals the principles by which God will judge us; and therefore is, and will remain to the end of the world, the true center of Christian union, and the supreme standard by which all human conduct, creeds and religious opinions should be tried.	The Holy Bible was written by men divinely inspired and is the record of God's revelation of Himself to man. It is a perfect treasure of divine instruction. It has God for its author, salvation for its end, and truth, without any mixture of error, for its matter. It reveals the principles by which God judges us; and therefore is, and will remain to the end of the world, the true center of Christian union, and the supreme standard by which all human conduct, creeds, and religious opinions should be tried. The criterion by which the Bible is to be interpreted is Jesus Christ.	The Holy Bible was written by men divinely inspired and is God's revelation of Himself to man. It is a perfect treasure of divine instruction. It has God for its author, salvation for its end, and truth, without any mixture of error, for its matter. Therefore, all Scripture is totally true and trustworthy. It reveals the principles by which God judges us, and therefore is, and will remain to the end of the world, the true center of Christian union, and the supreme standard by which all human conduct, creeds, and religious opinions should be tried. All Scripture is a testimony to Christ, who is Himself the focus of divine revelation.
Luke 16:29-31; 2 Tim. 3: 15-17; Eph. 2:20; Heb. 1:1; 2 Peter 1:19-21; John 16:1 3-15; Matt. 22:29-31; Psalm 19:7-10; Psalm 119:1-8.	*Ex. 24:4; Deut. 4:1-2; 17:19; Josh. 8:34; Psalms 19:7-10; 119:11,89,105,140; Isa. 34:16; 40:8; Jer. 15:16; 36; Matt. 5:17-18; 22:29; Luke 21:33; 24:44-46; John 5:39; 16:13-15; 17:17; Acts 2:16ff.; 17:11; Rom. 15:4; 16:25-26; 2 Tim. 3:15-17; Heb. 1:1-2; 4:12; 1 Peter 1:25; 2 Peter 1:19-21.*	*Exodus 24:4; Deuteronomy 4:1-2; 17:19; Joshua 8:34; Psalms 19:7-10; 119: 11,89,105,140; Isaiah 34:16; 40:8; Jeremiah 15:16; 36:1-32; Matthew 5:17-18; 22:29; Luke 21:33; 24:44-46; John 5:39; 16:13-15; 17:17; Acts 2:16ff.; 17:11; Romans 15:4; 16: 25-26; 2 Timothy 3:15-17; Hebrews 1:1-2; 4:12; 1 Peter 1:25; 2 Peter 1:19-21.*
II. God	**II. God**	**II. God**
There is one and only one living and true God, an intelligent, spiritual, and personal Being, the Creator, Preserver, and Ruler of the universe, infinite in holiness and all other perfections, to whom we owe the highest love,	There is one and only one living and true God. He is an intelligent, spiritual, and personal Being, the Creator, Redeemer, Preserver, and Ruler of the universe. God is infinite in holiness and all other perfections. To him we	There is one and only one living and true God. He is an intelligent, spiritual, and personal Being, the Creator, Redeemer, Preserver, and Ruler of the universe. God is infinite in holiness and all other perfections. God is all

reverence, and obedience. He is revealed to us as Father, Son, and Holy Spirit, each with distinct personal attributes, but without division of nature, essence, or being.

Gen. 1:1; 1 Cor. 8:4-6; Deut. 6:4; Jer. 10:10; Isa. 48:12; Deut. 5:7; Ex. 3:14; Heb. 11:6; John 5:26; 1 Tim. 1:17; John 1:14-18; John 15:26; Gal. 4:6; Matt. 28:19.

owe the highest love, reverence, and obedience. The eternal God reveals Himself to us as Father, Son, and Holy Spirit, with distinct personal attributes, but without division of nature, essence, or being.

1. God the Father

God as Father reigns with providential care over His universe, His creatures, and the flow of the stream of human history according to the purposes of His grace. He is all powerful, all loving, and all wise. God is Father in truth to those who become children of God through faith in Jesus Christ. He is fatherly in his attitude toward all men.

Gen. 1:1; 2:7; Ex. 3:14; 6: 2-3; 15:11ff.; 20:1ff.; Levit. 22:2; Deut. 6:4; 32:6; 1 Chron. 29:10; Psalm 19: 1-3; Isa. 43:3,15; 64:8; Jer. 10:10; 17:13; Matt. 6:9ff.; 7:11; 23:9; 28:19; Mark 1: 9-11; John 4:24; 5:26; 14: 6-13; 17:1-8; Acts 1:7; Rom. 8:14-15; 1 Cor. 8:6; Gal. 4:6; Ephes. 4:6; Col. 1:15; 1 Tim. 1:17; Heb. 11:6; 12:9; 1 Peter 1:17; 1 John 5:7.

2. God the Son

Christ is the eternal Son of God. In His incarnation as Jesus Christ He was conceived of the Holy Spirit and born of the virgin Mary. Jesus perfectly revealed and did the will of God, taking upon Himself the demands and necessities of human nature and identifying Himself completely with mankind yet without sin. He honored the divine law by His personal obedience, and in His

powerful and all knowing; and His perfect knowledge extends to all things, past, present, and future, including the future decisions of His free creatures. To Him we owe the highest love, reverence, and obedience. The eternal triune God reveals Himself to us as Father, Son, and Holy Spirit, with distinct personal attributes, but without division of nature, essence, or being.

A. God the Father

God as Father reigns with providential care over His universe, His creatures, and the flow of the stream of human history according to the purposes of His grace. He is all powerful, all knowing, all loving, and all wise. God is Father in truth to those who become children of God through faith in Jesus Christ. He is fatherly in His attitude toward all men.

Genesis 1:1; 2:7; Exodus 3:14; 6:2-3; 15:11ff.; 20:1ff.; Leviticus 22:2; Deuteronomy 6:4; 32:6; 1 Chronicles 29:10; Psalm 19:1-3; Isaiah 43:3,15; 64:8; Jeremiah 10:10; 17:13; Matthew 6:9ff.; 7:11; 23:9; 28:19; Mark 1: 9-11; John 4:24; 5:26; 14: 6-13; 17:1-8; Acts 1:7; Romans 8:14-15; 1 Corinthians 8:6; Galatians 4:6; Ephesians 4:6; Colossians 1:15; 1 Timothy 1:17; Hebrews 11:6; 12:9; 1 Peter 1:17; 1 John 5:7.

B. God the Son

Christ is the eternal Son of God. In His incarnation as Jesus Christ He was conceived

1925 Baptist Faith and Message Statement (cont'd)	1963 Baptist Faith and Message Statement with 1998 Amendment (cont'd)	Current Baptist Faith and Message Statement (cont'd)
	death on the cross He made provision for the redemption of men from sin. He was raised from the dead with a glorified body and appeared to His disciples as the person who was with them before His crucifixion. He ascended into heaven and is now exalted at the right hand of God where He is the One Mediator, partaking of the nature of God and of man, and in whose Person is effected the reconciliation between God and man. He will return in power and glory to judge the world and to consummate His redemptive mission. He now dwells in all believers as the living and ever present Lord. *Gen. 18:1ff.; Psalms 2:7ff.; 110:1ff.; Isa. 7:14; 53; Matt. 1:18-23; 3:17; 8:29; 11:27; 14:33; 16:16,27; 17:5; 27; 28:1-6,19; Mark 1:1; 3:11; Luke 1:35; 4:41; 22:70; 24:46; John 1:1-18,29; 10:30,38; 11:25-27; 12:44-50; 14:7-11; 16:15-16,28;17:1-5, 21-22; 20:1-20,28; Acts 1:9; 2:22-24; 7:55-56; 9:4-5,20; Rom. 1: 3-4; 3:23-26; 5:6-21; 8:1-3,34; 10:4; 1 Cor. 1:30; 2:2; 8:6; 15:1-8,24-28; 2 Cor. 5:19-21; 8:9; Gal. 4:4-5; Ephes. 1:20; 3:11; 4:7-10; Phil. 2:5-11; Col. 1:13-22; 2:9; 1 Thess. 4:14-18; 1 Tim. 2:5-6; 3:16; Titus 2:13-14; Heb. 1:1-3; 4:14-15; 7:14-28; 9:12-15,24-28; 12:2; 13:8; 1 Peter 2:21-25; 3:22; 1 John 1:7-9; 3:2; 4:14-15; 5:9; 2 John 7-9; Rev. 1:13-16; 5:9-14; 12:10-11; 13:8; 19:16.*	of the Holy Spirit and born of the virgin Mary. Jesus perfectly revealed and did the will of God, taking upon Himself human nature with its demands and necessities and identifying Himself completely with mankind yet without sin. He honored the divine law by His personal obedience, and in His substitutionary death on the cross He made provision for the redemption of men from sin. He was raised from the dead with a glorified body and appeared to His disciples as the person who was with them before His crucifixion. He ascended into heaven and is now exalted at the right hand of God where He is the One Mediator, fully God, fully man, in whose Person is effected the reconciliation between God and man. He will return in power and glory to judge the world and to consummate His redemptive mission. He now dwells in all believers as the living and ever present Lord. *Genesis 18:1ff.; Psalms 2:7ff.; 110:1ff.; Isaiah 7:14; 53; Matthew 1:18-23; 3:17; 8:29; 11:27; 14:33; 16:16,27; 17:5; 27; 28:1-6,19; Mark 1:1; 3:11; Luke 1:35; 4:41; 22:70; 24:46; John 1:1-18,29; 10:30,38; 11:25-27; 12:44-50; 14:7-11; 16:15-16,28; 17:1-5, 21-22; 20:1-20,28; Acts 1:9; 2:22- 24; 7:55-56; 9:4-5,20; Romans 1:3-4; 3:23-26; 5: 6-21; 8:1-3,34; 10:4; 1 Corinthians 1:30; 2:2; 8:6;*

APPENDIX

3. God the Holy Spirit

The Holy Spirit is the Spirit of God. He inspired holy men of old to write the Scriptures. Through illumination He enables men to understand truth. He exalts Christ. He convicts of sin, of righteousness and of judgment. He calls men to the Saviour, and effects regeneration. He cultivates Christian character, comforts believers, and bestows the spiritual gifts by which they serve God through His church. He seals the believer unto the day of final redemption. His presence in the Christian is the assurance of God to bring the believer into the fulness of the stature of Christ. He enlightens and empowers the believer and the church in worship, evangelism, and service.

Gen. 1:2; Judg. 14:6; Job 26:13; Psalms 51:11; 139:7ff.; Isa. 61:1-3; Joel 2:28-32; Matt. 1:18; 3:16; 4:1; 12:28-32; 28:19; Mark 1:10,12; Luke 1:35; 4:1, 18-19; 11:13; 12:12; 24:49; John 4:24; 14:16-17,26; 15:26; 16:7-14; Acts 1:8; 2: 1-4,38; 4:31; 5:3; 6:3; 7:55; 8:17,39; 10:44; 13:2; 15:28; 16:6; 19:1-6; Rom. 8:9-11, 14-16,26-27; 1 Cor. 2:10-14; 3:16; 12:3-11; Gal. 4:6; Ephes. 1:13-14; 4:30; 5:18; 1 Thess. 5:19; 1 Tim. 3:16; 4:1; 2 Tim. 1:14; 3:16; Heb. 9:8,14; 2 Peter 1:21; 1 John 4:13; 5:6-7; Rev. 1:10; 22:17.

15:1-8,24-28; 2 Corinthians 5:19-21; 8:9; Galatians 4: 4-5; Ephesians 1:20; 3:11; 4: 7-10; Philippians 2:5-11; Colossians 1:13-22; 2:9; 1 Thessalonians 4:14-18; 1 Timothy 2:5-6; 3:16; Titus 2:13-14; Hebrews 1:1-3; 4:14-15; 7:14-28; 9:12-15, 24-28; 12:2; 13:8; 1 Peter 2:21-25; 3:22; 1 John 1:7-9; 3:2; 4:14-15; 5:9; 2 John 7-9; Revelation 1:13-16; 5:9-14; 12:10-11; 13:8; 19:16.

C. God the Holy Spirit

The Holy Spirit is the Spirit of God, fully divine. He inspired holy men of old to write the Scriptures. Through illumination He enables men to understand truth. He exalts Christ. He convicts men of sin, of righteousness, and of judgment. He calls men to the Saviour, and effects regeneration. At the moment of regeneration He baptizes every believer into the Body of Christ. He cultivates Christian character, comforts believers, and bestows the spiritual gifts by which they serve God through His church. He seals the believer unto the day of final redemption. His presence in the Christian is the guarantee that God will bring the believer into the fullness of the stature of Christ. He enlightens and empowers the believer and the church in worship, evangelism, and service.

Genesis 1:2; Judges 14:6; Job 26:13; Psalms 51:11; 139:7ff.; Isaiah 61:1-3; Joel 2:28-32; Matthew 1:18; 3:16; 4:1; 12:28-32; 28:19; Mark 1:10, 12; Luke 1:35; 4:1,18-19; 11:13; 12:12; 24:49; John

1925 Baptist Faith and Message Statement (cont'd)	1963 Baptist Faith and Message Statement with 1998 Amendment (cont'd)	Current Baptist Faith and Message Statement (cont'd)
		4:24; 14:16-17,26; 15:26; 16:7-14; Acts 1:8; 2:1-4,38; 4:31; 5:3; 6:3; 7:55; 8:17,39; 10:44; 13:2; 15:28; 16:6; 19: 1-6; Romans 8:9-11,14-16, 26-27; 1 Corinthians 2:10-14; 3:16; 12:3-11,13; Galatians 4:6; Ephesians 1:13-14; 4:30; 5:18; 1 Thessalonians 5:19; 1 Timothy 3:16; 4:1; 2 Timothy 1:14; 3:16; Hebrews 9:8,14; 2 Peter 1:21; 1 John 4:13; 5: 6-7; Revelation 1:10; 22:17.

III. The Fall of Man

Man was created by the special act of God, as recorded in Genesis. "So God created man in his own image, in the image of God created he him; male and female created he them" (Gen. 1:27). "And the Lord God formed man of the dust of the ground, and breathed into his nostrils the breath of life; and man became a living soul" (Gen. 2:7).

He was created in a state of holiness under the law of his Maker, but, through the temptation of Satan, he transgressed the command of God and fell from his original holiness and righteousness; whereby his posterity inherit a nature corrupt and in bondage to sin, are under condemnation, and as soon as they are capable of moral action, become actual transgressors.

Gen. 1:27; Gen. 2:7; John 1:23; Gen. 3:4-7; Gen. 3:22-24; Rom. 5:12,14,19, 21; Rom. 7:23-25; Rom. 11:18,22,32-33; Col. 1:21.

III. Man

Man was created by the special act of God, in His own image, and is the crowning work of His creation. In the beginning man was innocent of sin and was endowed by his Creator with freedom of choice. By his free choice man sinned against God and brought sin into the human race. Through the temptation of Satan man transgressed the command of God, and fell from his original innocence; whereby his posterity inherit a nature and an environment inclined toward sin, and as soon as they are capable of moral action become transgressors and are under condemnation. Only the grace of God can bring man into His holy fellowship and enable man to fulfil the creative purpose of God. The sacredness of human personality is evident in that God created man in His own image, and in that Christ died for man; therefore every man possesses dignity and is worthy of respect and Christian love.

III. Man

Man is the special creation of God, made in His own image. He created them male and female as the crowning work of His creation. The gift of gender is thus part of the goodness of God's creation. In the beginning man was innocent of sin and was endowed by his Creator with freedom of choice. By his free choice man sinned against God and brought sin into the human race. Through the temptation of Satan man transgressed the command of God, and fell from his original innocence whereby his posterity inherit a nature and an environment inclined toward sin. Therefore, as soon as they are capable of moral action, they become transgressors and are under condemnation. Only the grace of God can bring man into His holy fellowship and enable man to fulfill the creative purpose of God. The sacredness of human personality is evident in that God created man in His own image, and

Gen. 1:26-30; 2:5,7,18-22; 3; 9:6; Psalms 1; 8:3-6; 32: 1-5; 51:5; Isa. 6:5; Jer. 17:5; Matt. 16:26; Acts 17:26-31; Rom. 1:19-32; 3:10-18,23; 5:6,12,19; 6:6; 7:14-25; 8: 14-18,29; 1 Cor. 1:21-31; 15:19,21-22; Eph. 2:1-22; Col. 1:21-22; 3:9-11.

in that Christ died for man; therefore, every person of every race possesses full dignity and is worthy of respect and Christian love.

Genesis 1:26-30; 2:5,7,18-22; 3; 9:6; Psalms 1; 8:3-6; 32:1- 5; 51:5; Isaiah 6:5; Jeremiah 17:5; Matthew 16:26; Acts 17:26-31; Romans 1:19-32; 3:10- 18,23; 5:6,12,19; 6:6; 7:14- 25; 8:14-18,29; 1 Corinthians 1:21-31; 15:19,21-22; Ephesians 2:1-22; Colossians 1:21-22; 3:9-11.

IV. The Way of Salvation

The salvation of sinners is wholly of grace, through the mediatorial office of the Son of God, who by the Holy Spirit was born of the Virgin Mary and took upon him our nature, yet without sin; honored the divine law by his personal obedience and made atonement for our sins by his death. Being risen from the dead, he is now enthroned in Heaven, and, uniting in his person the tenderest sympathies with divine perfections, he is in every way qualified to be a compassionate and all-sufficient Saviour.

Col. 1:21-22; Eph. 1:7-10; Gal. 2:19-20; Gal. 3:13; Rom. 1:4; Eph. 1:20-23; Matt. 1:21-25; Luke 1:35; 2:11; Rom. 3:25.

V. Justification

Justification is God's gracious and full acquittal upon principles of righteousness of all sinners who believe in Christ. This blessing is bestowed, not in consideration of any works of righteousness which we have done, but through the redemption that

IV. Salvation

Salvation involves the redemption of the whole man, and is offered freely to all who accept Jesus Christ as Lord and Saviour, who by His own blood obtained eternal redemption for the believer. In its broadest sense salvation includes regeneration, sanctification, and glorification.

1. Regeneration, or the new birth, is a work of God's grace whereby believers become new creatures in Christ Jesus. It is a change of heart wrought by the Holy Spirit through conviction of sin, to which the sinner responds in repentance toward God and faith in the Lord Jesus Christ. Repentance and faith are inseparable experiences of grace. Repentance is a genuine turning from sin toward God. Faith is the acceptance of Jesus Christ and commitment of the entire personality to Him as Lord and Saviour. Justification is God's gracious and full acquittal upon principles of His righteousness of all sinners who repent and

IV. Salvation

Salvation involves the redemption of the whole man, and is offered freely to all who accept Jesus Christ as Lord and Saviour, who by His own blood obtained eternal redemption for the believer. In its broadest sense salvation includes regeneration, justification, sanctification, and glorification. There is no salvation apart from personal faith in Jesus Christ as Lord.

A. Regeneration, or the new birth, is a work of God's grace whereby believers become new creatures in Christ Jesus. It is a change of heart wrought by the Holy Spirit through conviction of sin, to which the sinner responds in repentance toward God and faith in the Lord Jesus Christ. Repentance and faith are inseparable experiences of grace.

Repentance is a genuine turning from sin toward God. Faith is the acceptance of Jesus Christ and commitment of the entire personality to Him as Lord and Saviour.

1925 Baptist Faith and Message Statement (cont'd)	1963 Baptist Faith and Message Statement with 1998 Amendment (cont'd)	Current Baptist Faith and Message Statement (cont'd)
is in and through Jesus Christ. It brings us into a state of most blessed peace and favor with God, and secures every other needed blessing. *Rom. 3:24; 4:2; 5:1-2; 8:30; Eph. 1:7; 1 Cor. 1:30-31; 2 Cor. 5:21.* ### VI. The Freeness of Salvation The blessings of salvation are made free to all by the gospel. It is the duty of all to accept them by penitent and obedient faith. Nothing prevents the salvation of the greatest sinner except his own voluntary refusal to accept Jesus Christ as teacher, Saviour, and Lord. *Eph. 1:5; 2:4-10; 1 Cor. 1:30-31; Rom. 5:1-9; Rev. 22:17; John 3:16; Mark 16:16.* ### VII. Regeneration Regeneration or the new birth is a change of heart wrought by the Holy Spirit, whereby we become partakers of the divine nature and a holy disposition is given, leading to the love and practice of righteousness. It is a work of God's free grace conditioned upon faith in Christ and made manifest by the fruit which we bring forth to the glory of God. *John 3:1-8, 1:16-18; Rom. 8:2; Eph. 2:1,5-6,8,10; Eph. 4:30,32; Col. 3:1-11; Titus 3:5.* ### VIII. Repentance and Faith We believe that repentance and faith are sacred duties, and also inseparable graces,	believe in Christ. Justification brings the believer into a relationship of peace and favor with God. 2. Sanctification is the experience, beginning in regeneration, by which the believer is set apart to God's purposes, and is enabled to progress toward moral and spiritual perfection through the presence and power of the Holy Spirit dwelling in him. Growth in grace should continue throughout the regenerate person's life. 3. Glorification is the culmination of salvation and is the final blessed and abiding state of the redeemed. *Gen. 3:15; Ex. 3:14-17; 6:2-8; Matt. 1:21; 4:17; 16:21-26; 27:22-28:6; Luke 1:68-69; 2:28-32; John 1:11-14,29; 3: 3-21,36; 5:24; 10:9,28-29; 15:1-16; 17:17; Acts 2:21; 4:12; 15:11; 16:30-31; 17: 30-31; 20:32; Rom. 1:16-18; 2:4; 3:23-25; 4:3ff.; 5:8-10; 6:1-23; 8:1-18,29-39; 10: 9-10,13; 13:11-14; 1 Cor. 1:18,30; 6:19-20; 15:10; 2 Cor. 5:17-20; Gal. 2:20; 3:13; 5: 22-25; 6:15; Ephes. 1:7; 2: 8-22; 4:11-16; Phil. 2:12-13; Col. 1:9-22; 3:1ff.; 1 Thess. 5:23-24; 2 Tim. 1:12; Titus 2:11-14; Heb. 2:1-3; 5:8-9; 9:24-28; 11:1-12:8,14; James 2:14-26; 1 Peter 1:2-23; 1 John 1:6-2:11; Rev. 3:20; 21:1-22:5.*	B. Justification is God's gracious and full acquittal upon principles of His righteousness of all sinners who repent and believe in Christ. Justification brings the believer unto a relationship of peace and favor with God. C. Sanctification is the experience, beginning in regeneration, by which the believer is set apart to God's purposes, and is enabled to progress toward moral and spiritual maturity through the presence and power of the Holy Spirit dwelling in him. Growth in grace should continue throughout the regenerate person's life. D. Glorification is the culmination of salvation and is the final blessed and abiding state of the redeemed. *Genesis 3:15; Exodus 3:14-17; 6:2-8; Matthew 1:21; 4:17; 16:21-26; 27:22-28:6; Luke 1:68-69; 2:28-32; John 1:11-14, 29; 3:3-21,36; 5:24; 10:9,28-29; 15:1-16; 17:17; Acts 2:21; 4:12; 15:11; 16:30-31; 17:30-31; 20:32; Romans 1:16-18; 2:4; 3:23-25; 4:3ff.; 5:8-10; 6:1-23; 8:1-18,29-39; 10:9-10,13; 13: 11-14; 1 Corinthians 1:18, 30; 6:19-20; 15:10; 2 Corinthians 5:17-20; Galatians 2:20; 3:13; 5:22-25; 6:15; Ephesians 1:7; 2:8-22; 4:11-16; Philippians 2:12-13; Colossians 1:9-22; 3:1ff.; 1 Thessalonians 5:23-24; 2 Timothy 1:12; Titus 2:11-14; Hebrews 2:1-3; 5:8-9; 9:24-28; 11:1-12:8,14; James 2:14-26; 1 Peter 1:2-23; 1 John 1:6-2:11; Revelation 3:20; 21:1-22:5.*

wrought in our souls by the regenerating Spirit of God; whereby being deeply convinced of our guilt, danger, and helplessness, and of the way of salvation by Christ, we turn to God with unfeigned contrition, confession, and supplication for mercy; at the same time heartily receiving the Lord Jesus Christ as our Prophet, Priest, and King, and relying on him alone as the only and all-sufficient Saviour.

Luke 22:31-34; Mark 1:15; 1 Tim. 1:13; Rom. 3:25,27,31; Rom. 4:3,9,12,16-17; John 16:8-11.

X. Sanctification

Sanctification is the process by which the regenerate gradually attain to moral and spiritual perfection through the presence and power of the Holy Spirit dwelling in their hearts. It continues throughout the earthly life, and is accomplished by the use of all the ordinary means of grace, and particularly by the Word of God.

Acts 20:32; John 17:17; Rom. 6:5-6; Eph. 3:16; Rom. 4:14; Gal. 5:24; Heb. 12:14; Rom. 7:18-25; 2 Cor. 3:18; Gal. 5:16,25-26.

IX. God's Purpose of Grace

Election is the gracious purpose of God, according to which he regenerates, sanctifies and saves sinners. It is perfectly consistent with the free agency of man, and comprehends all the means in connection with the end. It is a most glorious display of God's sovereign goodness, and is

V. God's Purpose of Grace

Election is the gracious purpose of God, according to which He regenerates, sanctifies, and glorifies sinners. It is consistent with the free agency of man and comprehends all the means in connection with the end. It is a glorious display of God's sovereign goodness, and is infinitely

V. God's Purpose of Grace

Election is the gracious purpose of God, according to which He regenerates, justifies, sanctifies, and glorifies sinners. It is consistent with the free agency of man, and comprehends all the means in connection with the end. It is the glorious display of God's sovereign goodness, and is infinitely wise,

1925 Baptist Faith and Message Statement (cont'd)	1963 Baptist Faith and Message Statement with 1998 Amendment (cont'd)	Current Baptist Faith and Message Statement (cont'd)
infinitely wise, holy, and unchangeable. It excludes boasting and promotes humility. It encourages the use of means in the highest degree. *Rom. 8:30; 11:7; Eph. 1:10; Acts 26:18; Eph. 1:17-19; 2 Tim. 1:9; Psalm 110:3; 1 Cor. 2:14; Eph. 2:5; John 6:44-45,65; Rom. 10:12-15.* **XI. Perseverance** All real believers endure to the end. Their continuance in welldoing is the mark which distinguishes them from mere professors. A special Providence cares for them, and they are kept by the power of God through faith unto salvation. *John 10:28-29; 2 Tim. 2:19; 1 John 2:19; 1 Cor. 11:32; Rom.8:30; 9:11,16; Rom. 5: 9-10; Matt. 26:70-75.*	wise, holy, and unchangeable. It excludes boasting and promotes humility. All true believers endure to the end. Those whom God has accepted in Christ, and sanctified by His Spirit, will never fall away from the state of grace, but shall persevere to the end. Believers may fall into sin through neglect and temptation, whereby they grieve the Spirit, impair their graces and comforts, bring reproach on the cause of Christ, and temporal judgments on themselves, yet they shall be kept by the power of God through faith unto salvation. *Gen. 12:1-3; Ex. 19:5-8; 1 Sam. 8:4-7,19-22; Isa. 5:1-7; Jer. 31:31ff.; Matt. 16:18-19; 21:28-45; 24:22,31; 25:34; Luke 1:68-79; 2:29-32; 19: 41-44; 24:44-48; John 1:12-14; 3:16; 5:24; 6:44-45,65; 10: 27-29; 15:16; 17:6,12,17-18; Acts 20:32; Rom. 5:9-10; 8:28-39; 10:12-15; 11:5-7, 26-36; 1 Cor. 1:1-2; 15:24-28; Ephes. 1:4-23; 2:1-10; 3:1-11; Col. 1:12-14; 2 Thess. 2:13-14; 2 Tim. 1:12; 2:10,19; Heb. 11:39-12:2; 1 Peter 1:2-5, 13; 2:4-10; 1 John 1:7-9; 2:19; 3:2.*	holy, and unchangeable. It excludes boasting and promotes humility. All true believers endure to the end. Those whom God has accepted in Christ, and sanctified by His Spirit, will never fall away from the state of grace, but shall persevere to the end. Believers may fall into sin through neglect and temptation, whereby they grieve the Spirit, impair their graces and comforts, and bring reproach on the cause of Christ and temporal judgments on themselves; yet they shall be kept by the power of God through faith unto salvation. *Genesis 12:1-3; Exodus 19:5-8; 1 Samuel 8:4-7,19-22; Isaiah 5:1-7; Jeremiah 31:31ff.; Matthew 16:18-19; 21:28-45; 24:22,31; 25:34; Luke 1:68-79; 2:29-32; 19:41-44; 24:44-48; John 1:12-14; 3:16; 5:24; 6: 44-45,65; 10:27-29; 15:16; 17:6, 12, 17-18; Acts 20:32; Romans 5:9-10; 8:28-39; 10:12-15; 11:5-7,26-36; 1 Corinthians 1:1-2; 15:24-28; Ephesians 1:4-23; 2:1-10; 3: 1-11; Colossians 1:12-14; 2 Thessalonians 2:13-14; 2 Timothy 1:12; 2:10,19; Hebrews 11:39-12:2; James 1:12; 1 Peter 1:2-5,13; 2: 4-10; 1 John 1:7-9; 2:19; 3:2.*
XII. The Gospel Church A church of Christ is a congregation of baptized believers, associated by covenant in the faith and fellowship of the gospel; observing the ordinances of Christ, governed by his laws, and exercising	**VI. The Church** A New Testament church of the Lord Jesus Christ is a local body of baptized believers who are associated by covenant in the faith and fellowship of the gospel, observing the two ordinances of	**VI. The Church** A New Testament church of the Lord Jesus Christ is an autonomous local congregation of baptized believers, associated by covenant in the faith and fellowship of the gospel; observing the two ordinances of

the gifts, rights, and privileges invested in them by his word, and seeking to extend the gospel to the ends of the earth. Its Scriptural officers are bishops, or elders, and deacons.

Matt. 16:18; Matt. 18:15-18; Rom. 1:7; 1 Cor. 1:2; Acts 2:41-42; 5:13-14; 2 Cor. 9:13; Phil. 1:1; 1 Tim. 4:14; Acts 14:23; Acts 6:3,5-6; Heb. 13:17; 1 Cor. 9:6,14.

Christ, committed to His teachings, exercising the gifts, rights, and privileges invested in them by His Word, and seeking to extend the gospel to the ends of the earth.

This church is an autonomous body, operating through democratic processes under the Lordship of Jesus Christ. In such a congregation, members are equally responsible. Its Scriptural officers are pastors and deacons.

The New Testament speaks also of the church as the body of Christ which includes all of the redeemed of all the ages.

Matt. 16:15-19; 18:15-20; Acts 2:41-42,47; 5:11-14; 6:3-6; 13:1-3; 14:23,27; 15: 1-30; 16:5; 20:28; Rom. 1:7; 1 Cor. 1:2; 3:16; 5:4-5; 7:17; 9:13-14; 12; Ephes. 1:22-23; 2:19-22; 3:8-11,21; 5:22-32; Phil. 1:1; Col. 1:18; 1 Tim. 3:1-15; 4:14; 1 Peter 5:1-4; Rev. 2-3; 21:2-3.

Christ, governed by His laws, exercising the gifts, rights, and privileges invested in them by His Word, and seeking to extend the gospel to the ends of the earth. Each congregation operates under the Lordship of Christ through democratic processes. In such a congregation each member is responsible and accountable to Christ as Lord. Its scriptural officers are pastors and deacons. While both men and women are gifted for service in the church, the office of pastor is limited to men as qualified by Scripture.

The New Testament speaks also of the church as the Body of Christ which includes all of the redeemed of all the ages, believers from every tribe, and tongue, and people, and nation.

Matthew 16:15-19; 18:15-20; Acts 2:41-42,47; 5:11-14; 6:3-6; 13:1-3; 14:23,27; 15: 1-30; 16:5; 20:28; Romans 1:7; 1 Corinthians 1:2; 3:16; 5:4-5; 7:17; 9:13-14; 12; Ephesians 1:22-23; 2:19-22; 3:8-11,21; 5:22-32; Philippians 1:1; Colossians 1:18; 1 Timothy 2:9-14; 3:1-15; 4:14; Hebrews 11:39-40; 1 Peter 5:1-4; Revelation 2-3; 21:2-3.

XIII. Baptism and the Lord's Supper

Christian baptism is the immersion of a believer in water in the name of the Father, the Son, and the Holy Spirit. The act is a symbol of our faith in a crucified, buried and risen Saviour. It is prerequisite to the privileges of a church relation and to the Lord's Supper, in which the members of the church,

VII. Baptism and the Lord's Supper

Christian baptism is the immersion of a believer in water in the name of the Father, the Son, and the Holy Spirit. It is an act of obedience symbolizing the believer's faith in a crucified, buried, and risen Saviour, the believer's death to sin, the burial of the old life, and the resurrection to walk in

VII. Baptism and the Lord's Supper

Christian baptism is the immersion of a believer in water in the name of the Father, the Son, and the Holy Spirit. It is an act of obedience symbolizing the believer's faith in a crucified, buried, and risen Saviour, the believer's death to sin, the burial of the old life, and the resurrection to walk in

1925 Baptist Faith and Message Statement (cont'd)	1963 Baptist Faith and Message Statement with 1998 Amendment (cont'd)	Current Baptist Faith and Message Statement (cont'd)
by the use of bread and wine, commemorate the dying love of Christ. *Matt. 28:19-20; 1 Cor. 4:1; Rom. 6:3-5; Col. 2:12; Mark 1:4; Matt. 3:16; John 3:23; 1 Cor. 11:23-26; 1 Cor. 10: 16-17,21; Matt. 26:26-27; Acts 8:38-39; Mark 1:9-11.*	newness of life in Christ Jesus. It is a testimony to his faith in the final resurrection of the dead. Being a church ordinance, it is prerequisite to the privileges of church membership and to the Lord's Supper. The Lord's Supper is a symbolic act of obedience whereby members of the church, through partaking of the bread and the fruit of the vine, memorialize the death of the Redeemer and anticipate His second coming. *Matt. 3:13-17; 26:26-30; 28:19-20; Mark 1:9-11; 14:22-26; Luke 3:21-22; 22:19-20; John 3:23; Acts 2:41-42; 8:35-39; 16:30-33; Acts 20;7; Rom. 6:3-5; 1 Cor. 10:16,21; 11:23-29; Col. 2:12.*	newness of life in Christ Jesus. It is a testimony to his faith in the final resurrection of the dead. Being a church ordinance, it is prerequisite to the privileges of church membership and to the Lord's Supper. The Lord's Supper is a symbolic act of obedience whereby members of the church, through partaking of the bread and the fruit of the vine, memorialize the death of the Redeemer and anticipate His second coming. *Matthew 3:13-17; 26:26-30; 28:19-20; Mark 1:9-11; 14:22-26; Luke 3:21-22; 22:19-20; John 3:23; Acts 2:41-42; 8:35-39; 16:30-33; 20:7; Romans 6:3-5; 1 Corinthians 10:16,21; 11: 23-29; Colossians 2:12.*
XIV. The Lord's Day The first day of the week is the Lord's day. It is a Christian institution for regular observance. It commemorates the resurrection of Christ from the dead and should be employed in exercises of worship and spiritual devotion, both public and private, and by refraining from worldly amusements, and resting from secular employments, works of necessity and mercy only excepted. *Ex. 20:3-6; Matt. 4:10; Matt. 28:19; 1 Tim. 4:13; Col. 3:16; John 4:21; Ex. 20:8; 1 Cor. 16:1-2; Acts 20:7; Rev. 1:1; Matt. 12:1-13.*	**VIII. The Lord's Day** The first day of the week is the Lord's Day. It is a Christian institution for regular observance. It commemorates the resurrection of Christ from the dead and should be employed in exercises of worship and spiritual devotion, both public and private, and by refraining from worldly amusements, and resting from secular employments, work of necessity and mercy only being excepted. *Ex. 20:8-11; Matt. 12:1-12; 28:1ff.; Mark 2:27-28; 16: 1-7; Luke 24:1-3,33-36; John 4:21-24; 20:1,19-28; Acts 20:7; 1 Cor. 16:1-2; Col. 2:16; 3:16; Rev. 1:10.*	**VIII. The Lord's Day** The first day of the week is the Lord's Day. It is a Christian institution for regular observance. It commemorates the resurrection of Christ from the dead and should include exercises of worship and spiritual devotion, both public and private. Activities on the Lord's Day should be commensurate with the Christian's conscience under the Lordship of Jesus Christ. *Exodus 20:8-11; Matthew 12:1-12; 28:1ff.; Mark 2:27-28; 16:1-7; Luke 24:1-3,33-36; John 4:21-24; 20:1,19-28; Acts 20:7; Romans 14:5-10; I Corinthians 16:1-2; Colossians 2:16; 3:16; Revelation 1:10.*

XIV. The Lord's Day

The first day of the week is the Lord's day. It is a Christian institution for regular observance. It commemorates the resurrection of Christ from the dead and should be employed in exercises of worship and spiritual devotion, both public and private, and by refraining from worldly amusements, and resting from secular employments, works of necessity and mercy only excepted.

Ex. 20:3-6; Matt. 4:10; Matt. 28:19; 1 Tim. 4:13; Col. 3:16; John 4:21; Ex. 20:8; 1 Cor. 16:1-2; Acts 20:7; Rev. 1:1; Matt. 12:1-13.

VIII. The Lord's Day

The first day of the week is the Lord's Day. It is a Christian institution for regular observance. It commemorates the resurrection of Christ from the dead and should be employed in exercises of worship and spiritual devotion, both public and private, and by refraining from worldly amusements, and resting from secular employments, work of necessity and mercy only being excepted.

Ex. 20:8-11; Matt. 12:1-12; 28:1ff.; Mark 2:27-28; 16:1-7; Luke 24:1-3,33-36; John 4: 21-24; 20:1,19-28; Acts 20:7; 1 Cor. 16:1-2; Col. 2:16; 3:16; Rev. 1:10.

VIII. The Lord's Day

The first day of the week is the Lord's Day. It is a Christian institution for regular observance. It commemorates the resurrection of Christ from the dead and should include exercises of worship and spiritual devotion, both public and private. Activities on the Lord's Day should be commensurate with the Christian's conscience under the Lordship of Jesus Christ.

Exodus 20:8-11; Matthew 12:1-12; 28:1ff.; Mark 2:27-28; 16:1-7; Luke 24:1-3,33-36; John 4:21-24; 20:1,19-28; Acts 20:7; Romans 14:5-10; I Corinthians 16:1-2; Colossians 2:16; 3:16; Revelation 1:10.

XXV. The Kingdom

The Kingdom of God is the reign of God in the heart and life of the individual in every human relationship, and in every form and institution of organized human society. The chief means for promoting the Kingdom of God on earth are preaching the gospel of Christ, and teaching the principles of righteousness contained therein. The Kingdom of God will be complete when every thought and will of man shall be brought into captivity to the will of Christ. And it is the duty of all Christ's people to pray and labor continually that his Kingdom may come and his will be done on earth as it is done in heaven.

Dan. 2:37-44; 7:18; Matt. 4:23; 8:12; 12:25; 13:38,43; 25:34; 26:29; Mark 11:10; Luke 12:32; 22:29; Acts 1:6; 1 Cor. 15:24; Col. 1:13; Heb.

IX. The Kingdom

The kingdom of God includes both His general sovereignty over the universe and His particular kingship over men who willfully acknowledge Him as King. Particularly the kingdom is the realm of salvation into which men enter by trustful, childlike commitment to Jesus Christ. Christians ought to pray and to labor that the kingdom may come and God's will be done on earth. The full consummation of the kingdom awaits the return of Jesus Christ and the end of this age.

Gen. 1:1; Isa. 9:6-7; Jer. 23:5-6; Matt. 3:2; 4:8-10,23; 12:25-28; 13:1-52; 25:31-46; 26:29; Mark 1:14-15; 9:1; Luke 4:43; 8:1; 9:2; 12:31-32; 17:20-21; 23:42; John 3:3; 18:36; Acts 1:6-7; 17:22-31; Rom. 5:17; 8:19; 1 Cor. 15:24-28; Col. 1:13; Heb.

IX. The Kingdom

The Kingdom of God includes both His general sovereignty over the universe and His particular kingship over men who willfully acknowledge Him as King. Particularly the Kingdom is the realm of salvation into which men enter by trustful, childlike commitment to Jesus Christ. Christians ought to pray and to labor that the Kingdom may come and God's will be done on earth. The full consummation of the Kingdom awaits the return of Jesus Christ and the end of this age.

Genesis 1:1; Isaiah 9:6-7; Jeremiah 23:5-6; Matthew 3:2; 4:8-10,23; 12:25-28; 13:1-52; 25:31-46; 26:29; Mark 1:14-15; 9:1; Luke 4:43; 8:1; 9:2; 12: 31-32; 17:20-21; 23:42; John 3:3; 18:36; Acts 1:6-7; 17: 22-31; Romans 5:17; 8:19; I Corinthians 15:24-28;

1925 Baptist Faith and Message Statement (cont'd)	1963 Baptist Faith and Message Statement with 1998 Amendment (cont'd)	Current Baptist Faith and Message Statement (cont'd)
12:28; Rev. 1:9; Luke 4:43; 8:1; 9:2; 17:20-21; John 3:3; John 18:36; Matt. 6:10; Luke 23:42.	11:10,16; 12:28; 1 Peter 2:4-10; 4:13; Rev. 1:6,9; 5:10; 11:15; 21-22.	Colossians 1:13; Hebrews 11:10,16; 12:28; 1 Peter 2:4-10; 4:13; Revelation 1:6,9; 5:10; 11:15; 21-22.

XV. The Righteous and the Wicked

There is a radical and essential difference between the righteous and wicked. Those only who are justified through the name of the Lord Jesus Christ and sanctified by the Holy Spirit are truly righteous in his sight. Those who continue in impenitence and unbelief are in his sight wicked and are under condemnation. This distinction between the righteous and the wicked holds in and after death, and will be made manifest at the judgment when final and everlasting awards are made to all men.

Gen. 3:19; Acts 13:36; Luke 23:43; 2 Cor. 5:1,6,8; Phil. 1:23; 1 Cor. 15:51-52; 1 Thess. 4:17; Phil. 3:21; 1 Cor. 6:3; Matt. 25:32-46; Rom. 9: 22-23; Mark 9:48; 1 Thess. 1:7-10; Rev. 22:20.

XVI. The Resurrection

The Scriptures clearly teach that Jesus rose from the dead. His grave was emptied of its contents. He appeared to the disciples after his resurrection in many convincing manifestations. He now exists in his glorified body at God's right hand. There will be a resurrection of the righteous and the wicked. The bodies of the righteous will conform to the glorious spiritual body of Jesus.

X. Last Things

God, in His own time and in His own way, will bring the world to its appropriate end. According to His promise, Jesus Christ will return personally and visibly in glory to the earth; the dead will be raised; and Christ will judge all men in righteousness. The unrighteous will be consigned to hell, the place of everlasting punishment. The righteous in their resurrected and glorified bodies will receive their reward and will dwell forever in heaven with the Lord.

Isa. 2:4; 11:9; Matt. 16:27; 18:8-9; 19:28; 24:27,30,36,44; 25:31-46; 26:64; Mark 8:38; 9:43-48; Luke 12:40,48; 16:19-26; 17:22-37; 21:27-28; John 14:1-3; Acts 1:11; 17:31; Rom. 14:10; 1 Cor. 4:5; 15:24-28,35-58; 2 Cor. 5:10; Phil. 3:20-21; Col. 1:5; 3:4; 1 Thess. 4:14-18; 5:1ff.; 2 Thess. 1:7ff.; 2; 1 Tim. 6:14; 2 Tim. 4:1,8; Titus 2:13; Heb. 9:27-28; James 5:8; 2 Peter 3:7ff.; 1 John 2:28; 3:2; Jude 14; Rev.

X. Last Things

God, in His own time and in His own way, will bring the world to its appropriate end. According to His promise, Jesus Christ will return personally and visibly in glory to the earth; the dead will be raised; and Christ will judge all men in righteousness. The unrighteous will be consigned to Hell, the place of everlasting punishment. The righteous in their resurrected and glorified bodies will receive their reward and will dwell forever in Heaven with the Lord.

Isaiah 2:4; 11:9; Matthew 16:27; 18:8-9; 19:28; 24:27,30,36,44; 25:31-46; 26:64; Mark 8:38; 9:43-48; Luke 12:40,48; 16:19-26; 17:22-37; 21:27-28; John 14:1-3; Acts 1:11; 17:31; Romans 14:10; 1 Corinthians 4:5; 15:24-28,35-58; 2 Corinthians 5:10; Philippians 3:20-21; Colossians 1:5; 3:4; 1 Thessalonians 4:14-18; 5:1ff.; 2 Thessalonians 1:7ff.; 2; 1 Timothy 6:14; 2 Timothy 4:1,8; Titus 2:13; Hebrews 9: 27-28; James 5:8; 2 Peter 3:7ff.; 1 John 2:28; 3:2; Jude 14; Revelation 1:18; 3:11; 20: 1-22:13.

1 Cor. 15:1-58; 2 Cor. 5:1-8; 1 Thess. 4:17; John 5:28-29; Phil. 3:21; Acts 24:15; John 20:9; Matt. 28:6.

XVII. The Return of the Lord

The New Testament teaches in many places the visible and personal return of Jesus to this earth. "This same Jesus which is taken up from you into heaven, shall so come in like manner as ye have seen him go into heaven." The time of his coming is not revealed. "Of that day and hour knoweth no one, no, not the angels in heaven, but my Father only" (Matt. 24:36). It is the duty of all believers to live in readiness for his coming and by diligence in good works to make manifest to all men the reality and power of their hope in Christ.

Matt. 24:36; Matt. 24:42-47; Mark 13:32-37; Luke 21: 27-28; Acts 1:9-11.

XXIII. Evangelism and Missions

It is the duty of every Christian man and woman, and the duty of every church of Christ to seek to extend the gospel to the ends of the earth. The new birth of man's spirit by God's Holy Spirit means the birth of love for others. Missionary effort on the part of all rests thus upon a spiritual necessity of the regenerate life. It is also expressly and repeatedly commanded in the teachings of Christ. It is the duty of every child of God to seek constantly to win the lost to Christ by personal effort and by all

XI. Evangelism and Missions

It is the duty and privilege of every follower of Christ and of every church of the Lord Jesus Christ to endeavor to make disciples of all nations. The new birth of man's spirit by God's Holy Spirit means the birth of love for others. Missionary effort on the part of all rests thus upon a spiritual necessity of the regenerate life, and is expressly and repeatedly commanded in the teachings of Christ. It is the duty of every child of God to seek constantly to win the lost to Christ by personal effort

XI. Evangelism and Missions

It is the duty and privilege of every follower of Christ and of every church of the Lord Jesus Christ to endeavor to make disciples of all nations. The new birth of man's spirit by God's Holy Spirit means the birth of love for others. Missionary effort on the part of all rests thus upon a spiritual necessity of the regenerate life, and is expressly and repeatedly commanded in the teachings of Christ. The Lord Jesus Christ has commanded the preaching of the gospel to all nations. It is the duty of every child of God

1925 Baptist Faith and Message Statement (cont'd)	1963 Baptist Faith and Message Statement with 1998 Amendment (cont'd)	Current Baptist Faith and Message Statement (cont'd)
other methods sanctioned by the gospel of Christ.

Matt. 10:5; 13:18-23; 22:9-10; 28:19-20; Mark 16:15-16; 16:19-20; Luke 24:46-53; Acts 1:5-8; 2:1-2,21,39; 8:26-40; 10:42-48; 13:2,30-33; 1 Thess. 1-8. | and by all other methods in harmony with the gospel of Christ.

Gen. 12:1-3; Ex. 19:5-6; Isa. 6:1-8; Matt. 9:37-38; 10:5-15; 13:18-30,37-43; 16:19; 22:9-10; 24:14; 28:18-20; Luke 10:1-18; 24:46-53; John 14:11-12; 15:7-8,16; 17:15; 20:21; Acts 1:8; 2; 8:26-40; 10:42-48; 13:2-3; Rom. 10:13-15; Ephes. 3:1-11; 1 Thess. 1:8; 2 Tim. 4:5; Heb. 2:1-3; 11:39-12:2; 1 Peter 2:4-10; Rev. 22:17. | to seek constantly to win the lost to Christ by verbal witness undergirded by a Christian lifestyle, and by other methods in harmony with the gospel of Christ.

Genesis 12:1-3; Exodus 19:5-6; Isaiah 6:1-8; Matthew 9:37-38; 10:5-15; 13:18- 30, 37-43; 16:19; 22:9-10; 24:14; 28:18-20; Luke 10:1-18; 24:46-53; John 14:11-12; 15:7-8,16; 17:15; 20:21; Acts 1:8; 2; 8:26-40; 10:42-48; 13:2-3; Romans 10:13-15; Ephesians 3:1-11; 1 Thessalonians 1:8; 2 Timothy 4:5; Hebrews 2:1-3; 11:39-12:2; 1 Peter 2:4-10; Revelation 22:17. |
| ### XX. Education

Christianity is the religion of enlightenment and intelligence. In Jesus Christ are hidden all the treasures of wisdom and knowledge. All sound learning is therefore a part of our Christian heritage. The new birth opens all human faculties and creates a thirst for knowledge. An adequate system of schools is necessary to a complete spiritual program for Christ's people. The cause of education in the Kingdom of Christ is coordinate with the causes of missions and general benevolence, and should receive along with these the liberal support of the churches.

Deut. 4:1,5,9,13-14; Deut. 6:1,7-10; Psalm 19:7-8; Prov. 8:1-7; Prov. 4:1-10; Matt. 28:20; Col. 2:3; Neh. 8:1-4. | ### XII. Education

The cause of education in the kingdom of Christ is coordinate with the causes of missions and general benevolence and should receive along with these the liberal support of the churches. An adequate system of Christian schools is necessary to a complete spiritual program for Christ's people.

In Christian education there should be a proper balance between academic freedom and academic responsibility. Freedom in any orderly relationship of human life is always limited and never absolute. The freedom of a teacher in a Christian school, college, or seminary is limited by the preeminence of Jesus Christ, by the authoritative nature of the Scriptures, and by the distinct purpose for which the school exists. | ### XII. Education

Christianity is the faith of enlightenment and intelligence. In Jesus Christ abide all the treasures of wisdom and knowledge. All sound learning is, therefore, a part of our Christian heritage. The new birth opens all human faculties and creates a thirst for knowledge. Moreover, the cause of education in the Kingdom of Christ is coordinate with the causes of missions and general benevolence, and should receive along with these the liberal support of the churches. An adequate system of Christian education is necessary to a complete spiritual program for Christ's people.

In Christian education there should be a proper balance between academic freedom and academic responsibility. Freedom in any orderly relationship of human life is always limited |

Deut. 4:1,5,9,14; 6:1-10; 31:12-13; Neh. 8:1-8; Job. 28:28; Psalms 19:7ff.; 119:11; Prov. 3:13ff.; 4:1-10; 8:1-7,11; 15:14; Eccl. 7:19; Matt. 5:2; 7:24ff.; 28:19-20; Luke 2:40; 1 Cor. 1:18-31; Eph. 4:11-16; Phil. 4:8; Col. 2:3,8-9; 1 Tim. 1:3-7; 2 Tim. 2:15; 3:14-17; Heb. 5:12-6:3; James 1:5; 3:17.

and never absolute. The freedom of a teacher in a Christian school, college, or seminary is limited by the preeminence of Jesus Christ, by the authoritative nature of the Scriptures, and by the distinct purpose for which the school exists.

Deuteronomy 4:1,5,9,14; 6:1-10; 31:12-13; Nehemiah 8:1-8; Job 28:28; Psalms 19:7ff.; 119:11; Proverbs 3:13ff.; 4:1-10; 8:1-7, 11; 15:14; Ecclesiastes 7:19; Matthew 5:2; 7:24ff.; 28:19-20; Luke 2:40; 1 Corinthians 1: 18-31; Ephesians 4:11-16; Philippians 4:8; Colossians 2:3, 8-9; 1 Timothy 1:3-7; 2 Timothy 2:15; 3:14-17; Hebrews 5:12-6: 3; James 1:5; 3:17.

XXIV. Stewardship

God is the source of all blessings, temporal and spiritual; all that we have and are we owe to him. We have a spiritual debtorship to the whole world, a holy trusteeship in the gospel, and a binding stewardship in our possessions. We are therefore under obligation to serve him with our time, talents and material possessions; and should recognize all these as entrusted to us to use for the glory of God and helping others. Christians should cheerfully, regularly, systematically, proportionately, and liberally, contribute of their means to advancing the Redeemer's cause on earth.

Luke 12:42; 16:1-8; Titus 1:7; 1 Peter 4:10; 2 Cor. 8:1-7; 2 Cor. 8:11-19; 2 Cor. 12:1-15; Matt. 25:14-30; Rom. 1:8-15; 1 Cor. 6:20; Acts 2:44-47.

XIII. Stewardship

God is the source of all blessings, temporal and spiritual; all that we have and are we owe to Him. Christians have a spiritual debtorship to the whole world, a holy trusteeship in the gospel, and a binding stewardship in their possessions. They are therefore under obligation to serve Him with their time, talents, and material possessions; and should recognize all these as entrusted to them to use for the glory of God and for helping others. According to the Scriptures, Christians should contribute of their means cheerfully, regularly, systematically, proportionately, and liberally for the advancement of the Redeemer's cause on earth.

Gen. 14:20; Lev. 27:30-32; Deut. 8:18; Mal. 3:8-12; Matt. 6:1-4,19-21; 19:21;

XIII. Stewardship

God is the source of all blessings, temporal and spiritual; all that we have and are we owe to Him. Christians have a spiritual debtorship to the whole world, a holy trusteeship in the gospel, and a binding stewardship in their possessions. They are therefore under obligation to serve Him with their time, talents, and material possessions; and should recognize all these as entrusted to them to use for the glory of God and for helping others. According to the Scriptures, Christians should contribute of their means cheerfully, regularly, systematically, proportionately, and liberally for the advancement of the Redeemer's cause on earth.

Genesis 14:20; Leviticus 27: 30-32; Deuteronomy 8:18; Malachi 3:8-12; Matthew 6:1-4, 19-21; 19:21; 23:23; 25:14-29;

1925 Baptist Faith and Message Statement (cont'd)	1963 Baptist Faith and Message Statement with 1998 Amendment (cont'd)	Current Baptist Faith and Message Statement (cont'd)
	23:23; 25:14-29; Luke 12:16-21, 42; 16:1-13; Acts 2:44-47; 5:1-11; 17:24-25; 20:35; Rom. 6:6-22; 12:1-2; 1 Cor. 4:1-2; 6:19-20; 12; 16:1-4; 2Cor. 8-9; 12:15; Phil. 4: 10-19; 1 Peter 1:18-19.	Luke 12:16-21,42; 16:1-13; Acts 2:44-47; 5:1-11; 17:24-25; 20:35; Romans 6:6-22; 12:1-2; 1 Corinthians 4:1-2; 6:19-20; 12; 16:1-4; 2 Corinthians 8-9; 12:15; Philippians 4:10-19; 1 Peter 1:18-19.

XXII. Co-Operation

Christ's people should, as occasion requires, organize such associations and conventions as may best secure co-operation for the great objects of the Kingdom of God. Such organizations have no authority over each other or over the churches. They are voluntary and advisory bodies designed to elicit, combine, and direct the energies of our people in the most effective manner. Individual members of New Testament churches should co-operate with each other, and the churches themselves should co-operate with each other in carrying forward the missionary, educational, and benevolent program for the extension of Christ's Kingdom. Christian unity in the New Testament sense is spiritual harmony and voluntary cooperation for common ends by various groups of Christ's people. It is permissable and desirable as between the various Christian denominations, when the end to be attained is itself justified, and when such co-operation involves no violation of conscience or compromise of loyalty to Christ and his Word as revealed in the New Testament.

XIV. Co-Operation

Christ's people should, as occasion requires, organize such associations and conventions as may best secure co-operation for the great objects of the kingdom of God. Such organizations have no authority over one another or over the churches. They are voluntary and advisory bodies designed to elicit, combine, and direct the energies of our people in the most effective manner. Members of New Testament churches should co-operate with one another in carrying forward the missionary, educational, and benevelent ministries for the extension of Christ's kingdom. Christian unity in the New Testament sense is spiritual harmony and voluntary co-operation for common ends by various groups of Christ's people. Co-operation is desirable between the various Christian denominations, when the end to be attained is itself justified, and when such cooperation involves no violation of conscience or compromise of loyalty to Christ and his Word as revealed in the New Testament.

Ex. 17:12; 18:17ff.; Judg. 7:21; Ezra 1:3-4; 2:68-69;

XIV. Cooperation

Christ's people should, as occasion requires, organize such associations and conventions as may best secure cooperation for the great objects of the Kingdom of God. Such organizations have no authority over one another or over the churches. They are voluntary and advisory bodies designed to elicit, combine, and direct the energies of our people in the most effective manner. Members of New Testament churches should cooperate with one another in carrying forward the missionary, educational, and benevolent ministries for the extension of Christ's Kingdom. Christian unity in the New Testament sense is spiritual harmony and voluntary cooperation for common ends by various groups of Christ's people. Cooperation is desirable between the various Christian denominations, when the end to be attained is itself justified, and when such cooperation involves no violation of conscience or compromise of loyalty to Christ and His Word as revealed in the New Testament.

Exodus 17:12; 18:17ff.; Judges 7:21; Ezra 1:3-4; 2:68-69; 5:14-15; Nehemiah 4; 8:1-5; Matthew

Ezra 1:3-4; 2:68-69; 5:14-15;
Neh. 4:4-6; 8:1-4; Mal. 3:10;
Matt. 10:5-15; 20:1-16; 22:
1-10; Acts 1:13-14; 1:21:26;
2:1,41-47; 1 Cor. 1:10-17;
12:11-12; 13; 14:33-34,40;
16:2; 2 Cor. 9:1-15; Eph. 4:
1-16; 3 John 1:5-8.

5:14-15; Neh. 4; 8:1-5; Matt.
10:5-15; 20:1-16; 22:1-10;
28:19-20; Mark 2:3; Luke
10:1ff.; Acts 1:13-14; 2:1ff.;
4:31-37; 13:2-3; 15:1-35;
1 Cor. 1:10-17; 3:5-15; 12;
2 Cor. 8-9; Gal. 1:6-10; Eph.
4:1-16; Phil. 1:15-18.

10:5-15; 20:1-16; 22:1-10;
28:19-20; Mark 2:3; Luke
10:1ff.; Acts 1:13-14; 2:1ff.;
4:31-37; 13:2-3; 15:1-35; 1
Corinthians 1:10-17; 3:5-15; 12;
2 Corinthians 8-9; Galatians
1:6-10; Ephesians 4:1-16;
Philippians 1:15-18.

XXI. Social Service

Every Christian is under obligation to seek to make the will of Christ regnant in his own life and in human society to oppose in the spirit of Christ every form of greed, selfishness, and vice; to provide for the orphaned, the aged, the helpless, and the sick; to seek to bring industry, government, and society as a whole under the sway of the principles of righteousness, truth and brotherly love; to promote these ends Christians should be ready to work with all men of good will in any good cause, always being careful to act in the spirit of love without compromising their loyalty to Christ and his truth. All means and methods used in social service for the amelioration of society and the establishment of righteousness among men must finally depend on the regeneration of the individual by the saving grace of God in Christ Jesus.

Luke 10:25-37; Ex. 22:10,14;
Lev. 6:2; Deut. 20:10; Deut.
4:42; Deut. 15:2; 27:17; Psalm
101:5; Ezek. 18:6; Heb. 2:15;
Zech. 8:16; Ex. 20:16; James
2:8; Rom. 12-14; Col. 3:12-17.

XV. The Christian and the Social Order

Every Christian is under obligation to seek to make the will of Christ supreme in his own life and in human society. Means and methods used for the improvement of society and the establishment of righteousness among men can be truly and permanently helpful only when they are rooted in the regeneration of the individual by the saving grace of God in Christ Jesus. The Christian should oppose in the spirit of Christ every form of greed, selfishness, and vice. He should work to provide for the orphaned, the needy, the aged, the helpless, and the sick. Every Christian should seek to bring industry, government, and society as a whole under the sway of the principles of righteousness, truth, and brotherly love. In order to promote these ends Christians should be ready to work with all men of good will in any good cause, always being careful to act in the spirit of love without compromising their loyalty to Christ and his truth.

Ex. 20:3-17; Lev. 6:2-5;
Deut. 10:12; 27:17; Psalm
101:5; Micah 6:8; Zech.
8:16; Matt. 5:13-16,43-48;
22:36-40; 25:35; Mark 1:
29-34; 2:3ff.; 10:21; Luke

XV. The Christian and the Social Order

All Christians are under obligation to seek to make the will of Christ supreme in our own lives and in human society. Means and methods used for the improvement of society and the establishment of righteousness among men can be truly and permanently helpful only when they are rooted in the regeneration of the individual by the saving grace of God in Jesus Christ. In the spirit of Christ, Christians should oppose racism, every form of greed, selfishness, and vice, and all forms of sexual immorality, including adultery, homosexuality, and pornography. We should work to provide for the orphaned, the needy, the abused, the aged, the helpless, and the sick. We should speak on behalf of the unborn and contend for the sanctity of all human life from conception to natural death. Every Christian should seek to bring industry, government, and society as a whole under the sway of the principles of righteousness, truth, and brotherly love. In order to promote these ends Christians should be ready to work with all men of good will in any good cause, always being careful to act in the spirit of love without compromising their loyalty to Christ and His truth.

1925 Baptist Faith and Message Statement (cont'd)	1963 Baptist Faith and Message Statement with 1998 Amendment (cont'd)	Current Baptist Faith and Message Statement (cont'd)
	4:18-21; 10:27-37; 20:25; John 15:12; 17:15; Rom. 12-14; 1 Cor. 5:9-10; 6:1-7; 7:20-24; 10:23-11:1; Gal. 3:26-28; Eph. 6:5-9; Col. 3:12-17; 1 Thess. 3:12; Philemon; James 1:27; 2:8.	*Exodus 20:3-17; Leviticus 6:2-5; Deuteronomy 10:12; 27:17; Psalm 101:5; Micah 6:8; Zechariah 8:16; Matthew 5:13-16,43-48; 22:36-40; 25:35; Mark 1:29-34; 2:3ff.; 10:21; Luke 4:18-21; 10:27-37; 20:25; John 15:12; 17:15; Romans 12-14; 1 Corinthians 5:9-10; 6:1-7; 7:20-24; 10:23-11:1; Galatians 3:26-28; Ephesians 6:5-9; Colossians 3:12-17; 1 Thessalonians 3:12; Philemon; James 1:27; 2:8.*

XIX. Peace and War / XVI. Peace and War / XVI. Peace and War

XIX. Peace and War	XVI. Peace and War	XVI. Peace and War
It is the duty of Christians to seek peace with all men on principles of righteousness. In accordance with the spirit and teachings of Christ they should do all in their power to put an end to war.	It is the duty of Christians to seek peace with all men on principles of righteousness. In accordance with the spirit and teachings of Christ they should do all in their power to put an end to war.	It is the duty of Christians to seek peace with all men on principles of righteousness. In accordance with the spirit and teachings of Christ they should do all in their power to put an end to war.
The true remedy for the war spirit is the pure gospel of our Lord. The supreme need of the world is the acceptance of his teachings in all the affairs of men and nations, and the practical application of his law of love.	The true remedy for the war spirit is the gospel of our Lord. The supreme need of the world is the acceptance of His teachings in all the affairs of men and nations, and the practical application of His law of love.	The true remedy for the war spirit is the gospel of our Lord. The supreme need of the world is the acceptance of His teachings in all the affairs of men and nations, and the practical application of His law of love. Christian people throughout the world should pray for the reign of the Prince of Peace.
We urge Christian people throughout the world to pray for the reign of the Prince of Peace, and to oppose everything likely to provoke war.	*Isa. 2:4; Matt. 5:9,38-48; 6:33; 26:52; Luke 22:36,38; Rom. 12:18-19; 13:1-7; 14:19; Heb.12:14; James 4:1-2.*	*Isaiah 2:4; Matthew 5:9,38-48; 6:33; 26:52; Luke 22:36,38; Romans 12:18-19; 13:1-7; 14:19; Hebrews 12:14; James 4:1-2.*
Matt. 5:9,13-14,43-46; Heb. 12:14; James 4:1; Matt. 6:33; Rom. 14:17,19.		

XVIII. Religious Liberty / XVII. Religious Liberty / XVII. Religious Liberty

XVIII. Religious Liberty	XVII. Religious Liberty	XVII. Religious Liberty
God alone is Lord of the conscience, and he has left it free from the doctrines and commandments of men which are contrary to his Word or	God alone is Lord of the conscience, and He has left it free from the doctrines and commandments of men which are contrary to His Word or not	God alone is Lord of the conscience, and He has left it free from the doctrines and commandments of men which are contrary to His Word or not

not contained in it. Church and state should be separate. The state owes to the church protection and full freedom in the pursuit of its spiritual ends. In providing for such freedom no ecclesiastical group or denomination should be favored by the state more than others. Civil government being ordained of God, it is the duty of Christians to render loyal obedience thereto in all things not contrary to the revealed will of God. The church should not resort to the civil power to carry on its work. The gospel of Christ contemplates spiritual means alone for the pursuit of its ends. The state has no right to impose penalties for religious opinions of any kind. The state has no right to impose taxes for the support of any form of religion. A free church in a free state is the Christian ideal, and this implies the right of free and unhindered access to God on the part of all men, and the right to form and propagate opinions in the sphere of religion without interference by the civil power.

Rom. 13:1-7; 1 Peter 2:17; 1 Tim. 2:1-2; Gal. 3:9-14; John 7:38-39; James 4:12; Gal. 5:13; 2 Peter 2:18-21; 1 Cor. 3:5; Rom. 6:1-2; Matt. 22:21; Mark 12:17.

contained in it. Church and state should be separate. The state owes to every church protection and full freedom in the pursuit of its spiritual ends. In providing for such freedom no ecclesiastical group or denomination should be favored by the state more than others. Civil government being ordained of God, it is the duty of Christians to render loyal obedience thereto in all things not contrary to the revealed will of God. The church should not resort to the civil power to carry on its work. The gospel of Christ contemplates spiritual means alone for the pursuit of its ends. The state has no right to impose penalties for religious opinions of any kind. The state has no right to impose taxes for the support of any form of religion. A free church in a free state is the Christian ideal, and this implies the right of free and unhindered access to God on the part of all men and the right to form and propagate opinions in the sphere of religion without interference by the civil power.

Gen. 1:27; 2:7; Matt. 6:6-7; 24:16:26; 22:21; John 8:36; Acts 4:19-20; Rom. 6:1-2; 13:1-7; Gal. 5:1,13; Phil. 3:20; 1 Tim. 2:1-2; James 4:12; 1 Peter 2:12-17; 3: 11-17; 4:12-19.

XVIII. The Family
(1998 Amendment)

God has ordained the family as the foundational institution of human society. It is composed of persons related to one another by marriage, blood, or adoption.

contained in it. Church and state should be separate. The state owes to every church protection and full freedom in the pursuit of its spiritual ends. In providing for such freedom no ecclesiastical group or denomination should be favored by the state more than others. Civil government being ordained of God, it is the duty of Christians to render loyal obedience thereto in all things not contrary to the revealed will of God. The church should not resort to the civil power to carry on its work. The gospel of Christ contemplates spiritual means alone for the pursuit of its ends. The state has no right to impose penalties for religious opinions of any kind. The state has no right to impose taxes for the support of any form of religion. A free church in a free state is the Christian ideal, and this implies the right of free and unhindered access to God on the part of all men, and the right to form and propagate opinions in the sphere of religion without interference by the civil power.

Genesis 1:27; 2:7; Matthew 6:6-7, 24; 16:26; 22:21; John 8:36; Acts 4:19-20; Romans 6:1-2; 13:1-7; Galatians 5:1,13; Philippians 3:20; 1 Timothy 2:1-2; James 4:12; 1 Peter 2:12-17; 3:11-17; 4:12-19.

XVIII. The Family

God has ordained the family as the foundational institution of human society. It is composed of persons related to one another by marriage, blood, or adoption. Marriage is the uniting of one man and one woman in covenant commitment for a lifetime.

1925 Baptist Faith and Message Statement (cont'd)	1963 Baptist Faith and Message Statement with 1998 Amendment (cont'd)	Current Baptist Faith and Message Statement (cont'd)
	Marriage is the uniting of one man and one woman in covenant commitment for a lifetime. It is God's unique gift to provide for the man and the woman in marriage the framework for intimate companionship, the channel for sexual expression according to biblical standards, and the means for procreation of the human race. The husband and wife are of equal worth before God, since both are created in God's image. The marriage relationship models the way God relates to His people. A husband is to love his wife as Christ loved the church. He has the God-given responsibility to provide for, to protect, and to lead his family. A wife is to submit herself graciously to the servant leadership of her husband even as the church willingly submits to the headship of Christ. She, being in the image of God as is her husband and thus equal to him, has the God-given responsibility to respect her husband and to serve as his helper in managing the household and nurturing the next generation. Children, from the moment of conception, are a blessing and heritage from the Lord. Parents are to demonstrate to their children God's pattern for marriage. Parents are to teach their children spiritual and moral values and to lead them, through consistent lifestyle example and loving discipline, to make choices based on biblical truth.	It is God's unique gift to reveal the union between Christ and His church and to provide for the man and the woman in marriage the framework for intimate companionship, the channel of sexual expression according to biblical standards, and the means for procreation of the human race. The husband and wife are of equal worth before God, since both are created in God's image. The marriage relationship models the way God relates to His people. A husband is to love his wife as Christ loved the church. He has the God-given responsibility to provide for, to protect, and to lead his family. A wife is to submit herself graciously to the servant leadership of her husband even as the church willingly submits to the headship of Christ. She, being in the image of God as is her husband and thus equal to him, has the Godgiven responsibility to respect her husband and to serve as his helper in managing the household and nurturing the next generation. Children, from the moment of conception, are a blessing and heritage from the Lord. Parents are to demonstrate to their children God's pattern for marriage. Parents are to teach their children spiritual and moral values and to lead them, through consistent lifestyle example and loving discipline, to make choices based on biblical truth. Children are to honor and obey their parents.

Children are to honor and obey their parents.

Gen. 1:26-28; 2:18-25; 3:1-20; Ex. 20:12; Deut. 6:4-9; Josh. 24:15; 1 Sam. 1:26-28; Ps. 51:5; 78:1-8; 127; 128; 139:13-16; Prov. 1:8; 5:15-20; 6:20-22; 12:4; 13:24; 14:1; 17:6; 18:22; 22:6,15; 23:13-14; 24:3; 29:15,17; 31:10-31; Eccl. 4:9-12; 9:9; Mal. 2:14-16; Matt. 5:31-32; 18:2-5; 19: 3-9; Mark 10:6-12; Rom. 1:18-32; 1 Cor. 7:1-16; Eph. 5:21-33; 6:1-4; Col. 3:18-21; 1 Tim. 5:8,14; 2 Tim. 1:3-5; Titus 2:3-5; Heb. 13:4; 1 Pet. 3:1-7.

Genesis 1:26-28; 2:15-25; 3:1-20; Exodus 20:12; Deuteronomy 6:4-9; Joshua 24:15; 1 Samuel 1:26-28; Psalms 51:5; 78:1-8; 127; 128; 139:13-16; Proverbs 1:8; 5:15-20; 6:20-22; 12:4; 13:24; 14:1; 17:6; 18:22; 22:6,15; 23:13-14; 24:3; 29:15,17; 31:10-31; Ecclesiastes 4:9-12; 9:9; Malachi 2:14-16; Matthew 5:31-32; 18:2-5; 19:3-9; Mark 10:6-12; Romans 1:18-32; 1 Corinthians 7:1-16; Ephesians 5:21-33; 6:1-4; Colossians 3:18-21; 1 Timothy 5:8,14; 2 Timothy 1:3-5; Titus 2:3-5; Hebrews 13:4; 1 Peter 3:1-7.

BIBLIOGRAPHY

Ammerman, Nancy T. *Baptist Battles—Social Changes & Religious Conflicts in the Southern Baptist Convention*. New Brunswick, NJ: Rutgers University Press, 1990.

———, ed. *Southern Baptists Observed: Multiple Perspectives on a Changing Denomination*. Knoxville: The University of Tennessee Press, 1993.

Barnhart, Joe Edward. *The Southern Baptist Holy War*. Austin: Texas Monthly Press, 1986.

Basden, Paul A., ed. *Has Our Theology Changed? Southern Baptist Thought Since 1845*. Nashville: Broadman & Holman Publishers, 1994.

Baugh, John F. *The Battle for Baptist Integrity*. Austin, TX: The Battle for Baptist Integrity, Inc., n.d.

Beale, David O. *Southern Baptist Convention—House on the Sand?* Greenville, SC: Unusual Publications, 1985.

Bland, Thomas A., ed. *Servant Songs*. Macon, GA: Smyth & Helwys Publishing, Inc., 1994.

Bush, L. Russ, and Tom J. Nettles. *Baptists and the Bible*. Chicago: Moody Press, 1980.

Copeland, E. Luther. *The Southern Baptist Convention and the Judgment of History: The Taint of an Original Sin*. Lanham, MD: University Press of America, 1995.

Cothen, Grady C. *The New SBC: Fundamentalism's Impact on the Southern Baptist Convention*. Macon, GA: Smyth & Helwys Publishing, Inc., 1995.

———. *What Happened to the Southern Baptist Convention? A Memoir of the Controversy*. Macon, GA: Smyth & Helwys Publishing, Inc., 1993.

Davis, Jimmy Thomas. "Organizational Ideographs: A Case Study of the Recent Rise of Southern Baptist Fundamentalism." PhD diss., Bloomington: Indiana University, 1987.

Elliott, Ralph H. *The "Genesis Controversy" and Continuity in Southern Baptist Chaos: A Eulogy for a Great Tradition*. Macon, GA: Mercer University Press, 1992.

Farnsley, Arthur Emery, II. "Majority Rules: The Politicization of the Southern Baptist Convention." PhD diss., Emory University, 1990.

———. *Southern Baptist Politics: Authority and Power in the Restructuring of an American Denomination*. University Park: The Pennsylvania State University Press, 1994.

Ferguson, Robert U., Jr., ed. *Amidst Babel, Speak the Truth*. Macon, GA: Smyth & Helwys Publishing, Inc., 1993.

Fletcher, Jesse C. *The Southern Baptist Convention: A Sesquicentennial History*. Nashville: Broadman & Holman Publishers, 1994.

Garrett, James Leo, Jr. *"Are Southern Baptists 'Evangelicals?'"* Macon, GA: Mercer University Press, 1983.

Gourley, Bruce. *The Godmakers: A Legacy of the Southern Baptist Convention*. Franklin, TN: Providence House Publishers, 1996.

Harvey, Paul William. *Southern Baptists and Southern Culture, 1865–1920*. 2 vols. Berkeley: University of California, 1992.

Hefley, James C. *The Conservative Resurgence in the Southern Baptist Convention*. Hannibal, MO: Hannibal Books, 1991.

———. *The Truth in Crisis: Bringing the Controversy Up-to-Date*. Hannibal, MO: Hannibal Books, 1987.

———. *The Truth in Crisis: Conservative Resurgence or Political Takeover?* Hannibal, MO: Hannibal Books, 1988.

———. *The Truth in Crisis: The Controversy in the Southern Baptist Convention*. Dallas: Criterion Publications, 1986.

———. *The Truth in Crisis: The "State" of the Denomination*. Hannibal, MO: Hannibal Books, 1989.

———. *The Truth in Crisis: The Winning Edge*. Hannibal, MO: Hannibal Books, 1990.

Humphreys, Fisher. *The Way We Were: How Southern Baptist Theology Has Changed and What It Means to Us All*. New York: McCracken Press, 1994.

James, Gordon. *Inerrancy and the Southern Baptist Convention*. Dallas: Southern Heritage Press, 1986.

James, Rob, and Gary Leazer. *The Takeover in the Southern Baptist Convention*. 8th edition. Decatur, GA: Baptists Today, 1994.

James, Robison B., ed. *The Unfettered Word*. Waco, TX: Word, Inc., 1987.

James, Robison B., and David S. Dockery, eds. *Beyond the Impasse? Scripture, Interpretation and Theology in Baptist Life*. Nashville: Broadman Press, 1992.

Johnson, James Benson, II. "Academic Freedom and the Southeastern Baptist Theological Seminary Experience, 1979–1989." PhD diss., The College of William and Mary, 1994.

Kell, Carl L., and L. Raymond Camp. *In the Name of the Father: The Rhetoric of the New Southern Baptist Convention.* Carbondale: Southern Illinois University Press, 1999.

Leonard, Bill J. *God's Last and Only Hope: The Fragmentation of the Southern Baptist Convention.* Grand Rapids: Wm. B. Eerdmans Publishing Co., 1990.

Lindsell, Harold. *The Battle for the Bible.* Grand Rapids: Zondervan Publishing House, 1976.

McBeth, H. Leon. *The Baptist Heritage.* Nashville: Broadman, 1987.

McNabb, Freddie, III. "Inerrancy and Beyond: The Controversy in the Southern Baptist Convention." MA thesis, University of Southern Mississippi, 1991.

Morgan, David T. *The New Crusades, The New Holy Land: Conflict in the Southern Baptist Convention, 1969–1991.* Tuscaloosa: University of Alabama Press, 1996.

Neely, Alan, ed. *Being Baptist Means Freedom: The Southern Baptist Alliance Publishers.* Charlotte, NC: Southern Baptist Alliance, 1988.

Nettles, Thomas J. *By His Grace and for His Glory.* Grand Rapids: Baker Book House, 1986.

Noll, Mark A. *The Scandal of the Evangelical Mind.* Grand Rapids: Wm. B. Eerdmans Publishing Co., 1994.

Parker, Gary E. *Principles Worth Protecting.* Macon, GA: Smyth & Helwys Publishing, Inc., 1993.

Paschall, Henry Franklin. *Identity Crisis in the Church: The Southern Baptist Convention Controversy.* Nashville: Gospel Progress Inc., 1993.

Patterson, Paige. *The Proceedings of the Conference on Biblical Inerrancy 1987.* Nashville: Broadman Press, 1987.

Pool, Jeff B. *Against Returning to Egypt: Exposing and Resisting Creedalism in the Southern Baptist Convention.* Macon, GA: Mercer University Press, 1998.

———, ed. *Sacred Mandates of Conscience: Interpretations of the Baptist Faith and Message.* Macon, GA: Smyth & Helwys, 1997.

Pressler, Paul. *A Hill on Which to Die.* Nashville: Broadman & Holman, 1999.

Queen, Edward L., II. *In the South the Baptists Are the Center of Gravity.* Brooklyn, NY: Carlson Publishing Co., 1991.

Rosenberg, Ellen M. *The Southern Baptists: A Subculture in Transition.* Nashville: Broadman Press, 1987.

Shurden, Walter B. *The Baptist Identity: Four Fragile Freedoms.* Macon, GA: Smyth & Helwys Publishing, Inc., 1993.

———. *The Doctrine of the Priesthood of Believers.* Nashville: Broadman Press, 1987.

———. *Going for the Jugular: A Documentary History of the SBC Holy War.* Macon, GA: Mercer University Press, 1996.

———. *Not a Silent People: Controversies That Have Shaped Southern Baptists.* Updated edition. Macon, GA: Smyth & Helwys Publishing, Inc., 1995.

———. "The Struggle for the Soul of the SBC: Reflections and Interpretations." In *The Struggle for the Soul of the SBC: Moderate Responses to the Fundamentalist Movement,* edited by Walter B. Shurden, 275–90. Macon, GA: Mercer University Press, 1993.

———, ed. *Proclaiming the Baptist Vision: The Bible.* Macon, GA: Smyth and Helwys Publishing, Inc., 1994.

———, ed. *Proclaiming the Baptist Vision: The Priesthood of All Believers.* Macon, GA: Smyth & Helwys Publishing, Inc., 1993.

———, ed. *The Struggle for the Soul of the SBC: Moderate Responses to the Fundamentalist Movement.* Macon, GA: Mercer University Press, 1993.

Shurden, Walter B., & Randy Shepley, eds. *Going for the Jugular—A Documentary History of the Southern Baptist Holy War.* Macon, GA: Mercer University Press, 1996.

Smith, Oran P. *The Rise of Baptist Republicanism.* New York: New York University Press, 1997.

Stone, William Stanley, Jr. "The Southern Baptist Convention Reformation, 1979–1990: A Social Drama (Social Movement)." PhD diss., Louisiana State University, 1993.

Sullivan, Clayton. *Called to Preach, Condemned to Survive.* Macon, GA: Mercer University Press, 1985.

Sullivan, James. *Baptist Polity as I See It.* Nashville: Broadman Press, 1983.

Tuck, William Powell. *Our Baptist Tradition.* Macon, GA: Smyth & Helwys Publishing, 1993.

Turner, Helen Lee. "Fundamentalism in the Southern Baptist Convention: The Crystallization of a Millennialist Vision." PhD diss., University of Virginia, 1990.

Wardin, Albert W. *Baptist around the World: A Comprehensive Handbook.* Nashville: Broadman & Holman Publishers, 1995.

Whitlock, David. "Southern Baptists and Southern Culture: Three Visions of a Christian America." PhD diss., Southern Baptist Theological Seminary, 1988.

Wiles, Dennis Ray. "Factors Contributing to the Resurgence of Fundamentalism in the Southern Baptist Convention 1979–1990." PhD diss., Southwestern Baptist Theological Seminary, 1992.

CONTRIBUTORS

WAYNE C. BARTEE has been Professor of History at Missouri State University in Springfield since 1967. He has served on the Missouri Baptist Historical Commission and the Missouri Baptist Convention Nominating Committee. In 1997, he and his family left the Southern Baptist church into which he had been born. He is now a member of University Heights Baptist Church, which cooperates with American Baptists and the Cooperative Baptist Fellowship, having served there as Chair of Deacons and Sunday School teacher.

JUNE BROWN is Professor of Reading, Missouri State University, Springfield, Missouri. Dr. Brown served as the Moderator of the Cooperative Baptist Fellowship of Missouri in 2002–3. After serving in a local church over thirty years, she moved her church membership when her freedom to worship freely and support CBF missions was denied. Her new church honors the historical heritage of the Baptist faith and encourages her to be a free and faithful Baptist.

LAVONN D. BROWN is a retired Pastor, First Baptist Church, Norman, Oklahoma. He is working with the Cooperative Baptist Fellowship in Oklahoma.

RACHEL SMITH CHILDRESS is the Registrar and Director of Student Services at Lexington Theological Seminary, Lexington, Kentucky. She has an MA from that institution as well as a BA in Sociology from the University of Kentucky. Prior to serving at LTS, she held positions in state government and with a computer firm. Ms. Childress grew up as a Southern Baptist preacher's kid and has been a member at Central Baptist Church in Lexington since 1980. Central withdrew from the SBC and KBC in October 2000.

REBA COBB served on the administrative staff, Cooperative Baptist Fellowship, Atlanta. Ms. Cobb has been a strong voice for the moderate cause in the SBC controversy. She is a retired Baptist minister currently living in Louisville, Kentucky, where she enjoys being a community activist, world traveler, and devoted grandparent to Hunter and Clayton.

W. HENRY CROUCH, Retired, is Pastor Emeritus of the Providence Baptist Church in Charlotte, North Carolina. He pastored churches in Kentucky, Mississippi, and North Carolina and was first President of the Baptist Alliance.

CAROLYN WEATHERFORD CRUMPLER lives in Cincinnati, Ohio. She is a retired executive of WMU and SBC and is now serving, with her husband Joe, in their sixth pastorate since Joe's retirement in 1992. Carolyn has been active in the Cooperative Baptist Fellowship from its beginning, and she currently is moderator-elect for the North Central CBF. She serves on eight not-for-profit boards, several of which do the kind of ministry formerly associated with the "old SBC."

MICHAEL R. DUNCAN, who has pastored churches in Tennessee, Indiana, and Kentucky, is in his twenty-fifth year as pastor of Eminence Baptist Church, Eminence, Kentucky. He served two terms on the Executive Committee of the Kentucky Baptist Convention (1984–87 and 1997–2000). He has served as the Moderator of the Kentucky Baptist Fellowship (2001–2) and was elected in 2003 to serve a three-year term on the Cooperative Baptist Fellowship Coordinating Council. Following the 1998 Southern Baptist Convention, he announced to his congregation that he was no longer a Southern Baptist.

JAMES M. DUNN is professor of Christianity and public policy, Wake Forest University Divinity School, Winston-Salem, North Carolina. He has served the Divinity School since its opening in 1999. Before that, he was executive director of the Baptist Joint Committee on Public Affairs, 1980–99, in Washington, D.C. He has been president of *Bread for the World* and chairman of the Ethics Commission of the Baptist World Alliance, and is now chairman of the Whitsitt Historical Society.

TRACY DUNN-NOLAND pastors Fellowship of Believers Church in Hereford, Texas. She is a graduate of Baylor University and Brite Divinity School. She was ordained by and served Spring Creek Baptist Church in Oklahoma City. She and her husband Rob are the out-of-breath parents of six-year-old Anna and four-year-old Aaron.

Originally from Pennsylvania, MARK FLEMING moved to North Carolina in 1987 to attend graduate school at the University of North Carolina at Greensboro. In 1995, he and his wife, Angela, a Greensboro native, sought a church in which to start their family. They found College Park Baptist—a loving, progressive church that nurtures women in the ministry and lay members and children—as active worship leaders. In 1998, while Mark was serving his first term as a deacon, the congregation voted to leave the SBC.

GREGORY L. HANCOCK is Manager, Employee Communication, Ashland, Inc., Lexington, Kentucky. He was pastor of Latonia Baptist Church in Covington, Kentucky, and served as managing editor for the moderate-voice newspaper *The Call* during the 1970s and 1980s. Two years after the paper ceased publication, Hancock joined the staff of the Kentucky Baptist Convention as Director of the Communications Division. In 1990, he accepted a position as chief executive officer for a nondenominational organization and never returned to vocational ministry. He remains a member of a Baptist church that has severed ties with the Southern Baptist Convention.

PASCAL L. HOVIS is a lifelong Baptist and a member of Baptist churches of both large and small membership throughout North Carolina for more than sixty of his seventy-three years. He states, "It saddens me to see what has happened within the Southern Baptist Convention. No longer is there 'unity in diversity' within the SBC, and the 'priesthood of the individual believer' is a thing of the past. While most Baptists agree on the essentials of Christianity, now there is only one interpretation of the less important matters in the Bible, dictated by those who have succeeded in taking control through the appointive powers of the presidency. Those in control of the SBC do not want to discuss these minor issues; their only desire is to dictate."

J. R. HUDDLESTUN is pastor of Heritage Baptist Fellowship, Canton, Georgia. He has served on Baptist state executive committees and boards for the SBC in the pioneer areas of Kansas and Nebraska. He served as pastor there and in Georgia. He withdrew from the state and national Baptist Conventions because of positions on the doctrinal, ethical, and historical benchmarks of Baptist heritage.

S. L. HARRIS lives in San Angelo, Texas. He is a retired pastor, campus minister, and college and university teacher and administrator. He concluded his active ministry as Associate Pastor/Director of the Counseling Ministry, First Baptist Church, Brownwood, Texas.

ALAN G. JOLLY, retired, Bowling Green, Kentucky. Alan served as Coordinator of Training and Marketing Planning for the Book Store Division, Baptist Sunday School Board, Nashville, from 1987 to 1992. He has served as President and CEO of Jolly Communications, handling national media for the Home Mission Board's "Good News, God Loves You" campaign and serving as consultant for the "Good News, Kenyans, God Loves You" campaign in the Kentucky Baptist Convention Partnership. He was a part-time instructor at Western Kentucky University; Charter Member of Westport Road Baptist Church, Louisville, Kentucky; and is a member of First Baptist Church, Bowling Green, Kentucky.

FRANK KENDALL is retired after working for Exxon and its affiliates for thirty-eight years. He has taught Sunday School at various churches for twenty-five years and currently teaches and is a Deacon at College Park Baptist Church in

Greensboro, North Carolina. College Park withdrew from the Southern Baptist Convention in 1998 as the SBC continued to move further from historic Baptist principles.

GLADYS S. LEWIS is Professor of English at the University of Central Oklahoma, Edmond. She has been deeply involved in Baptist life, both church and denominational, all of her adult life. From 1959 to 1970, she and her surgeon husband, Wilbur, were medical missionaries in Asuncion, Paraguay. In denominational areas, she was a member of the Board of Trustees, Southwestern Baptist Theological Seminary, from 1974 to 1984; member of the Committee on Order of Business, Southern Baptist Convention, from 1979 to 1981; and a writer for Woman's Missionary Union into the 1990s.

RICK MCCLATCHY is Coordinator of the Cooperative Baptist Fellowship of Texas. He has served as pastor of churches in Texas and Oklahoma, taught at Baptist colleges and seminaries, and has served as Coordinator of the CBF in Oklahoma.

MICHAEL K. OLMSTED is Senior Pastor, University Heights Baptist Church, Springfield, Missouri, where he has served for twenty years. He has pastored SBC churches in Oklahoma, Texas, Mississippi, Alabama, New Mexico, California, and Missouri. He has served on two Baptist state executive boards, chaired major committees, and was chairman of a Baptist college trustee board. Dr. Olmsted severed his ties with the SBC because of their unethical behavior and departure from historical Baptist distinctives.

EDWIN FLEETWOOD PERRY SR. holds degrees from Wake Forest University, Wake Forest, North Carolina (1938), and from Andover Newton Theological School, Boston (1942). He was a part of the seventeen-member "Gatlinburg Gang" formed in opposition to the Fundamentalist takeover of the Southern Baptist Convention. He is Pastor Emeritus of Broadway Baptist Church, Louisville, Kentucky, where he served as pastor for thirty-one years.

CECIL E. SHERMAN, retired, pastor of churches throughout the South, is currently teaching part-time at Southern Baptist Theological Seminary, Richmond, Virginia, and writing materials for Smith and Helwys publishing house, Macon, Georgia. Dr. Sherman was a leading voice for the moderate Southern Baptist position. He served as the first Coordinator of the Cooperative Baptist Fellowship.

PAUL D. SIMMONS is Clinical Professor, Department of Family and Community Medicine, University of Louisville School of Medicine, and Adjunct Professor in the Department of Philosophy. He is an ordained Baptist minister and Director of the Center for Ethics: Ministry, Medicine and Business. He was professor of Christian Ethics at Southern Baptist Theological Seminary from 1970 to 1993, where he also served as Director of the Clarence Jordan Center for Christian Ethical Concerns from 1977 to 1992.

RONALD D. SISK is Professor of Homiletics and Christian Ministry at North American Baptist Seminary, Sioux Falls, South Dakota. He has served on the staff of the Christian Life Commission of the SBC and as a pastor in California,

Kentucky, and Texas. He entered the American Baptist Churches along with his congregation in 1996 and transferred his ordination to that body the next year.

GEORGE STEINCROSS relates the developing story of state/national convention concerns in Missouri—a story without a foreseeable conclusion. He lives in Liberty, Missouri.

JOE E. TRULL is Editor, *Christian Ethics Today,* and Pastor, the Baptist Church of Driftwood, Austin, Texas. From 1985 to 1999 he was Professor of Christian Ethics at New Orleans Baptist Theological Seminary, after serving for twenty years as pastor of churches in Oklahoma, Texas, and Virginia. Dr. Trull chose early retirement from seminary teaching rather than submit to new doctrinal and ethical requirements.

EMERSON CLEVELAND (E.C.) WATSON JR. retired in 1990 after fifty years of ministry. He was Pastor, Director of Associational Missions, and Associate in the Sunday School Board in North Carolina; Consultant on Associational Administration for the Home Mission Board; and Director of the Missions Department, Mission Division, Coordinated Planning, and Executive Assistant to the Executive Director (consecutively) in South Carolina.

DAWN DARWIN WEAKS is Senior Pastor of First Christian Church (Disciples of Christ), Rowlett, Texas. She previously served both Baptist and Christian churches throughout Texas. She was ordained by Royal Lane Baptist Church in Dallas. Her sermons and worship materials are widely published. She is a graduate of Baylor University and Brite Divinity School. She and her husband Joe are the proud parents of a four-year-old and a two-year-old.

FRED WERHAN is the retired pastor of Hominy Baptist Church, Candler, North Carolina (1973–95), a CBF church that has disassociated with the SBC. He holds MDiv and DMin degrees from Vanderbilt Divinity School and a BA from Carson-Newman College. He is now a strong Baptist advocate for the inclusion of gay and lesbian persons, which he contends is the religious/social issue of our day, as was the racial issue for a previous generation.

ELEANOR B. WILLIAMSON, a long-time member of First Baptist Church, Springfield, Missouri (1946–97), became a member of University Heights Baptist Church, Springfield, in her senior years. Her story reflects the experiences of many senior members of a Southern Baptist church in the recent upheaval in the Southern Baptist Convention. Ms. Williamson was the first Southern Baptist to agree to write for this book. She passed away on July 10, 2004.

JOE YELTON is Pastor, Hominy Baptist Church, Candler, North Carolina. Dr. Yelton tells a story of deeply felt sadness over the SBC matter.

INDEX

A

Allen, Jimmy R., xviii, xxvi
Allen, Wayne, 22, 110
American Baptists, 37, 63, 65, 74, 101
American Bible Society, xxi
Anderson College, 95–96
Anthony, Susan B., 13
Armstrong, Annie, xxi, 135
Associated Baptist Press, 37
autonomy (local church), 14, 16, 30, 39, 50, 61, 65, 68, 74, 87, 97, 128
Aytoun, William, 115

B

Baker, Larry, 22
Baker, Robert A., xxvii
Baptist Alliance, 90–91, 122
Baptist Courier, 98
Baptist distinctive, 73, 87, 91
Baptist General Convention of Oklahoma, 61

Baptist General Convention of Texas (BGCT), xxvii–xxix, 82
Baptist Medical-Dental Fellowship, 48
Baptist Press, xvii, xxii, 37
Baptist Student Union, xii–xiii, 71
Baptist Theological Seminary, Richmond, Va., 37, 122, 188
Baptist Today, 134
Baptist Training Union (BTU), xii–xiii
Baptist World Alliance (BWA), xvii, xx
Baptist World Fellowship, xxvi, xxviii
Barnes, W. W., xxvii
Baylor University, xxviii, xxx, 32, 37
Brite Divinity School, 135
Broadman Bible Commentary, 103
Bruster, Bill, xxxvi, 83

C

Call, The, 77
Call to Concern (1979), 112
Calvinism, xxx–xxxi

Camp, Carolyn, xxxvi
Camp, L. Raymond, xxxiv, xxxvi, xxxviii
Campbell University, 37, 93
Campbell, Will, 104, 117
captivity, xxxviii, 39–42, 44–45, 47, 50
Carlson, E. Leslie, xxvii
Caroll, B. H., 15
Carson-Newman College, 147
Carter, Jimmy, 98
Cauthen, Baker James, xvi–xvii
CBF Global Missions, 62, 68
CBF National Council, 64
Central Baptist Seminary, 37
Chafin, Kenneth, xxxviii
Chapman, Morris, 74
Christian Ethics Today, 39, 151
Christian Life Commission (SBC), xviii, xxix–xxx, 22, 99, 148
Cole, A. Harold, 95
Conner, W. T., xxvi–xxvii
Cooperative Baptist Fellowship (CBF), xxi, xxxvi, 15, 35, 60, 62, 64, 68, 70, 74, 95, 100–101, 104–5, 122, 124–25, 131, 141, 144
Cooperative Program (SBC), xiii–xiv, xxi, 14, 17–18, 59, 62, 93–94, 96, 121–22
Criswell Bible College, 18
Criswell Center for Biblical Studies, xxxiv, 72
Criswell, W. A., xxix, 72
Currie, David, 82–83

D
Dalai Lama, 107
Daley, C. R., 122
Dana, H. E., xxvi
Dawson, J. M., xxviii–xxix
Denominational Study Committee, 22

Dilday, R. H., xxvi, 64, 100
Dipboye, Larry, 77–78
Draper, Jimmy, xx, 124

E
ecclesiology, 9, 42
Elliott, L. R., xxvi
Estep, William R., xxvii
Eubanks, Ralph T., xliii
evangelical, 2, 108n2, 110, 135. *See also* fundamentalism
exodus, 39, 42–47, 50, 103–5

F
Falwell, Jerry, 126
Ferguson, Milton, xxvi, 47
Florida Baptist Convention, xiii–xiv
Florida State University, xiii
Folio, 143
Forbis, Jean, xli
Foreign Mission Board (SBC), xvi, xxi, 21, 50, 73, 121, 148
FORUM, 122
fundamentalism, xxvi, xxviii–xxix, xxxiv–xxxv, 3–4, 14, 32, 41, 60, 68, 70, 74, 78–79, 84, 94–95, 97, 99, 108, 126, 144; faction, xxviii, xxxiv, 2–3, 22–23, 32, 56, 65, 72–75, 79, 82–85, 87–91, 96, 99–100, 110, 116–18, 121–22, 126, 140–41, 143; movement, 13–14, 78, 118; takeover, 15, 32, 48, 81, 87, 90, 144, 146. *See also* evangelical

G
Gardener Webb University, 37
Gatlinburg, Tenn., 32, 60, 121, 123–24; "Gatlinburg Gang," 121, 123
Glorieta Assembly, 55–56, 59
Golden Gate Seminary, 100, 130

Graham, Billy, 72
Gray, Elmer, xli
Gyatso, Tenzin, 107

H
Hardin-Simmons University, xxviii, 37
Hobbs, Herschel, 14, 73, 29, 152
Hoffer, Eric, 118
Home Mission Board (SBC), xvii–xviii, 96
Honeycutt, Roy, xix, 23, 113

I
inerrancy (Biblical), xxxiv–xxxv, 3, 14, 65, 88, 121
inerrant, xxxiv, xxxvi–xxxvii, 4
infallibility, 3, 6
infallible, 78
Inter-Agency Council, xvii

J
John Leland School of Theology, 37

K
Kelley, Charles, 147–48

L
Leavell, Landrum P., 129, 148, 150
Lee, David, xli
legalism, 70, 74
Lemke, Steve, 147, 149
Lewis, Joseph P., 113
liberalism, 4, 18, 73

M
Maston, T. B., xxvi, xxx, 147
MBC Historical Commission, 65
McAfee School of Theology, 37
McBride, Jerold, xxvii
McCall, Abner V., xxx
McKinney, B. B., xxv

McNeely, Edwin, xxv–xxvi, xxxi
Message of Genesis, The, 139
Miller, Acker C., xxx
moderate: agenda, 88–90; cause, 87, 91; faction, xxxix, 2–5, 32–33, 36–37, 60, 62, 64, 78, 81–82, 87–91, 95–98, 100, 118, 130, 139–40, 144; leadership, 37, 87, 90–91
Mohler, Al, 23, 74, 100
Moon, Lottie, xxi–xxiii, 135
Moral Majority, 126
Moyers, Bill D., xxvi
Mullins, E. Y., xix, 5, 109
Myers, Phillip E., xli

N
New Orleans Baptist Theological Seminary, xiv, 129, 147–48, 151
Newman, A. H., xxvi
Niebuhr, H. Richard, xxvi
Norris, J. Frank, xxvi–xxix, xxxi
North American Baptist Fellowship, xx–xxi
Northern Baptist Convention, 126

O
O'Brien, William R., xxvi
Open Windows, xxii

P
Parks, Keith, xxvi, 65, 73
Patterson, Paige, xxxiv, 72, 74, 130
Peace Committee, 4, 33, 129, 131
Pilgrimage, 27, 39, 47–48, 50, 78
Pinson, Bill, xxvi
Pressler, Paul, xxxiv, 32, 60, 72, 130
Price, John Milburn, xv, xxvi
priesthood of the believer, xxxvi–xxxvii, 30, 39, 47–48, 50, 68, 87, 109, 128

R

Rauschenbusch, Walter, xxvi
Ray, Sally J., xli
Republican Party, 126
Resolution on Women (1984), xviii
Reynolds, I. E., xxv
rhetoric, xxxiii–xxxix, 31, 47, 100
Rhetorics of Southern Baptist Life, xxxv
Ridgecrest Assembly, xiii–xiv, 59, 63
Rogers, Adrian, xviii, xxxiii, 23, 31, 122
Roman Catholic Church, 1–2, 9, 41,
    100, 145

S

SBC Ministers' Wives Association, xxi
SBC Today, 77, 89–90
Scarborough, L. R., xxv
Schneider, J. M., 116
separation of church and state, xxviii,
    xxxi, 15, 65, 68, 74, 113, 117
Sheer, Lynn, 13
Shurden, Walter B., xxxiv, 36
soul competency, 8, 18, 39, 41, 50,
    108, 128
soul liberty, 39, 41–42, 49–50
South Carolina Baptist Convention,
    94–95
Southeastern Baptist Theological
    Seminary, 18
Southern Baptist Convention (SBC):
    1970 meeting, Denver, Colo., 103;
    1979 meeting, Houston, Tex., xviii,
    xxvi, xxxiii, 14, 17, 31, 64, 104,
    125, 129, 143; 1981 meeting, Los
    Angeles, Calif., 17, 32, 72; 1982
    meeting, New Orleans, La., 88;
    1984 meeting, Kansas City, Mo.,
    xviii, 60; 1988 meeting, San
    Antonio, Tex., xix, 32, 64; 1989
    meeting, Las Vegas, Nev., xix, 64,
    90, 95; 1990 meeting, New Orleans,
    La., xix, 4, 17, 32, 36, 38; 1998
    Family Amendment, 148, 150

Southern Baptist Theological Seminary
    (Southern Seminary, SBTS), 21–23,
    29, 93–94, 99, 101, 104, 110–11,
    118, 139, 144
Southern Baptist Women in Ministry
    (SBWIM), 143
Southwestern Baptist Theological
    Seminary, xxv–xxvi, xxxi, 32
Stagg, Frank, xv
Stanley, Charles, 72
Strange, Olen, xv
Summers, Ray, xxvi
Sumners, Bill, xli

T

takeover: crowd, xxvi, xxx; fundamen-
    talist, 32, 60, 81, 87, 90, 121, 146;
    group, 123–26; plot, 143; of SBC,
    xvii–xviii, xxvii, xxxiii, xxxvi, xli–xlii,
    14–15, 19, 56, 73–74, 78–79, 104,
    107, 140, 144
Texas Baptist Committed (TBC), 82
total culture, 2, 8–9
Toy, Crawford, xxiii
Truett, George W., xxviii, 14
Truett Theological Seminary, 37

U

Union University, Jackson, Tenn., 104

V

Valentine, Foy D., xxvii, 63, 151
Vestal, Daniel, xix, 36, 60

W

Wake Forest University, 37, 93
Ware, Browning, xxvi
Western Recorder, 112, 122
White, K. Owen, 139
Williams, Charles B., xxvi
Williams, Roger, xxvii, 49, 108
Women's Missionary Union (WMU),
    xi–xxii, 14, 16, 48, 50, 60